Anna Mitchell

Women Take Their Place in State Legislatures

The Creation of Women's Caucuses

TEMPLE UNIVERSITY PRESS

Philadelphia • Rome • Tokyo

TEMPLE UNIVERSITY PRESS
Philadelphia, Pennsylvania 19122
tupress.temple.edu

Library of Congress Cataloging-in-Publication Data

Names: Mahoney, Anna Mitchell, 1978– author.
Title: Women take their place in state legislatures : the creation of women's
caucuses / Anna Mitchell Mahoney.
Description: Philadelphia : Temple University Press, [2018] | Includes
bibliographical references and index.
Identifiers: LCCN 2018018509 (print) | LCCN 2018020702 (ebook)
| ISBN 9781439915981 (ebook) | ISBN 9781439915967 (cloth : alk. paper)
| ISBN 9781439915974 (pbk. : alk. paper)
Subjects: LCSH: Women legislators—United States. | Women—Political
activity—United States. | Politics, Practical—United States. | Caucus.
| Feminism—United States.
Classification: LCC HQ1236.5.U6 (ebook) | LCC HQ1236.5.U6 M34
2018 (print) | DDC 320.082/0973—dc23
LC record available at https://lccn.loc.gov/2018018509

♾ The paper used in this publication meets the requirements of the American
National Standard for Information Sciences—Permanence of Paper for Printed
Library Materials, ANSI Z39.48-1992

Printed in the United States of America

9 8 7 6 5 4 3 2 1

For Elsa,

who will one day take her own place

wherever she chooses

CONTENTS

ACKNOWLEDGMENTS

This is the story of women strategically making their mark on state legislatures, deciding together how and when they will be seen and heard. By writing this book, I am similarly making my mark, and I could not have done so without the assistance of many mentors, colleagues, friends, and family members. I happily acknowledge them and their support here.

First, I thank all the men and women who participated in my study, especially Kathy Crotty and Laura Hoeppner, who were particularly gracious with their time and introductions. I also acknowledge all women legislators who work to represent their constituents throughout the fifty states in sometimes less than ideal conditions. I admire them greatly for raising their hands and answering the call to serve their communities. I hope this project illuminates their experience and contributes to the improved status of women in public office.

I also thank Aaron Javsicas and the staff at Temple University Press. Aaron, who showed great patience throughout the proposal and submission process, expressed early enthusiasm for the project that bolstered my confidence that the manuscript would one day become a book.

Many institutions and individuals made it possible for me to conduct this research. Initially, my training at Rutgers University was supported by fellowships granted by the Eagleton Institute of Politics, headed by Dr. Ruth Mandel, and the Department of Political Science. I am also grateful to the American Association of University Women for the American Dissertation Fellowship, which supported this work in a previous form. Alice Bragaw's investment in women's education made my fellowship and therefore this book possible. In addition, I thank my colleagues at Douglass Residential College, whose commitment to women's leadership continues to inspire me.

This project was guided by a wonderful dissertation committee, including Drs. Kira Sanbonmatsu, Sue Carroll, Beth Leech, Alan Rosenthal, and Gary Moncrief. Kira Sanbonmatsu managed to teach me when I didn't even know it was happening. When I thought I had done my best, she still pushed. When I thought I was done, she knew that I wasn't. This project became a reality because she recognized the merit of my curiosity about women and political parties and nurtured it into a proposal, a research project, a dissertation, and finally a book. I cannot thank her enough for her time, patience, and thoughtful input. Sue Carroll eased my entrance into graduate school. She connected me with financial support as soon as I was admitted and even picked me up when I got lost on campus on my first visit. No one has ever challenged me the way she has. I thank her for thinking I was worth it. Beth Leech has mentored me in countless ways, including teaching me how to ask for what I deserve. I thank her for that skill, which will serve me well for the rest of my career. Alan Rosenthal's genuine interest in my questions about state legislatures reassured me that this project was worth pursuing, and the many insights that he offered throughout my writing improved the final product immensely. Gary Moncrief offered me tremendous encouragement and, even more importantly, his work on state legislatures will forever guide my own.

I also thank Dr. Irwin Gertzog for his research on the Congressional Caucus on Women's Issues, which was of great help to me throughout this project, and for the notes he provided when this book was just a concept. Sarah Childs, who introduced me to the European version of caucuses, has been a wonderful mentor and an enthusiastic supporter. Her work has changed the way I look at legislatures and has broadened my view of women's representation.

I relied on the expertise of many people during the completion of this book. Chris Clark has been an outstanding colleague, always supportive of my work, and it has been a joy to know someone who shares my interest in state caucuses. He contributed a great deal to this project by tracking down his fair share of caucus-origin dates and by sharing such legislative data as the origin dates for black caucuses in the states. I thank Katie Ziegler and the rest of the staff at the National Conference of State Legislatures, who provided information on legislatures that made my analysis possible. Many legislative staffers, archivists, and librarians helped me uncover the story of women's caucuses. Their sometimes invisible work unearthed incredible stories. Similarly, many Center for American Woman and Politics (CAWP) staffers deserve my thanks. Debbie Walsh, who has always supported this project, facilitated my attendance at the 2009 National Conference of State Legislatures' Legislative Summit. Chelsea Hill and Gilda Morales provided me with tailored data on women legislators that enriched my findings. Finally, Kathy Kleeman served as a valued discussant at an early stage of the project, providing vital attention and suggestions. My decision to attend Rutgers University was due to my desire to work with CAWP, and it has been one of the most important and best decisions in my life.

I must acknowledge my Tulane University family as well. Since I joined Tulane and Newcomb College Institute in 2014, Sally J. Kenney has been a tireless advocate for me and for my scholarship. Supportive of this project from the start, Sally offered excellent feedback at the dissertation stage and beyond. She believed in me when I did not believe in myself and offered me the space and time I needed to complete this work. When she hired me, she also gave me the gift of wonderful colleagues, many of whom not only offered input on the manuscript but also, more importantly, politely endured years of complaint and self-deprecation.

I thank my colleagues in the Tulane University Political Science Workshop, who assisted with the book proposal and an early chapter. Their welcoming me into the group greatly bolstered my confidence and my sense of humor. Two noteworthy participants went above and beyond to support this work. Words cannot express my debt to Mirya Holman and Geoff Dancy. Mirya has read this book many times in many forms. She was instrumental in shaping the case-study chapters and in reminding me that just because I wrote it down once doesn't mean it stays. Mirya, who has been my champion—for which I thank her—also included me in the Gender and Political Psychology Writing Group, which kept me invigorated, writing, and on task. Many of the members of this inspiring group of scholars also read and edited several chapters. Also, at Tulane, I will be forever grateful to Geoff Dancy, who came to my assistance in the eleventh hour, when I needed it most.

My faithful research assistants at Tulane University, Mariana Deluera Canchola, Tatiana DeRouen, Emma Hurler, Rebecca Kelly, Jaqueline Landry, and Kate Rohr, have been a joy to work with—intellectually curious, passionate women leaders in their own right and kindly forgiving of my habitual rescheduling.

This book would not have come to fruition without the love and genius of my friends. I thank my entire cohort, especially Johanna Dobrich, Marika Dunn, Ben Dworkin, and Kevin McQueeney. Other noteworthy friends include Amanda Crabb, Ingrid Reed, and Kate Rose. I thank Amanda for answering my crazy calls and always believing in me, Ingrid for her support and for helping me to develop as a scholar, and Kate for sustaining me with daily communiques of little consequence or understanding to anyone else but us. To Kate's credit, she also married the incredible photographer David Rose, who provided the cover art for this book. He captured exactly what I asked for, and I appreciate it.

I am grateful to all the women-and-politics faculty and students at Rutgers University, including Dana Brown, Nadia Brown, Janna Ferguson, Erin Heidt-Forsythe, Danielle Gougon, Aiisha Harden, Jennifer Miller, Mary Nugent, Danielle Pritchett, Wendy Wright, and especially Sara Angevine and Kelly Dittmar. Sara offered me counsel on my analysis and reminded me that being kind to myself was more important than acquiring a technical skill. Kelly has been with me every step of the way, and anyone who knows her appreciates that keeping up with her pace is quite a challenge. She has been my travel agent, ice-cream concierge, and role model these past twelve years. All the members of the Rutgers University women-and-politics community offered comments on early drafts of the book, encouragement when I thought the process would never end, and valuable mentorship that will carry me through the rest of my career. I must also thank Dr. Cynthia Daniels for providing, when it was sorely needed, leadership of the department that changed the environment and reset our priorities. Cyndi has made a mark on the discipline by creating institutional change that paved a slightly easier road for the next young women scholars to follow.

My family supported me on this journey in many ways. In particular, my sister Patricia served as my editor and biggest fan, for which I am forever grateful. My brother, Michael, and sister Delia kept me sane over the years through their love and laughter. My parents taught me to read and to love it, never to be ashamed of being a smart girl, and to count on their always welcoming me home and giving me the strength to leave it to follow my dreams. It has meant a great deal to me that the Mahoneys, who have always taken me seriously as a scholar and a person, enabled me to pursue my work by caring for me and my family each and every step of the way.

Notably, I must thank my son, Patrick, and my daughter, Elsa, for not caring one whit whether I finished this book or not, and all the women—including Parul Shah, those at Kiddie Korner, and those at Newcomb Child Care Center—who cared for them along the way. I could not have succeeded without their crucial, tender nurturing. And to my husband, I lovingly express my thanks for simply everything.

Finally, this project is the direct result of all the foremothers in the discipline of political science who fought to create a space so that I could study the subjects that I so passionately pursue. Their sacrifices and struggles changed academia in ways that allowed me to be here and do this.

Any errors that may have found their way into this book are mine alone.

WOMEN TAKE THEIR PLACE
IN STATE LEGISLATURES

1

WOMEN TAKE THEIR PLACE
IN LEGISLATURES

> Bands of brothers create informal trust networks that
> shape governing institutions. The extent to which
> bands of sisters—or bands of brothers and sisters—
> also do the same, warrants close attention.
>
> —GEORGIA DUERST-LAHTI, "Governing Institutions,
> Ideologies, and Gender"

On February 28, 2012, three-term senator Olympia Snowe (R) announced that she would retire from the U.S. Senate. She was dissatisfied with her work environment within Congress. Partisanship had made government unfriendly and ineffective. She vowed to find new ways to "best serve the people of Maine" (Steinhauer 2012). Senator Snowe did not leave the Senate without first trying to change it. She and her female colleagues had tried to avoid the pitfalls of heightened polarization by participating in women-only activities to foster camaraderie across the aisle and keep debate civil (Carlson 2012). Unlike Representatives Margaret Heckler (R-MA) and Elizabeth Holtzman (D-NY), who created the Congressional Caucus for Women's Issues (CCWI) in 1977 to organize Congress' response to women's policy issues raised by second-wave activism and improve women representatives' effectiveness, Senator Barbara Mikulski (D-MD) created a Senate organization in the late 1980s, commonly referred to as the Supper Club, to better the quality of life for the legislators themselves (Carlson 2012). While Mikulski's club was social in nature, observers have credited its participants with ending the 2013 government shutdown (Stolberg 2015a) and cosponsoring legislation at a higher rate than their male counterparts or women in the U.S. House (Stolberg 2015b). Bipartisan policy is sometimes a by-product, though not the objective, of this group. Similarly, the CCWI's commitment to bipartisan policy achievement has ebbed and flowed over time.

Women legislators are strategic actors making decisions about their legislative strategy in specific political contexts. The CCWI and Supper Club each emerged in distinct political and institutional contexts within Congress and produced groups with different goals and activities. The CCWI is a congressional member organization registered with the House Administration Committee with officially recognized bipartisan leaders, while the Supper Club is an informal gathering over dinner, sometimes in the senators' own homes (Carlson 2012; Women's Policy 2016). Women legislators founded the CCWI during the second wave of the women's movement in the United States in order to address women's issues they felt party and committee leaders had previously ignored as well as to increase their own influence and effectiveness.[1] They were responding to a political environment that was ripe for attention to particular constituents' needs. They faced unique challenges in the House and the gender dynamics therein.[2] Women created the senators' Supper Club, on the other hand, during a different political climate for women with different needs. Their primary goal was not to address women's issues but rather to improve their own working environment, "to restore some of the natural camaraderie" (Carlson 2012).

This book traces the development of women's state legislative caucuses and the influence that both gender and party have on women's ability to organize collectively. An increase in partisanship at the federal and state levels has raised questions about whether American democracy is at serious risk. The polarization of political parties has stymied Congress's work and made "compromise" among our deliberative bodies a dirty word. Scholars and pundits alike often cite women legislators as an exception to the partisan rule, with their male colleagues corroborating women's claims of collegiality and bottom-line practicality. Women's caucuses at the state and federal level are evidence of such bipartisanship, but sweeping generalizations about women's political noblesse or high expectations of these organizations to represent all women would be misplaced within institutions traditionally organized around political parties.

Using over 180 interviews with state legislators and their staff, I map the location and types of women's caucuses across the United States. State-level variables such as party control, proportion of women in the legislature, and professionalism do not adequately explain why women organize where they do. Case studies provide the best vehicle for exploring the motivations of caucus creators and participants. Similarly, I use data from my interviews to understand why women created the types of organizations they did across the states and why women in some states do not organize around their gender at all.

Women create organizations on the basis of a shared gender identity in order to achieve both personal and collective goals. They do this within legislatures that mask the effects of gender while incentivizing political party affinity over any other identity.[3] Understanding how and why women form state legislative caucuses offers insights into broad questions regarding gendered institutions, collective action, and political party governance. The norms of legislatures disadvantage women through practice and policy, simultaneously acting as catalyst and deterrent for the creation of women's caucuses. By considering these groups within an institutional context, I examine party reactions to legislators who attempt to identify around a characteristic other than party and document what strategies women choose in which contexts. I also uncover the challenges they face as they represent their constituents and develop professionally as individuals.

Women's caucuses are examples of collective action *within* institutions. As such, I argue that the components of collective action (opportunities, resources, and frames) available to legislators organizing women's caucuses are contingent on the legislative environment, and are often gendered. With women's caucuses at the center of the analysis and by employing a feminist institutional frame—which analyzes formal and informal processes that reflect, structure, and reinforce gendered patterns of power within institutions—I expand the current conception of organizing in legislatures and reveal previously perceived neutral processes as gendered (Kenny 2007).

Through case studies that examine four attempts—two successful and two unsuccessful—to create women's legislative caucuses in New Jersey, Colorado, Pennsylvania, and Iowa, I uncover the strategies that women legislators employ to both thrive within male-dominated legislatures and harness their collective power to influence the institution and its policies. I find that savvy entrepreneurs, specific institutional features such as Democratic Party control, existence of other caucuses, and low levels of partisanship facilitate successful women's organizing. These findings indicate that party and gender intersect to facilitate and constrain legislators' pursuit of political power and influence.

Within this investigation, I asked four central questions: (1) What are the specific opportunities, resources, and frames that women legislators use to create women's caucuses? (2) How and why do some women legislators choose a policy mission for their caucus rather than limiting their focus to a social network for members? (3) How do women legislators overcome the challenges to their collective identification as women within male-dominated and partisan institutions? (4) Why do some attempts at creating women's caucuses fail while others succeed?

As the first comprehensive analysis of women's caucus attempts in state legislatures, my work gives voice to women's experience within state legislatures. This book illuminates the daily interactions among officeholders that create and reinforce gender norms that limit all legislators' ability to serve their constituencies effectively. It is a comprehensive study of how political parties and gender shape legislative behavior, including women's organizing and men's reactions to it, and I offer remedies to the more negative aspects of increasing partisanship. Finally, my analysis can serve women legislators who are considering creating a caucus by offering them a list of potential assets to consider and obstacles to circumvent as they organize.

WOMEN'S CAUCUSES AS WOMEN'S POLITICAL HISTORY

The first women to serve as state legislators were three Republicans elected to the Colorado House of Representatives in 1894. Since then, thousands of women have served in state senates and houses in all fifty states. Their proportions in 2017 varied between a high of 40 percent in Arizona and Vermont to a low of 11.1 percent in Wyoming (CAWP 2017b). Questions about these women reflect the cultural expectations of gender norms and traditional inquiries of political science. While some studies ask, "Do women matter?" (Berkman and O'Connor 1993; Bratton 2002; Saint-Germain 1989; Swers 1998; Welch 1985), others ask, "When and how do they matter?" (Beckwith 2007; Holman 2014; Osborn 2002; Poggione 2004; Reingold 1996; C. Rosenthal 2000; Stanley and Blair 1991; Thomas 1991). As our understanding of gender as a concept has evolved, scholars have begun to ask how gender as a constitutive process, shaping our views of what it means to be a man or a woman, affects those who enter public office (Hawkesworth 2003; Kenney 1996; Sanbonmatsu 2006).[4] My analysis of women's attempts at collective action within legislatures exposes this process and illustrates the gendered nature of political parties and state legislatures.

Twenty-two women's caucuses existed at the state legislative level in the United States as of 2016. In my research, I have found them in every region of the country, in Republican-controlled and Democrat-controlled legislatures. They are present in states with average proportions of women legislators as well as in those at the high and low poles of the scale. They are found all over the map, with several in conservative southern states. Some caucuses are very formal with bylaws, officers, and dues, while others are less so. Most notably, their objectives vary, with some formulating policy agendas, others taking issues as they come, and others with no policy focus at all. Caucus activities are varied as well, with many taking part in distributing scholarships, hosting campaign trainings, or sponsoring events to commemorate women's contributions to their states' political history. The diversity of women's caucuses is reflective of their diverse political contexts. Women tailor their organizations to meet their states' specific needs and in response to the gender and partisan norms of their political environments. Those norms necessitate different priorities from other types of legislative caucuses, with a majority of women's caucuses declining to set legislative agendas. Their decisions to forgo policy in pursuit of other goals reflect that women's experiences within legislatures are distinct due to their gender, necessitating unique organizations. A cohort of legislators from rural or coastal areas of the state (who often form caucuses) does not have needs beyond policy in the way women legislators do. My analysis of caucus formation clarifies the legislative behavior of men and women and the elasticity of partisan and gender norms within political institutions.

Representative Julia McClune Emery of Connecticut founded the first known women's caucus, the Order of Women Legislators (OWL), in 1927. She would go on to form the National Order of Women Legislators (NOWL) in 1938 when President Franklin D. Roosevelt received over thirty women legislators for tea in Washington, D.C. The purpose of this national nonpartisan organization was to "promot[e] a spirit of helpfulness" among women members of state legislatures, acting as a "'clearing house for information,' and promoting the election of competent women to public office" (National Order of Women Legislators Records). These early pioneers set priorities that many women's caucuses still share today; the gendered nature of legislatures persists as women often remain marginalized from traditional information channels and elective office.

The Center for American Women and Politics (CAWP) began monitoring women's presence in public office in 1971. A year later, Senator Rosalie Abrams (D), Delegate Pauline Menes (D), and others formed the Women Legislators of Maryland, the oldest sustaining women's caucus, following the NOWL model, after abhorrent treatment by their male colleagues. Georgia Sorenson highlights the last straw as perceived by the women legislators of the day:

> The increasing presence of women in the Maryland legislature had begun to create some stresses and pressures. While their numbers and tenure had increased, women had been entirely shut out of key positions in both the Senate and the House. Delegate Pauline Menes pointed out this lack of representation when she criticized her party's leadership for its failure to appoint any women to the key standing committees in the House of Delegates. The Speaker of the House, Thomas Hunter Lowe, responded by appointing Delegate Menes "Chairman of the Ladies' Rest Room Committee." Delegate Menes recognized, however, that this obvious slight could be put to her advantage. She interpreted her appointment as committee chair as grounds for her attendance at the weekly leadership meetings held by the Speaker and President of the Senate. She was refused admittance because her presence would "make the men feel uncomfortable" and since there was "really no reason for the Chairman of the

Ladies' Rest Room Committee to attend anyway." (Sorenson 2000)

The WLM was formed in direct reaction to bias against women inside the institution. This excerpt highlights women's increased presence in the legislature, their exclusion from leadership and information flows, and male condescension as contributing to the development of a women's organization. In addition to their dissatisfaction with the status of women inside the institution and the lack of attention paid to issues they felt were of vital importance, the establishment of the black caucus in 1971 was also cited by the legislators as inspiration. It signaled to Menes and others that organizing around identity was legitimate.

The Massachusetts Caucus of Women Legislators (MCWL) was created in 1975 to pass the state's equal rights amendment. Legislators organized around this issue, and the state constitution was amended in 1976 to change the existing language of "all men are born free and equal" to "all people" are so created (Sainsbury-Wong, Wilson, and Vangeli 2011). In Massachusetts today, caucus leadership is decided alphabetically with leaders serving two years and the position moving to the next name alphabetically, regardless of seniority, with one chair from the House and one from the Senate. The caucus has several subcommittees that host informational meetings on issues, but there is no consensus agenda created at the beginning of the session. It has staff, creates a quarterly newsletter, and its members pay dues. The stated mission of the MCWL has been "to enhance the economic status and equality of women and to encourage and foster women in all levels of government" (MCWL 2018). This caucus was created to address women's issues within the legislature and continues to do so today without a formal agenda.

These caucus creation stories share elements with the cases I examine here. Bias against women was a useful frame in the case of Maryland in 1972 and in New Jersey in 2009.[5] While both caucuses in the 1970s were formed to be policy oriented, the caucuses of today find challenges associated with this purpose. Some organizers choose to postpone that goal in order to get a group off the ground, as in Colorado, while others push forward sometimes with success, as in New Jersey (however short-lived). Still others are not able to establish a group with policy as a goal as in Pennsylvania. In Iowa, even when the purpose was left up to the participants, leaving open the possibility for a social caucus only, one failed to materialize.

Partisanship has always been a challenge for women seeking to solidify their influence through bipartisan collective action. At a 1982 conference hosted by CAWP, women legislators from eighteen states convened to share best practices about caucus formation as well as other legislative and elective strategies. Carol Mueller (1984) reported that, among these conference attendees, women in fourteen states were actively meeting as a group, one state had already had a group that had faded out, and two additional states were in the early stages of organizing.

In Mueller's (1984) first accounting of women's caucuses, she quotes one Maine legislator as saying, "We're not a caucus-oriented state. We're a partisan state and we love our political parties" (160), juxtaposing women's caucuses and political parties. Within a partisan environment, women legislators must weigh the costs and benefits of bipartisan organizing. Boris Shor and Nolan McCarty (2011) find wide variation in polarization at the state legislative level. My analysis of bipartisan organizing across the fifty states contextualizes those findings and indicates potential deviations from the national trend of polarization.

DEFINING WOMEN'S ORGANIZING IN LEGISLATURES

Before I can anticipate which factors influence caucus creation or how caucuses might engage the legislative process, I must first define my terms. Clarifying which behaviors count as caucusing has been important in previous scholarship because these conceptual decisions narrow or expand our understanding of women's organizing. For my purposes, I define a women's caucus as a bipartisan, institutionalized association of legislators that seeks to improve women's lives.

For my purposes, a *bipartisan* association is open to members of any political party. Norms of legislative behavior suggest that party leaders reward loyalty and conformity within legislatures (Francis 1985; Hedlund 1984; Kanthak 2009). Women legislators who draw attention to their gender rather than their party by forming these groups are challenging the party system that traditionally governs the legislative process. I argue that organizations in which legislators prioritize gender over party are alternative mechanisms that challenge party control of legislative agendas and allegiances. In some rare cases, these caucuses may consist of legislators of only one party at some points in time. As long as the group is open to all, year-to-year membership may vary according to which women are in office at the time.

By *institutionalized,* I refer to a structure that enables the group to function and be recognized by other nonmembers as a group. While some organizations are very sophisticated with multiple leadership positions, formal bylaws, and regular meeting schedules, the minimum requirement for my criteria is an identifiable leader. A leader facilitates meetings and communicates information, which makes even the most basic activities of a group possible.

Seeking to improve women's lives is understood broadly, and includes efforts on behalf of women constituents through legislation or more informal mechanisms, as well as efforts to improve the lives of women legislators themselves. In setting this as a criterion, I am requiring that at least some of the activities of the group be focused on addressing issues of gender. It is common for women to create and be the majority of members of other caucuses, like Kids' Caucuses, for example, and while scholars should examine their proclivity toward these issues, this type of organization would not qualify as a women's caucus because the primary issue of concern is not women.

Because I allow for such broad purposes, I capture a variety of activities within my definition. Examples of legislation sought on behalf of women constituents might include women's health initiatives like funding for breast and cervical cancer screening (as in Hawaii). More informal examples include establishing a breastfeeding area in the capitol building (New York), or women legislators appearing as a group in the front row of the gallery to support victims of sexual violence who had experienced inappropriate questioning by male committee members during a formal hearing (Maryland). Some groups may hold legislative hearings, make bill endorsements, offer resolutions, or hold public events. Finally, efforts to improve the lives of women legislators could include advocating for more gender equity

in leadership positions and committee appointments (Massachusetts). Other possible purposes may be mentoring (other legislators
or women at large), candidate recruitment/training, granting scholarships, or socializing that boosts morale.

To be clear, within my definition, the absence of a caucus does not
mean that women in the state have no organizational ties. In many
states, women have important relationships, sometimes as roommates
or lunch mates. These social networks are important and play a role
in how women work together within legislatures. Caucuses, however,
are groups with some formality of structure and purpose, although
these structures may be varied and their purposes broadly defined.
I also acknowledge that individual women may work to improve the
lives of women and be successful. I am studying here the examples
in which women choose to join together consistently to undertake
these activities. I do not include official recognition by the legislature
as part of my criteria. States vary in whether or not formal filing for
legislative organizations is necessary. Many legislatures have no process by which the institution can confer official recognition. Caucuses
may be recognizable by legislators without official recognition by the
institution and therefore I do not consider it a criterion.

My definition of a women's caucus is more expansive than that in
previous scholarship on the subject. At the congressional level, caucuses are alternative organizing mechanisms to committees and parties
that prove important for legislation (Hammond 1998). The National
Conference of State Legislatures, which monitors women's organizing,
goes a step further and defines a formal women's caucus as one that
meets weekly or monthly during session, hires staff, is policy oriented,
and/or pays dues. Informal caucuses are primarily social in nature,
meet less regularly than formal caucuses, and do not necessarily have
a legislative agenda (Oliver 2005). While Susan Hammond (1998) requires policy interest, the National Conference of State Legislatures
(NCSL) differentiates between those caucuses that seek to influence
policy and those that are primarily social. My research in state legislatures has uncovered variations even between these two categories,
indicating that not all formally structured women's caucuses engage
in policy work, while some with very informal structures may do so.
Further, not all women's caucuses engage specifically in the creation of

public policy and none of them do it in the same ways. It is for these reasons that I have chosen to consider a broader range of purposes and structures in evaluating women's caucuses.

WHY CAUCUSES MATTER FOR LEGISLATURES AND LEGISLATORS

Caucuses are significant aspects of legislative life that deserve closer study. Congressional caucuses are important tools for voicing public concerns in Congress (Hammond 1998). Similarly, state legislative caucuses are alternative organizing mechanisms important to state policy agendas. They provide a space for legislators to create policy priorities apart from those that committees and parties determine. Consequently, relationships and skills created by caucus participation assist members in pursuing public policies regardless of whether those policies are caucus priorities. This benefit indicates that identity-based caucuses may improve legislative function by equipping their members with useful political skills that can be applied broadly beyond those issues of concern to the specific constituents of an identity caucus.

It is important to understand the potential benefits caucuses bring to both individual legislators and the legislative institution as a whole. Caucuses allow legislators to express certain identities, thereby signifying themselves as experts in certain legislative areas and advocates for certain constituencies. They help fellow members build relationships and gain information useful for accomplishing their goals. Caucuses also provide opportunities for leadership. Depending on the proportion of women in the majority party, the presence of a women's caucus may correlate to higher proportions of women in leadership positions, thus increasing their status within the institution, getting them closer to the reins of power themselves (Kanthak and Krause 2012).

Identity caucuses also have an important symbolic power to signal governmental legitimacy to their constituents and amplify the voice of marginalized citizens. For example, states with influential black caucuses tend to have higher black voter turnout, indicating a relationship between caucus presence and political behavior (Clark 2010). Across the states, black caucuses have included both public policy and community engagement as priorities (Sullivan and Winburn 2011).

Because of the historical exclusion of marginalized groups from political institutions, their establishment of caucuses has not only policy but also efficacy implications for their constituents. Identity caucuses can also, however, act as gatekeepers and define insiders and outsiders in ways that complicate collaboration and unity (Lemi 2017). Who is allowed to participate in these groups defines not only the organization but also individual members of the legislature and influences the racing and gendering of institutions.[6]

Women's caucuses are a gendered opportunity structure within legislatures that potentially increases the ability of women to act on behalf of their constituents (Reingold and Schneider 2001). Social movement scholars characterize opportunity structures as those that cause political decision makers to alter their views of different groups such that shifting opinions allow for movement strategies to be successful. Gendered political opportunities would be those that shift elite opinions about the proper roles for women (McCammon et al. 2001). Women's caucuses are a signal of "women's institutional strength" (Tolbert and Steuernagel 2001, 15) and can increase the number of women in leadership positions (Kanthak and Krause 2012). However, caucus participation also risks backlash from male colleagues and party leaders who hold positional and informal power. This book examines the context in which risk might be minimized for women legislators seeking to shift the gendered expectations of legislative institutions.

If the gendered or partisan nature of the legislature restricts women's ability to form such groups, women's ability to legislate and represent women may be constrained. As a constitutive process, gender operates within institutions in conjunction with other identity categories, such as race, to shape the legislative behavior available to members—legitimizing some political strategies (like caucusing) and eliminating others. Within my analysis, I investigate specifically the tension for women between their gender and party identities in the pursuit of their legislative goals by examining more closely women's relationship to each other and their political parties. State legislatures are following the national trend of heightened polarization, but this trend varies across the states (Shor and McCarty 2011). By examining the context in which women's bipartisan caucuses emerge, we can better understand both the effects of party polarization on women legislators and women legislators' potential influence on the polarization of the legislature itself. My evaluation of women legislators' decisions to organize or not tells us about not only about women's legislative behavior but also the institutional norms, both formal and informal, that men and women alike enforce and enact.

Attention to institutions illustrates the benefits women's organizing may bring to legislatures. Because political party is so important within legislative life, it is crucial to understand how women legislators integrate party identity with the other identities that they bring with them to the legislature and that are constituted therein. Bipartisan women's caucuses offer a unique opportunity to analyze how individuals manage intersectional political identities within partisan and gendered institutions. This analysis can help explain not only women's legislative behavior but also the ways institutions perpetuate both partisan and gender norms throughout time and place. In examining the stability of congressional norms, Barbara Hinckley (1971) described institutions in this way:

> Institutions, by definition, exist over time. They are human creations, existing through stable patterns of interaction among individuals and groups. Actions are defined, refined, and supported with the passage of time. They become regularized, routinized, stabilized. Expectations about who does what and who should do what are formed and influence subsequent actions, and so on. (7)

Hinckley's (1971) depiction explains how gendered norms are both enforced and perpetuated within legislatures, and can delay or discourage women from rocking the boat. At the same time, it offers hope that the creation of women's caucuses might disrupt those stable patterns and alter the inner workings of the institution.

Women's caucuses make three significant interventions to legislative institutions. First, by creating a legislative organization that signifies gender as politically salient, women legislators challenge the false gender neutrality of politics, which, as Iris Young (2000) explains, distorts political reality and therefore outcomes:

> Where some structural social groups have dominated political discussion and decision-making, these social perspectives have usually defined political priorities, the terms in which they have been discussed, and the account of social relations that frames the discussion. At the same time these perspectives are not experienced as only one way to look at issues, but rather often taken as neutral and universal. (144)

By centering women legislators' organizing behaviors, I make visible male dominance within these institutions that many consider androgynous. Observers may note this male advantage in the social norms of legislatures where men call out women for speaking in groups larger than pairs, where men exclude women from social gatherings where they actually make the deals, and through more formal processes where party leaders concentrate women legislators in less powerful committee appointments and exclude them from leadership positions. Examples of these practices are illustrated in the creation story of women's legislative caucuses and make legislatures legible as gendered institutions.

Second, the establishment of women's caucuses inside male-dominated legislative institutions can provide a safe space for marginalized legislators to support each other, as well as help develop and refine legislative initiatives. Many legislators' descriptions of caucuses mirror S. Laurel Weldon's (2004) subaltern public spheres "where marginalized groups are better able to organize and express themselves more freely" (5). Caucuses are a way to counteract institutional norms that may require women to play a man's game, adopt a particular political persona, or adhere to someone else's definition of appropriate political priorities. Under certain conditions, women's caucuses may be the site of transformation within institutions described by Mary Fainsod Katzenstein (1998) as "protected spaces or habitats where activists can meet, share experiences, receive affirmation, and strategize for change" (35).

Finally, as one type of organization within what Weldon (2004) calls the feminist civil society, women's caucuses may contribute to making "democratic policymaking processes more inclusive of women's voices and reflective of their perspectives by providing a forum for them into the broader public sphere. . . . [T]he development of feminist civil society greatly enriches feminist and democratic politics and should improve state responsiveness to women's concerns" (2). As conduits for advocacy organizations into the legislature, women's caucuses may contribute to better representation for many different constituencies. These potential interventions are significant and indicate the importance of these organizations beyond the adoption (or not) of women-friendly policy. By defining caucuses as policy-seeking only, we limit our ability to account for organizations' larger effect on institutions.

ANALYZING WOMEN'S ORGANIZING IN U.S. STATE LEGISLATURES

I seek to explain and ameliorate the marginalization of women within and by legislatures through feminist institutionalism, analyzing formal and informal processes that reflect, structure, and reinforce gendered patterns of power within institutions (Kenney 1996; Kenny 2007; Mackay, Kenny, and Chappell 2010). To do so, it is necessary to observe and document the processes by which this marginalization occurs and the potential opportunities for equalizing the gender power balance for more inclusive participation and more fair representation by and for women. Women not only are acted on within gendered legislatures, they also can play a role in the restructuring of those institutions and legislative behaviors by accentuating or downplaying their feminine identity. By caucusing around their gender, women are gendering the practices and norms of the legislature (Krook and Mackay 2011; Lovenduski 1998). This book investigates specifically those institutional aspects that facilitate or constrain women's creation of legislative caucuses, moving us toward a better understanding of the different ways women legislators practice gender in various local contexts.

Understanding how the strategic employment of gender happens in different institutional contexts is useful to political science because it can shed light on the importance of context in the outcomes of legislatures. Beyond the formal organization of legislatures, informal rules invoke systems that serve to produce and reproduce gender inequality. Women's caucuses may be one way to subvert this inequality, as Georgia Duerst-Lahti (2002) explains, "Based upon trust, loyalty, unspoken rules, and reciprocity, informal associations and processes often circumvent, even supersede, processes and practices of the formal organization" (382).

While all state legislatures are gendered institutions, I do not find that gender affinity is a tool that women legislators universally invoke or uniformly implement. Nor do I find that it is guaranteed to work in the same ways across different environments.[7] Similarly, understanding how and why women employ gender in their own legislative behaviors demonstrates the multiplicity of "women's interests" and enriches our understanding of women's representation.

To accomplish these goals, I conducted cases studies of all women legislators' attempts at caucus creation made between 2006 and 2010. During this time frame, four attempts occurred in New Jersey, Colorado, Pennsylvania, and Iowa. My case studies test hypotheses about women's caucus creation, employing personal interviews and analysis of media coverage when available. Case studies are the best way to determine the reasons why caucuses emerge in some environments and not in others because this investigation can take into account various contextual factors that contribute to or prohibit the development of a caucus. By taking a step beyond identifying and categorizing women's caucuses, I am able to hear in women's own words why they made the decisions they did, what obstacles they perceived and the strategies they chose to face them, and to what they attribute their success and failure. I also document the enforcement of gender and political party norms by women and men legislators in reaction to women's organizing, recognizing that gender is not something only women do or inhabit.

Identifying where women form caucuses and when they are successful is important for understanding when and where women identify collective action as a useful strategy for representation. Similarly, identifying those contexts in which collective action has been unsuccessful and detrimental to women's representation is also necessary to appreciate the quality of women's representation across the states. Social movement theorists consider political opportunity, mobilizing structures, and frames to be explanatory of collective action outside of institutions (McAdam, McCarthy, and Zald 1996). Evidence within the literature suggests that women legislators share many things that motivate them to act collectively and mobilize *within* legislatures. Generally, findings suggest that women share common issue interests, more moderate or liberal positions on existing policies, and legislate differently than their male counterparts (CAWP 2001; Dodson 1991; Thomas 1991; Thomas and Welch 1990). For example, CAWP (2001) reports that "within both parties, women are more likely than men to support more liberal or moderate positions on a variety of issues, including abortion, hate crimes, civil unions for gays and lesbians, and racial preferences in job hiring and school admissions" (8).

Studies regarding women's legislative style also indicate that organizing caucuses may be an extension of their approaches to work. Women demonstrate more inclusive behaviors, spend more time on constituent service, collaborate with others more, and are perceived by other legislators as opening up the political process by bringing in historically underserved groups and making political processes more public (CAWP 2001; Epstein and Powell 2005; C. Rosenthal 1997). On the basis of these commonalities, caucusing may be an extension of these legislative behaviors.

The fact that women's caucuses exist in some states but not in others may not be a function of opportunities, resources, and frames only. These factors' "effects are interactive" (McAdam, McCarthy, and Zald 1996, 8) and, as Lee Ann Banaszak (1996) explains, interpretation of these three factors by actors may explain different results for the same phenomenon. Caucuses may be unevenly distributed across the fifty states because women legislators have different perceptions of the political landscape of their legislature, their own gendered identity, and the political consequences of their gendered identity. While some women legislators may not wish to organize, others who do may perceive the political opportunities, resources, and frames available to them differently, explaining the variation in the success and failure of women's caucuses across states.

By examining the creation of women's caucuses we can better understand the partisan and gendered nature of state legislatures. I find that political party shapes the options and strategies available to women legislators. Previous work on women's substantive representation has found that Democratic and Republican women do not always share public policy priorities or positions, and my study corroborates that their decisions about how to legislate is also influenced by their party identification (Osborn 2012). This project also analyzes how men react to women's presence in the legislature and the role they think gender should play in politics. While women are still tokens in many state legislatures with their difference magnified, men's gender identity is rendered invisible, masking their disproportionate representation in the body in general and within leadership positions specifically.[8]

My analysis demonstrates the gendered nature of partisanship. Building on previous scholarship (Freeman 1986; Osborn 2012), this study documents the navigating women legislators do in order to balance their partisan and gendered identities within legislatures. Legislatures have established party as the premier political identity; however, many women legislators think gender is also important. Their experiences in the world and the legislature are heavily determined by their identity as women, which often relegates them to particular committees and excludes them from leadership positions. To leverage this identity, some women have sought to create gender specific spaces within legislatures. Often this is a consequence of the bias they experience, within not only the legislature but also their respective parties (for example, in New Jersey).

Gender plays an important role in legislative behavior, influencing the decisions legislators make and the judgments they make about their colleagues' behavior. A bipartisan organization that validates gender as a significant political identity disrupts the prioritization of political party within legislatures. I find that women's caucuses call attention to women's political contributions indirectly or directly (as in Colorado) making visible the androcentrism of the legislature and political party ideologies that pigeonhole women's interests as "special" interests. Caucuses also, however, reify women's difference, often with members reverting to the language of difference to justify their existence and narrow priorities. Women legislators draw stark comparisons between their own work ethic and that of their male colleagues who do not share the second shift as primary caregivers at home and who do not have to work as hard within the legislature to see results.

While women legislators create women's caucuses, they do so in reaction to or in conversation with men's behaviors and decision making. It was New Jersey's male partisans who ignored and discouraged women politically, enabling Senator Loretta Weinberg (D) to exploit their actions as a frame for organizing. It was male dominance of the agenda that motivated Representative Karen Middleton (D) in Colorado to rally women together. In Pennsylvania, however, it was women who scuttled the attempt at a caucus because it was women, feeling slighted by a newcomer and harboring bitter partisan resentments, who sabotaged the attempt there. The Democratic Party leadership, at least officially, supported efforts to organize subgroups, which inspired Representative Vanessa Lowery Brown, even though the informal rules enforced by men and women within that institution won out. In Iowa, party leaders on both sides, Democrat and Republican, have long discouraged the creation of alternative groups and even a very senior woman entrepreneur could not overcome her status as an outsider to get things off the ground. Again, informal rules were violated—not any formal ones.

If we are to understand how women represent women (or anyone else, for that matter) within legislatures, we must better understand the role women's caucuses play, why they take different forms across the states, and why some women do not organize around their gender identity at all. Identifying where and why women organize in legislatures can determine if such groups contribute to improved quality of life for women both inside and outside the institution.

OVERVIEW

Chapter 2 establishes the theoretical framework for the project, explaining gender as a process and behavior that legislators act out. I argue that the existing conceptions of caucuses are problematic for women who, due to gendered and partisan legislative norms, often create caucuses without an explicit policy focus or formal structure. In order to placate party leadership or convince tepid participants that the caucus is "safe," women legislators often prioritize networking among women, cataloguing women's history, or promoting other women (through scholarships, mentoring, and so on) as acceptable motivations to organize. By reconceptualizing and broadening what counts as a women's caucus, I offer a more accurate accounting of these groups across the country and suggest that policy impact may come from unexpected places. In particular, I demonstrate how partisan identification and gender identification present potential caucus entrepreneurs with a web of challenges that must be negotiated in order to successfully organize.

In Chapter 3, I report findings that reveal a number of types of women's caucuses previously unaccounted for across the fifty states. I present legislators' explanations of why they created the particular type of caucus within their state and offer evidence of why women in some states do not caucus. This diversity validates my claim that women's organizing is contextual, and demonstrates the dynamic nature of gender as practiced in state legislatures with varying levels partisanship. Descriptive statistics paint only a partial picture and miss the important dynamics of these factors as determinative of caucus creation. This discrepancy establishes a need for the four case studies.

In Chapter 4, I examine the New Jersey case and document the ups and downs of caucus creation, telling the story of seasoned entrepreneurs taking advantage of a political opportunity only to be thwarted by partisanship. While an influx of new women elected to office provided the impetus for senior women legislators to organize a caucus, party loyalty divided them later, threatening the survival of the group and illustrating the role political party plays in constraining women's collective action.

Chapter 5 consists of the Colorado case, where a motivated entrepreneur sought to take advantage of the large number of women in office by founding a women's caucus. With her eye on the long game, she and her fellow early adopters compromised their own expectations for policy impact by establishing a social caucus, which would have bipartisan participation and possibly outlive their New Jersey counterpart's endeavor. A savvy entrepreneur and the continuity provided by staff enabled the Colorado women legislators to avoid the pitfalls of partisanship, which nevertheless constrained the options available to them for legitimate caucus objectives.

In Chapter 6, I analyze the Pennsylvania case, in which a political novice in an unfriendly environment failed to launch a caucus. Her fellow women legislators did not perceive a women's caucus as important to them or their constituents. Senior women legislators in a highly polarized legislature sabotaged the caucus attempt due to both mistrust of women across the aisle and a desire to maintain their own status within the institution, demonstrating again the role political parties and institutional norms play in constraining women's organizing.

Chapter 7 focuses on Iowa, where, despite a history of women's caucuses in the state, an experienced former legislator lending her support, and the support of the Commission for the Status of Women, the legislators did not successfully launch a women's caucus. Even with external support, the women inside the institution, lacking any strong gender consciousness and facing the discouragement of party leaders, chose not to resurrect an all-women group.

In Chapter 8, I review where women's caucuses have emerged since 2010 and indicate that they adhere to the expectations laid out here. Finally, this chapter offers a discussion on the usefulness of caucuses for both the representatives and the represented. I conclude that because these groups can benefit both women legislators and their constituents, it is crucial that we appreciate their emergence within partisan and gendered institutions, acknowledging that they may defy our previous conception of legislative caucuses.

2

MANY PATHS TO YES

The Creation of Women's Caucuses

Gender has consequences within legislatures, though they may vary across contexts. By caucusing, women legislators are strategically signifying their gender in a particular way but to a variety of ends. Women legislators' gendered identity interacts with their partisan identity (among others) to inform the decisions they make about how to best improve their own professional lives as well as the lives of their constituents. To best evaluate the role women play in the policy process, we must acknowledge the influence of partisan and gendered institutions on their behaviors and those of their colleagues.

Women's caucuses are a visible gendered practice wherein legislators signify gender as politically salient not only for constituents but also for themselves within male-dominated institutions.[1] By creating these organizations, or even just attempting them, women legislators are calling attention to the masked role that gender often plays in organizing legislatures and public policy. These caucus attempts may qualify as the crucial acts Drude Dahlerup (1988) calls for to bring about a significant change for women within masculine institutions.[2] Even if they do not dramatically alter the legislature, "small changes within the state may have significant consequences for social change" (Banaszak 2010, 19). In this book, I argue that the opportunities, resources, and frames available to legislators organizing women's caucuses are contingent on the legislative environment and are often gendered. In this chapter, I recast our current conception of organizing in legislatures by applying a feminist institutional frame, revealing previously perceived neutral processes as gendered.

SITUATING CAUCUSES WITHIN LEGISLATIVE INSTITUTIONS

New institutionalism as a theoretical framework assumes that institutions affect individual behavior and to varying degrees allows for the possibility that individual behavior, history, and ideas shape those institutions as well (Peters 2012; Lowndes and Roberts 2013). Legislatures are formalized political organizations that can be evaluated as institutions. U.S. legislatures offer a comparative opportunity to evaluate the features that transmit particular political values and create informal rules that shape individual behavior. Formal rules shape legislative behavior by determining who can speak, when, and on which subjects. Informal rules, however, may also function to determine who *should* speak, when, and on which subjects. Both formal and informal rules influence when and how women's caucuses occur, with partisan and gendered norms at the top of the list.

Political party membership influences these formal and informal rules and is extremely important in determining the behavior of legislators. The political party holding the majority of seats determines the leadership of the whole body as well as committees, manages the procedures by which action is taken (or not), and in large part controls the legislative agenda through these mechanisms (A. Rosenthal 2009). The ability of the majority party to maintain this level of control depends on their ability to remain a cohesive group. Individual legislators run under a party label for election and are ideologically tied to these organizations. Across the United States, however, the meaning of that party label and the level of cohesion within them varies (Shor and McCarty 2011).

Due to the central role they play in legislatures, political parties play a central role in the creation of women's caucuses. When a legislator enters the office, others expect he or she to behave as a loyal party member, if not exclusively at least primarily. Party affiliation can determine committee assignments, seating arrangements on the floor, office location, and access to a range of formal and informal resources. Party leaders incentivize women legislators, just like their male counterparts, to act as partisans beyond even what their ideological preferences might demand as "partisanship is so natural within the modern representative legislature that the only relevant question for legislators, it seems, is *how to be partisan*" (Muirhead 2014, 174).

Gendered institutions are those in which an individual's sex and gender performance affect their experience within that institution (Kenney 1996). Further, that identity interacts with others, such as race or ethnicity, and regulates appropriate behavior. Institutions have gendered cultures that produce and reproduce gender (Lovenduski 1998). Scholars have documented the gendered nature of legislatures, including the performance of gender, during campaigns (Dittmar 2015) as well as once in office (Barrett 1997; Carroll 2002; CAWP 2001). Scholars have also examined the distinct intersection of race and gender, demonstrated bias against women of color, and provided evidence of unique representative practices (Fraga et al. 2008; Hawkesworth 2003; Reingold and Smith 2014). Public policy analysis has further discovered the reproduction of gender from welfare policy to foreign policy (Enloe 2014; Nelson 1990). Gendered institutions are spaces in which men and women interact, following codes of conduct that shape and reshape their gendered identities. These interactions influence women legislators' own consciousnesses and behaviors, including whether and how to caucus. As Paul J. DiMaggio and Walter W. Powell (1991) indicate, "Institutions do not just constrain options; they establish the very criteria by which people discover their preferences" (11).

Some evidence suggests women have shared political behaviors and policy interests. Women legislators feel an obligation to represent women, they open politics to previously marginalized groups, and they are more likely to focus on issue areas deemed of particular interest to women (CAWP 2001). Most women legislators belong to women's organizations and offer them entre to the legislative arena (Carroll 2003). They also share some unique demographic characteristics relative to men legislators, including being better educated, older, less likely to be attorneys, less likely to be married, and less likely to have young children (CAWP 2001). They also approach the job distinctly from men who are more likely to perceive it as a career than women (CAWP

2001). The differences suggest alternative paths to public office, which many scholars have investigated (Fox and Lawless 2004; Carroll and Sanbonmatsu 2013). These variances from men result in different experiences within the legislature that serve as catalysts for caucus creation.

Women's experience outside the legislature can unite them once inside it. Many legislators cite the second-shift responsibilities[3] as conflicting with their ability to do their job in the same way as men. They often reference their different life experience as wives and mothers as uniquely qualifying them for public office. These different gendered experiences have political consequences that carry over to women's role as legislators, sometimes uniting them across party lines. It is not only Democratic women who take on the second shift or only Republican women who face bias on the campaign trail. Gender differences—good and bad—draw women together despite the organizational rules regarding political party affinity primacy.

THE PARADOX OF POLITICAL PARTY IDENTITY FOR WOMEN

Women embody both gender and party identities as they represent their constituents' interests. Organizing legislatures around partisan identities poses inherent contradictions for legislators who hold multiple politically salient identities, including gender, race, class, ability, and sexuality. Collective action, whether around partisan or gender identity, is problematic because conflicting interests compromise the efficiency of the collective (Olson 1965). Women legislators' interests are multifaceted and often conflict with their partisan interests, particularly for Republican women legislators whose party has faced accusations of waging a war on women and who may be violating their party's particular norms related to identity politics (Dodson 2006; Epstein 2011; Freeman 1986). This pressure suggests that the costs for women who organize and participate in a women's caucus at the expense of partisan norms may be different for Democratic and Republican women. These differences are reflective of the different gender norms of each party.

Women's caucuses are unique opportunities to observe these inherent contradictions because they are the only examples of truly bipartisan, identity-based caucuses. Members of a black caucus are almost always Democrats and do not require their members to suspend even momentarily their partisan identity in order to acknowledge another (King-Meadows and Schaller 2006). The same is true for LGBT and Latino caucuses (California Latino Caucus 2016; California Lesbian, Gay, Bisexual, Transgender Caucus 2016; New York Black, Puerto Rican, Hispanic and Asian Legislative Caucus 2016).[4] It is possible that these types of identity caucuses may emerge in states with more partisan diversity among potential members—expanding the opportunity to explore the dynamic relationship between these identities and partisanship in the future. For now, as we understand the primacy of partisan identification within legislatures and appreciate the political significance of one's gendered identity, an interesting puzzle emerges—how do we expect women legislators to align? Under what conditions would women legislators violate the norms of partisan behavior to act collectively as women across party lines? And under what circumstances will they be successful?

Gender and party uniquely constrain women who seek to act collectively. Shared values are not a given among women (Sigel 1996). Partisanship divides women, and the institution is designed for partisans (Osborn 2012). But we also see women working collectively during specific political eras or on specific issues, including the initial fight for the Equal Rights Amendment and, during the 1990s, on initiatives addressing inequality in health care for women. Appreciating both the push and pull women legislators face in seeking to leverage their power, what are the perfect conditions for a women's caucus?

CAUCUSES AS COLLECTIVE ACTION WITHIN INSTITUTIONS

While women's caucuses are not social movements, collective action theory can help to illustrate the conditions likely to produce such an organization within an institution. An examination of women's organizing within legislatures can benefit from social movement concepts that explain the conditions under which women may act collectively and deconstruct the barriers between women's activism inside and outside the state. Scholars have considered what feminist collective action looks like within the state and argue that artificially dividing feminists inside and outside the state obscures our ability to understand the hegemonic control of the state and the ability of activists to counteract it (Banaszak 2010; Katzenstein 1998).

In her analysis of feminism within institutions, Katzenstein (1998) argues that protest within institutions is not monolithic and that different feminist groups may have different goals and strategies as a consequence of their respective group perspectives and institutional norms. Obviously, not all women legislators are feminists and/or interested in protesting anything within legislatures. Similarly, women's caucuses may not be sites for protest within legislatures. In some cases they may be motivated to challenge the status quo, while in others they may be safe places for women to socialize with other women with no intention of rocking the boat of established norms and rules within the institution. However, Katzenstein's point helps to explain why women legislators, with seemingly much in common as a result of their gender, choose to form women's caucuses in some legislatures while in others they do not. Women's caucuses are probable sites of access for women's advocacy groups outside the institution, making them ripe for empirical study (Banaszak 2010). Further, legislators with ties to feminist organizations or women's organizations more generally are more likely to attend to women's policies, and women's caucuses would be an iteration of those memberships inside the state (Carroll 2003).

Political opportunity, mobilizing structures (resources), and frames make up the factors considered by social movement theorists to explain collective action (McAdam, McCarthy, and Zald 1996). I argue that the opportunities, resources, and frames available to women legislators who organize women's caucuses are contingent on the legislative environment and are often gendered. Political opportunities include specific instances that may have occurred in a legislature to motivate a caucus attempt at a particular time, including shifts in power dynamics between women legislators and their male colleagues. Other examples of political opportunities include differences in structures that may account for caucus attempt success or failure, like party control and polarization. In addition to these variables, I consider those specifically gendered opportunity structures that enhance women's power within the institution, such as the proportion of women in general and in leadership positions (Reingold and Schneider 2001). Resources include those provided by legislatures, including staff, office space, and material support, as well as resources from organizations outside of the legislature that have an interest in seeing women legislators create a caucus. Finally, frames are the shared beliefs of participants in a movement that hold organizations together and serve to recruit members.

Women's marginalization within male-dominated institutions often inspires them to organize, while it also constrains their ability to seize opportunities, marshal resources, and legitimize frames. Caucuses may be unevenly distributed across the fifty states because women legislators have different perceptions of the political landscape, their political party, their own gendered identity, the political consequences of their gendered identity, and how to get things done (Banaszak 2010). Collective identity also shapes the perceived strategies and tactics available to the group, while political context conditions the effectiveness of particular frames mobilized by activists seeking to influence political outcomes (McCammon et al. 2007; Polletta and Jasper 2001). These differences in collective identity and political context further explain why women in different states may enact different strategies for dealing with their gendered status within institutions. In particular, changes in gender relations defined by Joan Acker (1992) as "pervasive ordering of human activities, practices, and social structures in terms of differentiations between women and men" (567) can provide a gendered opportunity—an opening for women activists to successfully push for change (McCammon et al. 2001).

Caucus entrepreneurs respond to the political opportunities presented, marshal the appropriate resources, and select the appropriate frames to recruit participants and hold back opposition. Like policy entrepreneurs who champion a cause and bring legitimacy, connections, and persistence to an issue, successful caucus entrepreneurs also require these skills (Kingdon 2003). Skillful caucus entrepreneurs take advantage of political opportunities to marshal the right resources and messages that resonate with their colleagues.

To be successful, a caucus needs a savvy champion—one who knows when to rock the boat or when to use unobtrusive mobilization.[5] Caucuses may take different forms and may appear in some states but not in others because of women legislators' varying levels of comfort with making the move from unobtrusive mobilization to protest. In some states, even a social caucus may draw too much attention and risk forcing women legislators to "negotiate the often hazardous terrain where influence and access are traded against independence and critical distance" (Katzenstein 1998, 9). Although contested, critical mass is the theory that a certain threshold of women within an institution may affect substantive change (Dahlerup 2006). This theory is the subject of much debate within political science but as Katzenstein (1998) so concisely asserts, "Presence is not voice" (6) and many scholars caution that rules and processes constrain the objectives and actions of women within male-dominated institutions. Electing a woman is not the same thing as electing a feminist (Childs and Krook 2009). Current scholarship points us beyond what biological women do to consider critical actors (men or women) "who initiate policy proposals on their own and/or embolden others to take steps to promote policies for women, regardless of the numbers of female representatives" (Childs and Krook 2009, 138). Caucus entrepreneurs may be critical actors, but they may also time their attempts according to their perceptions of women's critical mass.

Being a critical actor and initiating a women's caucus carries with it risks for women legislators marginalized within masculine institutions. By drawing attention to women's place in the legislature and public policy, caucus entrepreneurs denaturalize masculine political norms. Rather than fitting in, these women intentionally stand out, in institutions that prioritize party identity above all others. Further, caucusing risks alienating men who are disproportionately in positions of power within the legislature, placing women's caucus entrepreneurs in a precarious position because "if one curtails risk-taking behavior because doing so renders one less trustworthy, the chances of being seen as a leader also diminish. Leaders must take risks and get out in front of followers, and followers must want to follow" (Duerst-Lahti 2002, 382).

Caucus entrepreneurs as the critical actors behind changing the gendered dynamics of legislatures must be deft politicians, reading both their environment and their colleagues astutely as "what constitutes nonnormative behavior, disrupts existing understandings, and challenges established roles is context specific" (Katzenstein 1998, 8). Like policy entrepreneurs who bear the cost of time, energy, and

risk to their reputations in pursuit of legislative goals, caucus entrepreneurs and their decisions are crucial to the success or failure of
women's organizing in legislatures (Kingdon 2003). My findings indicate that caucus launches are successful, not just because of a seren-
dipitous arrangement of political opportunities but rather because of
the actions of capable leaders who recognize the right opportunities,
use resources creatively, and frame the justifications appropriately for
their potential allies and opposition.

WHAT CHALLENGES DO WOMEN FACE IN ORGANIZING?

Formal and informal rules govern the legislative behavior of all representatives. Formal rules, which afford authority to those with positional
power, organize who manages committee hearings and who refers bills
where. Informal rules wherein party leaders set strategy for who will
be the face of particular bills determine who gets credit and sometimes
who gets blamed for legislative success or failure. Gender role expectations—like those requiring women to be likable and collegial while
preventing them from being aggressive or independent—influence
both men and women's legislative behavior. Establishing a women's
caucus may be more likely and advantageous in political environments
that have lower partisan expectations and are more accepting of women
occupying a political role in the first place. Violating these norms and
adopting partisan loyalty above all else may result in negative consequences for women when being likable and collegial is contradictory
with their legislative responsibilities. This dichotomy is particularly relevant in environments that allow less leeway for political women and
adhere to strict partisanship. Men, who hold most positional leadership
positions within parties and legislatures, reward and punish women
legislators who violate either gender role or partisan expectations.

The establishment of a women's caucus, then, is fraught with risk
because of the violation of partisan expectations that place party not
gender as the prime political identity within legislatures. If party leaders
keep women out of power, and women attribute this to their gender,
they may seek alternative mechanisms for increasing their power (desir-
ing, as all representatives do, career advancement, power, and policy),

which a women's caucus may offer. However, depending on how strong those party leaders are, women vary in how they establish these groups. In states where party leaders incorporate women into the power structure or where women do not meet a threshold number, women may choose to play by the formal or informal rules. In states where playing by the rules does not get you anywhere and women meet a threshold, they may seek to organize. How they do so is also a function of the strength of party leaders and ties. Where women are ideologically divided beyond reach, they may create a social caucus. Even if they can agree on policy, they may face strong party leaders, in which case they may choose the path of less resistance and form a social caucus. Meanwhile, where party leaders are weak or ideological differences small, they may decide to work openly together to achieve shared policy goals.

Forming a caucus is risky for all women legislators who may be tagged as disloyal. However, there is a particular risk for Republican women. Even by acknowledging gender as a salient political identity, Republican women are already in violation of their party's ideology. It is particularly dangerous for them to align with Democratic women, indicating the complicated dynamic between party and gender. In relatively low partisan environments, there is virtually no risk to Democratic women, while Republican women still have a hurdle to jump. There must be a sufficient number of women within the institution in order to have a caucus in the first place. And while the number of women in state legislatures has plateaued, this stagnation puts into relief the challenge of establishing women's caucuses in places where women's numbers are not improving.

Women's marginalization within legislatures both motivates and inhibits their ability to organize. Their shared experience of bias on the campaign trail or exclusion from the levers of power once in office can unite them. Similarly, the stress of holding office while doing a disproportionate share of household work is a common thread for women legislators. Under certain conditions, a caucus may be a solution to these shared challenges.

These disadvantages are specifically gendered while also conditioned by other identity factors, such as race or sexual orientation, and complicated by women's party affiliation. Both the dynamics of and challenges to women's caucus organizing are not wholly distinct from legislative organizing by other identities, such as race or sexuality. Non-white men and women legislators also confront institutional biases and imbalances of power, but these challenges are unique to their identities and may manifest differently in their behavior and organizing than do the gendered challenges that emerged from my research. Partisan effects also vary by identity groups. For example, black legislators and those who identify as LGBT are largely concentrated within the Democratic Party, reducing this important barrier to collective action around these identity markers. On the other hand, Latinx and Asian American legislators, whose identification may be more cross-party, as their numbers increase the facilitation of caucusing within legislatures, may find, like women, that partisan affiliation inhibits collective action. Women of color come to organizing along gender lines, with distinctive intersectional challenges (and motivations) that may further complicate the choices available to them in creating alliances with black male legislators in black caucuses or with white women (or other women of color) in women's caucuses. It is also possible that as parties shift, even black or LGBT legislators may face the same partisan challenges that women legislators currently face in organizing.

Broadly speaking, legislators who find themselves marginalized by their policy preferences or political ideology may also be motivated to caucus. Pooling their resources and delegating tasks would be to their advantage as it would for a women's caucus. They would also face some of the general challenges of collective action, like obtaining resources and recruiting members. They would not, however, face the additional hurdles created by the racing and gendering of legislative institutions. For example, the pressures to conform are high for legislators who do not exhibit white, male identities (Beckwith 2007; Hawkesworth 2003). Singling out themselves as a special group may be strategically disadvantageous in particular circumstances, but majority-identity members, may have more room to take the risk outside of traditional party or committee organization. Their descriptive identity lends their claims legitimacy rather than serving as further evidence for their deviance.

The prevailing norm of partisanship limits women's options to improve their gendered disadvantage. In the case of Republicans, the prevailing message is to deny the political salience of gender. The political futures of Democratic or Republican women who see gender as salient are tied to their role as loyal partisans, not necessarily as collegial bipartisan advocates for women. For some women, in some contexts, caucusing appears to be a lose-lose proposition.

When is forming a caucus a more attractive option? In heavily Democratic states where women are seen as a vital and powerful constituency, party leaders may not discourage their organizing because of the increased capital women in those environments hold and because the expected goals of such a group would not be threatening. Alternatively, party leaders may not see women's organizing under particularly harsh environments (those in which women hold low status, very conservative legislatures, and the like) as potentially threatening. Depending on the perceptions of the party leadership, it may be less costly for them to ignore women legislators interested in organizing a group that promises little threat to the overall agenda. Finally, even under hostile conditions where party leaders or male colleagues are very opposed to women's organizing, trusted savvy caucus entrepreneurs may be able to capitalize on women's feeling of marginalization and launch a caucus—even with opposition—if they are trusted by women of both parties and frame their attempt appropriately to resist opposition.

Scholars of collective action have considered the costs to organizing (Olson 1965; Katzenstein 1998). On top of the typical costs of time and resources, legislatures have unique sets of obstacles, including partisanship and leadership (whose interest is in party organizing to the exclusion of other affiliations). Some legislatures may also have lower levels of trust and lower levels of gender consciousness among legislators. Finally, some have preexisting norms about organizing any caucus that may lay the groundwork (or not) for women to organize.

In addition to costs that would face any legislative caucus, women legislators face additional gendered costs, including their historical political marginalization, their disproportionate household responsibilities, and a narrower repertoire of acceptable political behavior. To overcome these is not impossible, as I show in the following chapters, but it begs the question of how women ever create caucuses. Because the institution of the legislature is already established as partisan, the rules of the game are already set. Legislators are expected to caucus with their party, so there would have to be compelling reasons to violate the crucial formal and informal rules or very low barriers to entry or, most likely, both.

State legislatures are also raced institutions, and organizational norms that may constrain legislators of color from achieving influence within the institution may also have consequences for women's ability to act collectively. Mary Hawkesworth's (2003) theory of racing-gendering institutions posits that political processes particularly marginalize women of color. She describes the practices of racing-gendering when she states, "Through tactics such as silencing, stereotyping, enforced invisibility, exclusion, marginalization, challenges to epistemic authority, refusals to hear, legislative topic extinctions, and pendejo [stupid] games, Congresswomen of color are constituted as 'other'" (596). This differing experience for women of color means their perspective may not align with that of white women legislators.

Generally speaking, racial divides among women have been a challenge for the women's movement (Simons 1979; Anthias and Yuval-Davis 1983; Breines 2006). More specifically, Edith Barrett (1997) finds that within legislatures "white women see women as less able to accomplish their legislative tasks, either because of personal attributes or because of barriers to access" (138). Interestingly, black women do not share these feelings of inadequacy, but do agree with white women that they must work harder to prove themselves and juggle a complicated agenda that speaks to their broad constituencies and to specialized groups of women and minorities (140). These feelings indicate that women of color may be more interested in creating and participating in caucuses because of their more optimistic perspective on the likelihood of their success. They also may have the experience and skills gained from participation in black or Latino caucuses that would position them well as organizers of women's caucuses. The relationship between racial diversity and women's organizing is not a simple one, however.

The easiest opportunities for caucus entrepreneurs would be in low-cost environments where low levels of partisanship do not divide potential women participants or motivate party leadership to clamp down on alternative organizing. Successful framing may go a long way to ensure this by presenting the potential groups as nonthreatening. Preexisting trust and gender consciousness among legislators are the foundations for any potential organizing. And if other bipartisan caucuses are already present in a legislature—legitimizing these alternative organizations—it can take the wind out of the sail of any potential opposition. Further, women of color may provide a strong base of support for women's organizing.

HOW CAN THESE CHALLENGES BE OVERCOME?

Entrepreneurs who properly read informal and formal rules are crucial to the creation of a women's caucus. Those legislators who are able to identify which rules they must follow and which ones they can violate, and under what circumstances, are able to innovate without alienating critical audiences like women from other parties, more senior women, party leaders (men or women), or male colleagues. By accurately reading norms, caucus entrepreneurs can determine which frames are most likely to be successful in their legislature.

Relatedly, caucus entrepreneurs need to have their colleagues perceive them as legitimate leaders. They may be newcomers or more senior, but their colleagues must view them as people who are capable of corralling disparate groups of legislators, who are not out for personal credit only (politicians are willing to allow for personal gain to be a part of the story but not the entire one), and who will not put others at political risk. Successful entrepreneurs respond appropriately to the level of partisanship of their legislature. They must determine how much to ask of Republican women—are they for social camaraderie only, or can they be pushed on policy? They must also determine how much to realistically require Democratic women to forgo—time and capital are not limitless and to dedicate either to a women's caucus must have tangible rewards for Democratic partners. Those rewards do not have to be policy achievements, but if they are not, caucuses must provide some other carrot.

Caucus entrepreneurs must be able to get key leaders (both formal and informal, men and women) to approve, participate, or at least tacitly approve (or ignore) the caucus. This task requires proper framing for multiple audiences that include constituents and advocates. Caucus entrepreneurs must sell the caucus to potential participants by highlighting proposed priorities that resonate for women legislators in that state. If there is a shared sense of grievance against party leadership among women, this marginalization may be a unifying theme; however, if women do not feel marginalized, playing to their shared life experiences as women may be more successful. Participants want to know that their time and reputations are being spent wisely and do not pursue projects that do not fill a specific need. Similarly, party leaders at least need to be neutralized so that they do not discourage their members from participating. This mission can be accomplished again through framing. Caucus entrepreneurs can demonstrate respect by giving leaders a heads-up about their plans or can try to fly under the radar depending on the expected reaction. They may sell the caucus to leadership as nonthreatening and highlight the more benign benefits of a caucus, like social capital, rather than drawing attention to potential policy interventions.

Caucus entrepreneurs must also take advantage of opportunities. Just as in any collective action, women's caucus attempts in the following cases exploited grievances that women had against their male colleagues and party leaders and the enthusiasm of newly elected women. These attempts were most successful when the appropriate frame was matched to the political climate and when the entrepreneurs were perceived as legitimate leaders.

GENDERING THE STUDY OF LEGISLATIVE CAUCUSES

I argue that the partisan and gendered norms of the institution shape women legislators' decisions to caucus and subsequent strategies for organizing. This argument is situated within a feminist institutionalist framework that understands institutions like legislatures to be gendered and requires the application of gender as an analytic category to legislative practices and policies as a way to understand how political change does or does not occur (Krook and Mackay 2011). By offering women legislators a place to discuss their quality of life within the institution collectively, caucuses may facilitate the development of a feminist consciousness as well as a strategy for altering negative experiences that result from their gendered identity (Duerst-Lahti 2002).

It is within gendered legislatures that women legislators make the decision to signify their gender as politically salient or not. They do this (or not) through the issues they choose to prioritize, the framing of their political messages, the strategies and behaviors they enact, and, in some instances, through the formation of a women's caucus. Entrepreneurs decide to create a caucus (and colleagues to participate) within an institution that is, by default, gendered (Duerst-Lahti 2002; Kenney 1996). Men make up the majority of legislators, including state legislative leadership, and have built the processes and norms around their identities as breadwinners and fathers. Their role in public life is the norm, not something they fought for decades to achieve. They do not face the same double-binds as their women counterparts, who must balance competence with likability, ambition with humility (Eagly and Carli 2007; Jamieson 1995; Rhode 2016). It is likely then that the decision to draw attention to their gendered identity by creating a women's caucus is a careful calculation based in a context of specific gender rules and norms (Banaszak 2010). When and how women mark their gender in this way can help illustrate the diversity and elasticity of partisan and gender norms across the fifty U.S. state legislatures.

Women's gender identity influences the goals and structures of their organizing efforts within gendered political institutions. Political parties as the primary identity and the ideological organizers of legislators limit the legitimate frames available to women interested in acting collectively within legislatures. Institutional rules and norms also limit the permissible tactics of women legislators. Caucus entrepreneurs have to successfully navigate both political parties and institutional norms to create a women's caucus that may over time disrupt and expand what are legitimate tactics and frames for all legislators. By examining the creation of women's caucuses, I uncover the gendered nature of these constraints and lay the groundwork to better understand the behaviors of women legislators and the policies they produce or fail to produce. Beyond the traditional purpose of a caucus to directly influence the policy process, these organizations offer women a supportive environment—what Katzenstein calls "protected spaces"—from which to challenge the status quo, which has sometimes served to exclude women from full participation in the legislature (1998, 35). The remaining chapters of this book reflect this acknowledgment and investigate the creation of women's caucuses in the U.S. states.

3

FOR WOMEN, THERE IS NO
ONE WAY OR PLACE TO CAUCUS

L egislative conditions shape women legislators' decisions to organize around their gendered identity. Their unique experiences as women make it possible to conceive of an alternative
organization to traditional party institutions. Because the gender
and partisan expectations for women legislators are different in different legislative contexts, so are their decisions and strategies around
caucusing. Expanding the definition of caucuses to include organizations beyond those with a specific policy mission generates a much
richer picture of the legislative activity of women across the United
States.

INVESTIGATING WOMEN'S CAUCUSES

Most state legislatures do not formally recognize women's caucuses.
While some states have procedures for recognizing such groups, most
do not. As a result, when a group emerges, the institution does not
always record it in its proceedings or in any other archival holdings.
Similarly, because very few caucuses disband formally, no official record of their discontinuation is kept. As Hammond (1998) notes, the
fact that the organizations can fade in and out as necessary complicates the documentation of the life cycle of women's caucuses.

The first account of women's caucuses at the state level found that the main influences on the type of gender organizing in a state were fear of reactions by male colleagues, strength of partisanship, and existing divisions among women over such issues as the ERA and abortion (Mueller 1984). The analysis, however, was limited to the eighteen states that sent representatives to the conference, and no comprehensive study of women's caucuses has been undertaken since. CAWP began tracking the emergence of women's caucuses in 1986 in its newsletter, *CAWP News and Notes*. The center continued to do so intermittently until 1998, but no definitions or criteria for what constituted a caucus were established and the descriptions of the groups indicate wide variation in structure, priorities, and activities. The NCSL produced briefs on women's organizations in state legislatures in 2005, 2013, and 2017, which describe a wide range of organizations, including women's commissions and groups dedicated to women's state history. In 2005, the NCSL categorized women's caucuses into two groups—formal and informal (Oliver 2005). These early efforts to document women's organizing were crucial to my own investigation of women's caucuses, enabling me to pursue questions of origin, priorities, and process. Further, I sought to understand why some women chose to caucus and some did not. These questions required an original data collection.

In the fall of 2009, I began collecting data on the existence of women's caucuses within the fifty state legislatures. The result was 139 interviews: 39 personal interviews, including 34 at the NCSL's July 2010 Legislative Summit, and 100 telephone interviews. Questions were open-ended and included those directed at determining the type (if any) of organizing among women, as well as the motivations and challenges to organizing within the legislature. Six interviews are with women's caucus staff and three are with a legislator's personal staffer. Of the legislator interviews, ninety served in the lower chamber of the legislature, thirty-seven served in the upper chamber, and three served in the unicameral legislature of Nebraska (see Table 3.1). The partisan breakdown of legislator interviews is eighty-six Democrats, three Democratic Farmer Labor members, thirty-eight Republicans, and three nonpartisans, serving in Nebraska (see Table 3.2).[1] Through these interviews, I learned about the

TABLE 3.1. OCCUPATIONAL BREAKDOWN OF INTERVIEW SUBJECTS, 2011					
Lower chamber legislator*	Upper chamber legislator**	Unicameral legislator	Legislative staff	Caucus staff	Total
90	37	3	3	6	139

* Includes four former state representatives.
** Includes one former state senator.

TABLE 3.2. PARTISAN BREAKDOWN OF STATE LEGISLATOR INTERVIEW SUBJECTS, 2011				
Democrat*	Republican**	Democratic Farmer Labor	Nonpartisan	Total
86	38	3	3	130

* Includes four former state representatives.
** Includes one former state senator.

diversity of these groups in not only structure but also priorities and practices. While Hammond (1998) defined caucuses as policy-oriented groups and NCSL divided up women's groups on the basis of structure (Oliver 2005), my observations prompted a new approach that would capture the nuances of these organizations and acknowledge the wide range of strategies employed by women across state legislative cultures.

TYPOLOGY OF WOMEN'S CAUCUSES IN THE UNITED STATES

On the basis of my interview data, I categorized the states with women's caucuses into one of two groups, social and policy.

Social Caucuses

The first type of women's caucus is the *social caucus*. In these groups, women of all parties are invited to get together intermittently during the session, or outside of the session to be social or discuss politics. The social caucus has two major priorities. Women in these groups wish to build relationships with their fellow legislators. In some larger legislatures, women may not know any of the women in the other chamber or party. This type of group offers them an opportunity to get to know each other, which, as they report, assists them in pushing for their own individual legislation and helps them deal with the challenges they say are unique to women in the legislature. On some occasions, they may talk about how they manage their families and their jobs, or they may ask about how the other party has reacted to a bill they have put forth. This type of communication points to the second function of these groups: information sharing.

Information sharing may take a formal structure, such as having speakers or lobbyists address the group, or a more informal one, where the women tell each other about what they are working on and ask for advice. While information-sharing groups do not seek consensus or pressure members to vote together, they may have an indirect impact on policy despite their social priority. In particular, sharing within these groups may advantage minority party women, whose male counterparts may not have access to bipartisan collaboration. Further, the networks created within these groups may facilitate bill passage behind the scenes without the official adoption of any shared policy initiatives among participants. By not recognizing this function of social caucuses, scholars may miss opportunities to properly assess their impact.

Within a social caucus leaders are generally more senior legislators who are chosen by other women legislators or self-selected because of a particular commitment to developing and maintaining a caucus. They often hold the position for longer periods of time and do not necessarily stand for election by caucus members. Caucuses of this type may or may not have staff. Such a structure is not inherent to the type and is not a criterion for categorization. These groups do not take issue positions, which is their defining characteristic.

The Colorado Women's Legislative Caucus is an example of this type of group. It has four leaders, two from each house and party, a paid staff person, and funds that are administered by a local university. It is a highly institutionalized social caucus and has several meetings throughout the session. Many of these meetings are for planning events that recognize women's contributions to the state. They also host a website dedicated to the history of women in politics in Colorado. Because they are open to women of all parties, have an identifiable leadership, and undertake activities to support women, this state meets the criteria for a caucus, despite their mutual decision not to take formal policy positions.[2]

The most common explanation women offer for organizing a social caucus (as opposed to one that creates an agenda or takes policy positions) is that women in their state do not agree on issues and therefore a caucus with this mission would be unsuccessful. The second-most cited explanation is that women want a group that brings attention to women in the legislature and acknowledges their political contributions to the state, suggesting that a legislative purpose may be irrelevant to these legislators, or at least not a primary motivating frame. The desire for such attention is the consequence of a gendered legislature in which women are newcomers and often not considered a legitimate part of a state's political fabric. This type of activity differentiates identity caucuses from other types that do not share historical exclusion from government. By celebrating women's contributions, these caucuses highlight their structural disadvantage at the same time they redress it.

Policy Caucuses

The second type of women's caucus is the *policy caucus.* These groups are identified as such because they address specific legislation within a session. Like social caucuses, policy caucuses have elected leaders or those who traditionally take the lead to organize events. Within these caucuses, leadership structures are usually, but not always, more complicated, with some women holding specific official positions within the caucus. In some states, there are two to four cochairs, or chairs and vice chairs often including women from each party and chamber. Members usually elect leaders at the beginning of new sessions. Again, similar to social caucuses, policy groups may or may not have staff. However, the complexity of the leadership structure or the existence of staff is not what differentiates these groups from social caucuses. The difference is that these groups *do* take formal policy positions. Women's policy caucuses vary both in their approach to affect policy

TABLE 3.3. TYPES OF WOMEN'S CAUCUSES	
Caucus type	Activities on behalf of women
No gender organization	Individual, sporadic efforts may be made but are not organized by a leader.
Social	A group of women participate in mentoring, recruiting and training candidates, granting scholarships, socializing, advocating for more gender equity in leadership positions and committee appointments, public events, and informational meetings with lobbyists or women's organizations organized by one or more leaders.
Policy	A group of women participate in legislative hearings, bill endorsements, resolutions, public events, mentoring, recruiting and training candidates, granting scholarships, socializing, advocating for more gender equity in leadership positions and committee appointments, and informational meetings with lobbyists or women's organizations organized by one or more leaders.
Agenda setting	A group of women agree on a legislative agenda presented to legislative leadership or published more broadly at the beginning of a session organized by one or more leaders.
Ad hoc	A group of women take positions as issues that they agree on emerge and seek to influence, organized by one or more leaders, but there is no legislative agenda for the session. *Gender Open* Membership is open to both male and female legislators.

and whether or not they are gender exclusive. These categories may prove important in measuring the effectiveness of women's caucuses to influence legislative policy. Because some strategies may prove more effective than others, I divide policy caucuses as a category into two subgroups: *agenda setting* and *ad hoc.* For a complete listing of types of women's caucuses and their primary activities, see Table 3.3.

In what I call *agenda-setting caucuses,* women get together during or outside of the session to agree on the legislative agenda to present to legislative leadership or publish more broadly. Hawaii is an example of a state with a women's caucus with a legislative agenda. Their 2017 package consisted of twenty-three bills, including a bill for paid leave, a bill regarding the composition of police commissions (requiring that members have expertise on women's equality), and a bill requiring complaint and inspection reporting by child-care facilities (Hawaii Senate Majority Office 2017). This type of women's caucus most closely resembles the CCWI at the federal level when it was at its strongest.

Women's agenda-setting caucuses most closely emulate party caucuses in their creation of a legislative agenda prior to the session. By making their agendas public, legislators are able to demonstrate their commitment to the constituents affected by the policies they prioritize in these agendas, which also plays a role in constructing gender in the legislature. Setting the "women's caucus agenda" signals the political priorities of "women," thus deeming some policies appropriate or legitimate and leaving others out. How these agendas are created is an important area for scholars to consider, because the women legislators who are deciding this collective agenda are shaped by other identities, such as race, class, and sexual orientation. Their strategy may also be in concert with other legislative caucuses, such as the black, Hispanic, or LGBT caucuses, and so further investigation into how these groups interact is warranted. Such an analysis should center on women of color who are participants in multiple—and possibly contradicting—organizations. Agenda-setting caucuses are typically present in very Democratic legislatures. California, Hawaii, Maryland, and New York all have Democratic majorities in the lower chamber of 60 percent or more (NCSL 2017). In these legislatures, women were more likely to agree on issues enabling the development of a policy agenda. Similarly, three of these five states have high levels of professionalism, where formality in the formation of policy agendas would be common (Squire 2007).

Ad hoc caucuses take positions as the issues emerge, but there is no legislative agenda for the session. Florida is an example of an ad-hoc caucus state. The women legislators there may decide to formulate a position after an issue has arisen in the legislature. For instance, they may decide to add amendments to a piece of legislation already in progress, or they may decide mid-session to put forward their own bill. Often the legislation they try to influence is related to women's health. Women's health is a common issue for most women's caucuses that choose to deal with policy.[3]

Women in states with ad hoc caucuses explained that, as with social caucuses, women in their state were unlikely to agree on issues enough to warrant an agenda-setting caucus but that they wanted social ties to other women. Women in many of these states appreciated an alternative to other social events of the legislature, which often involved alcohol, which made them uncomfortable.[4] Women cite a lack of time as an obstacle to a more formal approach to issues, such as having a set legislative agenda, indicating that access to a resource like time shapes the type of organizing women legislators do. The case studies discussed in the following chapters include deeper discussions of time pressures on women legislators.

Within ad hoc caucuses, I discovered three *gender-open* caucuses, which focused on improving the lives of women but that allowed male legislators to join. The three gender-open caucuses identified through my research act as ad hoc caucuses and do not have set agendas, but they prefer to respond to issues as they emerge. It is possible that at another point in time, a gender-open caucus could change its strategy for improving the lives of women and become a subgroup of an agenda-setting or social caucus type.

In two states, these caucuses usually focus on women's health issues. Oregon has a Women's Health and Wellness Alliance, which includes both men and women legislators. The Texas House Women's Health Caucus is also open to legislators of both genders. Vermont's organization allows male participation, but its issue scope goes beyond women's health and has addressed military families and women in prisons.

While men are included in these groups, they do not elect leadership, serve as leaders, or set the priorities of the group. While no male participants of these groups are included in my subject pool, women legislators and staff who were tell me that men join to show their support for their women colleagues and the issues important to them and their constituents. Unlike in other places in the legislature, in these groups men tend to "hang back," according to one woman legislator. They do, however, pay dues to those groups that collect them. Their membership demonstrates the legitimacy of and expectation of men advocating for women, while their behavior within the group disrupts traditional, gendered legislative behavior. In this way, these caucuses and their male participants are reshaping the gender norms of the institutions. The women legislators in Oregon and Vermont explained that because there are so many women in the legislature, a gender-exclusive group was unnecessary.[5]

While women's social and policy caucuses may differ in their approaches to influencing legislation, both commonly recognize outstanding women in their states. Most caucuses hold an annual event honoring current women public servants or community activists or have an event that acknowledges the historical contributions of women. In some instances, women's caucuses provide merit scholarships to women or girls. These events act as reminders of the role women play in politics and the community. They remind legislators and the public of the right of women to be in public life. Participants describe them as "morale boosters." These activities may also indirectly impact policy and are deserving of further study.

Policy caucuses have a more direct impact on legislation. However, in recent years, their actions on specific legislation, have been more defensive than offensive. In previous years, these groups might have fought for the ERA (as in Massachusetts) or reform of sexual violence laws (Maryland), while today's women's caucuses are a line of defense against budget cuts that would disproportionately affect women and children. State budgets are in crisis, and women legislators feel responsible for protecting vulnerable populations. They do this by trying to reduce or block cuts to state welfare programs, child-care programs, and public health programs, for example.

I consider states that do not meet the criteria of identifiable leadership and activities to improve the lives of women as having no gender organization. Women in these states may get together informally throughout the session. In some cases, women lobbyists may organize annual events. For example, in Utah, in 2011, women legislators reported having a luncheon once a year. Democratic women usually spearheaded this effort, but they invited all women legislators in both houses. The women "felt it was important to get to know one another outside of the legislative or campaign sense."[6] One year, a Republican male legislator, who was disappointed to learn he was not allowed to attend, offered to pay for the lunch, despite his exclusion from it. This anecdote illustrates the novelty of a legislative space, created by a women's caucus, that excludes men, and it demonstrates one type of reaction to this exclusion. Was the offer to pay for lunch a genuine act of kindness or a gentle reminder of some women's historical dependence on men economically—a way for him to reassert traditional gender roles? In Utah, in 2011, no identifiable legislative leader organized this event or the women in this legislature more generally; therefore, it did not meet my criteria of a caucus. In 2016, however, this group formalized, demonstrating the fluidity of organizing within the states.

WHY SOME WOMEN LEGISLATORS DO NOT CAUCUS

In order to explain why women do not organize women's caucuses, I examined the interview data for explanations that pertained to political opportunities, resources, and frames. In some instances, women were satisfied with their experience in the legislature and their ability to enact their personal agendas without the need for a caucus. An example of this type of comment came from a legislator in Washington, who said, "When you have so much equality you don't want to rub it in, you need to be more inclusive—there is a progressive caucus that is women and men."[7]

Other positive explanations for the lack of a women's caucus were that women were in the legislative leadership already, and already worked together in a bipartisan fashion or had good personal relationships, making the need for any type of organization unnecessary. In 2011, Democratic women in Alabama, Montana, and Michigan organized as women within their party and felt this met their needs for gendered organization.[8] Women legislators may perceive caucuses as unnecessary when they do not feel excluded from leadership positions and do not desire more opportunities for social networking. In some states, women's groups outside the legislature provide resources to women inside the institution that enable the success of a caucus attempt, while in other noncaucus states, outside organizations, such as the Order of Women Legislators or Emerge America, serve the same purposes as a caucus and, according to those women, an internal organization like a caucus was redundant.[9]

Other explanations suggest that women may want a caucus but that there are forces, some from among women legislators and others from their colleagues or the institution of the legislature, that limit their choices. My evidence points to the constraint placed on women's ability to organize by political parties. Women in noncaucus states cite ideological differences on issues or a lack of interest among women as explanations for the lack of a gender organization. For example, a legislator in New Hampshire argued, "Just because you are women doesn't mean you have common values."[10] Democratic women often perceived Republican women in their state as unwilling or unable to participate. In some cases, Democrats cited ideological differences as holding Republican women back, but in others they perceived their counterparts as pressured by Republican leadership to not associate with them. For their part, Republican women did not acknowledge this pressure. In some instances, Republican women indicated that gender was not a relevant political category and therefore they were disinclined to participate in any such group.

The most common explanation for the lack of a caucus was a lack of interest among women. In these cases, gender was not politically salient for enough women to make a caucus work. This lack of gender consciousness, in most cases, reflected a difference of party, as Republican women were more likely to say they were not interested in organizing and Democratic women were most likely to be interested in creating a women's caucus (and likely to perceive Republican women as not interested). Party differences among women were the most often mentioned obstacles to women's organizing. Women's own choices not to caucus because of their lack of interest, initiative, or ideological differences are more common explanations than external opposition. Opposition by leadership or male colleagues was the least cited category of explanation. This absence may be because women are reluctant to report opposition or that it would influence their decisions or because it is an accurate assessment. Without more corroboration from women, it is difficult to parse out if Republican women are reluctant to participate because of their own objections or because of pressure from party leaders (which Democratic women perceive).

Women legislators in seven states expected that men in general or in leadership specifically would oppose an effort to organize a women's caucus. The states where women reported this expected opposition include South Dakota, North Dakota, Maine, and Kansas. In Delaware, Mississippi, and New Mexico, legislators reported a concern over male reactions in general. In Delaware, for example, one legislator said, "Women want to prove to men that they aren't radicals, queen bees."[11] In many states, regardless of caucus status, women reported that men were suspicious of any collegiality among women across party lines and intimidated by any social interactions, such as casual lunches or dinners, among women legislators. Most women characterize this treatment as light teasing and usually indicate that it does not bother them. It remains, however, that men who congregate on the floor together go unnoticed, while women regularly perceive men as closely monitoring their behavior. This gendered policing of behavior within legislatures is both a motivation and obstacle to caucusing. Women are reluctant to report that male colleagues are able to influence their legislative decisions and behaviors, however, and this reluctance is a challenge of this study. When are women free to choose not to caucus, and when does opposition exist they are unwilling to acknowledge?

Institutional barriers to women caucusing exist as well, including an absence of favorable political opportunities, such as a lack of a caucus culture in their state, too few women or lack of longevity of service in office, the lack of an entrepreneur, or a lack of resources. Women often cited time as a common missing resource. This lack of time was sometimes due to the legislative schedule but, in many cases, it was a result of women's dual obligations to office and home. Many of these factors emerge as crucial in the following case studies.

WHERE DO WOMEN ORGANIZE?

The first step in determining if caucuses contribute to improved quality of life for women inside and outside the institution is identifying where and under what the conditions women organize in legislatures. Identifying the legislatures open or closed to women's organizing can lead to a better understanding of how gender interacts with party organizations, types of legislative leadership structures, and political

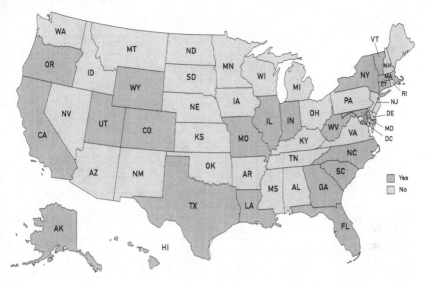

FIGURE 3.1. Caucus status by state in 2016. (Map created by Tatiana DeRouen.)

culture. In 2016, I found that the United States is almost evenly divided with twenty-two states having some type of women's caucus and twenty-eight states having no women's organization at all.

Figure 3.1 shows that caucuses extend across the entirety of the country and exist throughout each region. By census region, the West has seven states with caucuses and six without. The South has the most caucuses with eight throughout their states, and eight without. The Midwest has the fewest caucuses: three states with and nine states without them. Finally, the Northeast has four states with caucuses and five without. While western states were among the first to grant women's suffrage legislation in the country, and five of their thirteen state legislatures are highly ranked for the proportion of women in elective office (CAWP 2017b), they are split almost evenly in terms of caucus distribution. It is possible that with such high proportions of women in office, some women legislators see caucuses as unnecessary, while others take advantage of their numbers by organizing. The southern states, apart from Maryland, rank low for proportions of women in office yet have the most women's caucuses. It could be that their small numbers unify them or are a consequence

TABLE 3.4. DISTRIBUTION OF WOMEN'S CAUCUS TYPES ACROSS THE FIFTY STATES, 2016			
No caucus (28) 56%	Social (7) 14%	Policy: Ad hoc (10) 20%	Policy: Agenda (5) 10%
Alabama	Colorado	Alaska	California
Arizona	Illinois	Florida	Connecticut
Arkansas	Louisiana	Georgia	Hawaii
Delaware	Missouri	Indiana	Maryland
Idaho	South Carolina	Massachusetts	New York
Iowa	Utah	North Carolina	
Kansas	West Virginia	Wyoming	
Kentucky		*Gender Open*	
Maine		Oregon	
Michigan		Texas	
Minnesota		Vermont	
Mississippi			
Montana			
Nebraska			
Nevada			
New Hampshire			
New Jersey			
New Mexico			
North Dakota			
Ohio			
Oklahoma			
Pennsylvania			
Rhode Island			
South Dakota			
Tennessee			
Virginia			
Washington			
Wisconsin			

of the history of these states being one-party. In such states, factions of any type may be common (McGlennon 1998).

Table 3.4 notes the frequency of specific caucus types. Fourteen percent of states have a social caucus, while 30 percent have a policy caucus. Nationwide, 20 percent of caucuses are ad hoc policy caucuses, while 10 percent are agenda setting.

Ad hoc caucuses are the most common type and are found across the United States, as shown in Figure 3.2, which displays the states

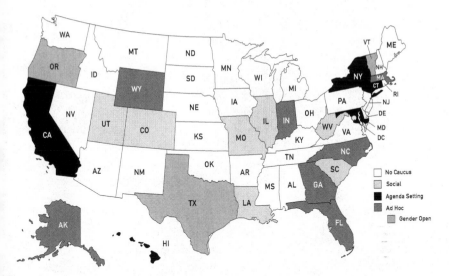

FIGURE 3.2. Caucus type (specific) by state in 2016. (Map created by Tatiana DeRouen.)

by caucus type. Social caucuses account for seven of the twenty-two states with caucuses (or 32 percent of caucus states), with agenda-setting types in five of the twenty-two caucus states (23 percent), and ad hoc caucuses in ten states (45 percent).

I have argued that there are three potential benefits to the creation of a women's caucus: the recognition of gender as politically significant, improvement in the quality of life for women legislators, and the improvement of representation as caucuses act as liaisons between community advocates and legislative bodies. It is vital, therefore, that scholars determine the most favorable contexts for these groups. Having identified where these organizations are, I now analyze the institutional features associated with them and identify the conditions that may favor women's organizing.

INSTITUTIONAL CONDITIONS ASSOCIATED WITH WOMEN'S CAUCUS FORMATION

The existence of women's caucuses is, in many senses, contrary to our theoretical expectations for how women should behave in male-dominated environments. When women represent both a numerical minority and a deviation from a long-standing norm, organizational and institutionalist political theories predict that women seek to minimize characteristics that differentiate them from their male counterparts (Beckwith 2007; Kanter 1977). Similarly, ideological differences among women would seem to make bipartisan women's caucuses unlikely (Dodson 2006; Osborn 2012). Since Representative Emery in Connecticut in 1927, women in thirty-two states have created these groups, despite backlash against the women's movement, pressure to conform within the institution, and their own ideological differences.

Beyond these challenges, norms and rules of the institution confine legislators. Political opportunity theory recognizes constraints and opportunities produced by allies, enemies, institutional structures, and political processes, which can mitigate or increase the costs of organizing and therefore influence the possibility of group creation (Banaszak 1996). The structural opportunities for caucus creation consist of the legislative environment and larger political context in which they emerge. Which legislative conditions create political opportunities that make women's organizing around a gendered identity more likely?

Political Opportunities

In defining what constitutes a political opportunity that contributes to the emergence of a social movement, Doug McAdam, John D. McCarthy, and Mayer N. Zald (1996) suggest that a change in at least one of four dimensions could be considered a political opportunity. These four dimensions are the openness or closure of the system itself, stability of elite alignments, the presence of allies, and the capacity for repression by the system. The ways in which legislatures are structured—the rules of the game—influence the decisions and behaviors of those seeking to work together outside of the traditional arrangements of political party and committees. I have argued that particular legislative conditions may be more advantageous to women's organizing than others and discuss here my expectations for which of these are most likely to be correlated with the creation of a women's caucus, including those characteristics that would affect the openness of the system and capacity for repression dimensions that McAdam, Mc-

Carthy, and Zald (1996) identify as crucial to political opportunities for change.[12]

Presence of Other Caucuses

The presence of other caucuses is an obvious indication that a legislature was open to women's organizing. Other types of caucuses beyond party caucuses lend legitimacy to alternative organizations and indicate an open system. Hammond (1998) cites that once one caucus is formed, others follow. This trend may be particularly true if other identity-based caucuses exist, thus making one's identity a legitimate political category. Maryland, for example, established its women's caucus in 1972 after the creation of the Congressional Black Caucus in 1971 and cited it as inspiration (Sorenson 2000). Identity caucuses include those based on characteristics such as race, gender, or sexual orientation, unlike issues caucuses, such as a sportsmen's caucus or an environmental caucus. It is appropriate to consider the presence of black caucuses because of the link between the civil rights and women's movements (Evans 1980; Freeman 1973). Therefore, I expect the following:

> H1: *Women's caucuses are more likely to form in states where other caucuses exist, particularly black caucuses.*

Democratic Party Control

Sixty percent of women in state legislatures are Democrats, and the Democratic Party has framed itself as the party most responsive to "women's issues" (CAWP 2017b; "The Democratic Party" 2010). Research by Jo Freeman (1986) and Debra L. Dodson (2006) indicates that the Republican Party is less tolerant of the expression of political identities beyond party. Further, as previously noted, Tracy Osborn (2003) finds that "a strong Republican party lessens cohesion [among women within a state legislature] and a strong Democratic party strengthens women's cohesion" (24). This research indicates that Democratic control may make legislatures more open both because of that party's association with identity politics since the realignment of the 1960s, indicating a tolerance for such organizing, and because of women's numerical presence within it. In my interviews, Democratic women were most often identified as the initiators of women's caucuses, which I discuss in Chapters 4–7. Therefore, I expect attempts in Democrat-controlled legislatures to be more successful than those in states where Republicans hold the majority. I expect a Democratic majority to be a positive political opportunity that caucus organizers take advantage of when timing their attempt.

H2: *Women's caucuses are more likely to form in legislatures with a Democratic majority.*

Proportion of Women in the Legislature

The presence of women serving in state legislatures is perhaps the most important political opportunity for organizing. Expanding on previous research by Rosabeth Moss Kanter, Karen Beckwith (2007) hypothesizes that in legislatures with fewer than 15 percent women, caucuses are less likely to emerge because of the pressure to conform to masculine norms. Without potential members, there is little need or opportunity for an organization. In legislatures with greater than 15 percent women, Beckwith hypothesizes that the creation of more women's caucuses is more likely.[13] Alternatively, in legislatures with large numbers of women, with percentages over thirty, legislators may not feel a need for an organization based on gender. In this sense, the positive political opportunity is present when a moderate proportion of women are present in a legislature. Therefore, I predict the following:

H3: *Caucuses are less likely to emerge in states in which the proportion of women is very high or very low.*

Resources to Get the Job Done

Resources are important for the successful launch of an organized group (Zald 1992; Cress and Snow 1996). They are a cache of support for legislators as they attempt to achieve their political and personal goals. Legislative institutions provide their members with general resources like staff, office space, and material support. Women may take advantage of these broad benefits in their attempt to create a women's caucus.

Professionalism

Professionalism in legislatures is "the capacity of both legislators and legislatures to generate and digest information in the policymaking process" (Squire 2007, 211). It is an important variable in legislative research because professionalism affects the types of legislators attracted to the position and the conditions under which certain candidates are successful. Similarly, it affects legislators once in office because of their access to particular resources, such as staff and session time. Hammond (1998) attributes the 1970s boom in congressional caucuses in part to rule changes that allocated more staff to be distributed equally among members. Additional staff allows legislators to have more contact with constituents and be more responsive to their concerns (Squire and Moncrief 2010). These resources make it more likely that women with more staff succeed in launching a caucus, particularly if women's issues are a constituent priority. More professional legislatures also have longer sessions. With more time spent at the state capital legislating, women legislators are more likely to have opportunities to associate with one another and have the time and proximity required for caucus activities. Further, women in more professional legislatures are more likely to work on women's-issue legislation, indicating that gender is a politically relevant category for them deserving of their legislative attention (Carroll and Taylor 1989).

Beth Reingold and Paige Schneider (2001) argue that the interaction between levels of professionalism and gender in the legislature is both positive and negative for women. While they cite Alan Rosenthal (1998), who finds that more professional legislatures produce more masculine norms, they also note Jeanie R. Stanley and Diane D. Blair's (1991) report that professionalism creates a more business-like environment in which an old-boys' network may be less able to exclude women. Ultimately, I expect the level of professionalism to affect women's ability to organize because of the additional resources associated with higher levels of professionalism.

H4: *Women's caucuses are less likely to emerge in legislatures with lower levels of professionalism than in other state legislatures.*

Term Limits

Scholars have analyzed term limits to determine their impact on legislators more generally as well as their specific impact on women. Generally, term limits contribute to a greater turnover in legislators at large, leading to a disintegration of the power of standing committees (Squire and Moncrief 2010). Joel A. Thompson and Gary Moncrief (1993) suggest that, because term limits increase the number of open seats in a legislature, these vacancies could help women who would be likely candidates for those seats. Susan J. Carroll and Krista Jenkins (2001), however, find that term limits on their own do not contribute to an increase in the number of women elected to legislatures but also require direct recruitment of women candidates by parties and other political organizations. Thompson and Moncrief (1993) also warn that term limits may have a negative effect on women's power within legislatures as senior women are termed out.

As a consequence of examining this research, I expect term limits to negatively affect women's abilities to create women's caucuses. Term limits shorten legislators' time in office and therefore may negatively affect their prioritization of gender work in the legislatures. Gender concerns may not be the top priority for every women legislator. With a shortened time horizon, women may prioritize other goals, thereby decreasing the number of women who might otherwise choose to participate in a caucus. Term limits could also affect the expertise levels of legislators. With less experience, women legislators may be lacking in the skills and institutional knowledge necessary to successfully launch a caucus. For these reasons, I expect the following:

H5: *Women's caucuses are less likely to emerge in states with term limits.*

To investigate these hypotheses, I undertook a second data collection with my colleague Chris Clark in July 2014. While my original data collection was able to identify existing caucuses, it did not determine the universe of caucuses that may have once existed in a state but were no longer active. This second data collection was targeted to establish if a caucus had ever existed in a state and, if so, the year it was founded. In a handful of cases, women's caucuses had websites that provided data on their emergence. *CAWP News and Notes,* a newsletter that provides information on women in politics, provided the caucus creation date for many states. In other instances, we consulted state legislators, both former and current, to determine when women's caucuses emerged. We also relied on data from state archives, state legislatures, and scholarly works. By determining the origin date for the thirty-two caucuses we discovered had been established between 1972 and 2009, we are able to identify some of the conditions present within the legislatures where women decided to act collectively.[14]

As indicated in Table 3.5, women created thirty-two original caucuses between 1972 and 2009. Twenty of them remained as of 2016, indicating that, once created, a majority of them were able to sustain themselves over time. The form a caucus took may have shifted, however, as the legislators themselves and their priorities did. As I have said, these organizations and legislators are flexible, molding caucuses to their own strategies and interests.

Out of the thirty-two caucuses, five (16 percent) were created in the 1970s. When these five were originally created they all had hopes of setting policy agendas and impacting legislation, but today only Maryland remains agenda setting. The others have readjusted their priorities and activities. Women legislators created sixteen of these women's caucuses in the 1980s. CAWP held the Tenth Anniversary Conference in 1982 (attended by Carol Mueller) and a discussion about how and whether to caucus was on the agenda. The value of an external organization is seen by the explosion in the number of women's caucuses during this decade. Seven (22 percent) were created in the 1990s but only three of those remain as of this writing. This is the worst maintenance record of any of the four decades.[15] Finally, four (or 13 percent) of women's caucuses were formed in the 2000s. For the percentage of caucuses formed within each time period, see Table 3.6.

An overwhelming majority of women's caucuses were created in states where a black caucus already existed.[16] I have hypothesized that their presence indicates something about the openness of the institution to identity organizing, which these women could have taken advantage of as well. Those black and women's caucuses founded most

TABLE 3.5. INSTITUTIONAL CONDITIONS AT TIME OF WOMEN'S CAUCUS FORMATION

State	Year of creation	Still present in 2016	Black caucus status	Party control	Proportion of women	Profession-alism score	Term limits
Maryland	1972	Yes	Yes (1970)	Dem	0.065	0.136	No
Oregon	1973	Yes	No	Dem	0.100	0.256	No
Florida	1975	Yes	No	Dem	0.081	0.307	No
Massachusetts	1975	Yes	Yes (1973)	Dem	0.057	0.467	No
Illinois	1979	Yes	Yes (1968)	Dem	0.110	0.344	No
Missouri	1980	Yes	Yes (1970)	Dem	0.086	0.266	No
Vermont	1980	Yes	No	Rep	0.189	0.13	No
Iowa	1981	No	No	Rep	0.120	0.266	No
North Carolina	1981	Yes	No	Dem	0.129	0.19	No
Virginia	1981	No	Yes (1978)	Dem	0.064	0.164	No
Kansas	1983	No	Yes (1975)	Rep	0.145	0.169	No
New York	1983	Yes	Yes (1966)	Split	0.104	0.407	No
Alaska	1985	Yes	Yes (1975)	Split	0.183	0.32	No
California	1985	Yes	Yes (1967)	Dem	0.125	0.526	No
Wisconsin	1985	No	Yes (1973)	Dem	0.189	0.249	No
Hawaii	1986	Yes	No	Dem	0.184	0.276	No
Louisiana	1986	Yes	Yes (1977)	Dem	0.035	0.185	No
Pennsylvania	1987	No	Yes (1973)	Split	0.063	0.336	No
Mississippi	1988	No	Yes (1976)	Dem	0.057	0.16	No
Rhode Island	1988	No	Yes (1986)	Dem	0.160	0.148	No
West Virginia	1988	Yes	No	Dem	0.157	0.125	No

State	Year of creation	Still present in 2016	Black caucus status	Party control	Proportion of women	Profession-alism score	Term limits
Georgia	1990	Yes	Yes (1973)	Dem	0.102	0.133	No
Arkansas	1991	No	Yes (1979)	Dem	0.074	0.105	No
Nebraska	1992	No	No	NP	0.184	0.186	No
Texas	1992	Yes	Yes (1973)	Dem	0.127	0.21	No
Delaware	1993	No	Yes (1977)	Split	0.145	0.192	No
Indiana	1993	Yes	Yes (1979)	Split	0.193	0.139	No
New Mexico	1997	No	No	Dem	0.268	0.053	No
South Carolina	2004	Yes	Yes (1973)	Rep	0.094	0.124	No
Wyoming	2006	Yes	No	Rep	0.156	0.054	No
Colorado	2009	Yes	Yes (1974)	Dem	0.370	0.202	Yes
New Jersey	2009	No	Yes (1979)	Dem	0.300	0.244	No

TABLE 3.6. TIME OF CAUCUS FORMATION			
Prior to 1980	**1980s**	**1990s**	**2000s**
5 (16%)	16 (50%)	7 (22%)	4 (13%)

closely together were in Maryland, Massachusetts, and Rhode Island. The largest time gap between the establishment of a black caucus and a women's caucus was in Colorado—thirty-five years. There is no instance of a women's caucus preceding the formation of a black caucus. Table 3.7 shows the presence or absence of a black caucus at the time of formation of the women's caucus.

When examining some of my expectations regarding structural opportunities for women's caucuses, one can see that an overwhelming majority were formed under Democratic control but five were formed during split control and five were formed under Republican

TABLE 3.7. BLACK CAUCUS STATUS AT TIME OF WOMEN'S CAUCUS FORMATION	
Present	Absent
22 (69%)	10 (31%)

TABLE 3.8. PARTY CONTROL AT TIME OF WOMEN'S CAUCUS FORMATION			
Democratic	Split	Republican	Nonpartisan
21 (66%)	5 (16%)	5 (16%)	1 (3%)

control, indicating that while it is more common under Democrats, women can organize under any partisan regime. Within this time period, two of the most recent caucuses were formed under Republican control as well as two more after 2016 (Utah and a revival in Texas). With Republicans sweeping state houses beginning in 2010, it is important to note that women's attempts at caucusing can be successful in Republican states. See Table 3.8.

I also hypothesized that women's numbers in the legislature would be an important factor in caucus creation and suggested that where women's numbers were very low or very high, a caucus would be less likely to form. Women would have trouble justifying the creation of an organization if numbers were low and might view a caucus as unnecessary when if token status was exceeded. As we can see from these thirty-two instances, most caucuses are formed when women's numbers are under 14 percent of the legislature—contradicting Beckwith's (2007) theory that token women would want to blend in with their environment. Very few caucuses are formed when women's numbers exceed 30 percent. See Table 3.9.

Resources are important for organizations, and two indicators of resources within legislatures are professionalism and potential time in office, which I operationalize as term limits. The former represents time in session and staff resources, while the latter allows for a longer horizon of time. Most women's caucuses are formed in legislatures with professionalism scores below .200, but the remaining 47 percent are created in moderately and highly professionalized legislatures. See Table 3.10. It is possible that the type of resources necessary for a

TABLE 3.9. PROPORTION OF WOMEN IN LEGISLATURE AT TIME OF WOMEN'S CAUCUS FORMATION		
0–14%	15–30%	> 30%
18 (56%)	13 (41%)	1 (3%)

TABLE 3.10. PROFESSIONALISM SCORE AT TIME OF WOMEN'S CAUCUS FORMATION		
0–0.200	0.210–0.300	> 0.300
17 (53%)	8 (25%)	7 (22%)

caucus to launch differs from session time and staff. Later in the case studies, I investigate resources that women's organizations outside the legislature may provide. Only one caucus was formed in a state with term limits—Colorado in 2009. Further discussion of term limits and the role of women's seniority follows in the case studies.

Unfortunately, these descriptive details do not tell us what the states that didn't form caucuses are like or if they are significantly different from caucus-forming states on these measures. Due to the ephemeral nature of women's caucuses, many sophisticated analyses are not possible at this time. Further analysis of the many other variables of interest, for which data are not available across all thirty-seven years is warranted. Finally, it is not possible to test in this way the importance of frames in collective action. Because these descriptive statistics are suggestive, and in order to better understand the role gender plays in the process of organizing within legislatures and test these and other variables qualitatively, I conducted four case studies between 2006 and 2010 in states where caucus attempts were underway.

PREVIEWING THE SUBSEQUENT CASE STUDIES

The case studies that follow in the next four chapters test hypotheses about women's caucus creation. Personal interviews and analysis of media coverage are implemented when available. (For demographic details about the interview subjects, see Table 3.11.) Cases were identified through telephone interviews in all fifty states, described previously, with state-level caucus attempts between 2006 and 2009 as

TABLE 3.11. INTERVIEW SUBJECT DEMOGRAPHICS				
State	Number of interview subjects	Party proportion	Number of staff	Number of legislative leaders
New Jersey (see Chapter 4)	12	6 Republicans, 5 Democrats	1	6 (2 male, 4 female)
Colorado (see Chapter 5)	13	2 Republicans, 10 Democrats	1	2 (male)
Pennsylvania (see Chapter 6)	10	5 Republicans, 5 Democrats	0	1 (male)
Iowa (see Chapter 7)	7	1 Republican, 5 Democrats	1	1 (female)

follows: New Jersey (2009), Colorado (2009), Pennsylvania (2009), and Iowa (2007). Interview participation rates in each state varied.

Review of media accounts of a caucus at the time of its emergence has allowed me to examine the frames used by caucus members in justifying their organization to other legislators and the public. These accounts were collected by internet research or were shared with me by caucus members or staff. In the case of New Jersey, additional media accounts were used to explain legislative battles in which the caucus became involved. In the Colorado case, I reviewed press coverage of their initial meeting and subsequent events. No press coverage was available for the two failed cases. For two cases, New Jersey and Colorado, I was able to observe caucus events as an invited participant.

My aim here is to discover the opportunities, resources, and frames that lead to caucus creation and therefore it is necessary to consider the context in which caucuses occur. Case studies are particularly conducive to this type of investigation (George and Bennett 2005). Case studies also allow for the discovery of new relevant variables and may identify important causal ones related to the creation of women's caucuses not necessarily anticipated by researchers. My investigation, which begins from the moment a caucus entrepreneur reaches out to another member, is able to capture this process comprehensively.

I center my hypotheses concerning caucus creation on the interaction of gender with other institutional variables within a legislature. I accomplish this analysis by implementing process tracing. Two primary advantages of process tracing, descriptive inference and exploring causal mechanisms within context, are a part of my project. David Collier (2011) notes the advantage of comparative case studies like mine that describe "a novel political and social phenomena" and "focuses on the unfolding of events . . . over time" (824). This focus on unfolding events allows for careful attention to the interaction of variables as a way to explain their causal significance. In addition to tracking the importance of the conditions observed in the preceding section, I consider the following hypotheses, again organized as political opportunities, resources and frames.

Political Opportunities

Party Competition

Strong party competition, where majorities are small and often changing, may inhibit women's caucus attempts. Party loyalty may be more prized in these environments, preventing women from fragmenting their legislative efforts between party (and sometimes competing) goals for women (Snyder and Groseclose 2000; Aldrich and Battista 2002). In highly competitive environments, party leaders are more likely to repress members and resist change. Therefore, I expect the following:

> H6: *Party competition constrains women's ability to organize a caucus.*

Party Polarization

Partisanship more generally may also influence the success of women's caucus attempts. As noted by several scholars, the political category "women" is diverse in ideology and issue priority (Osborn 2012; Hawkesworth et al. 2001; Huddy, Cassese, and Lizotte 2008; Dodson 2006). Specifically, Hawkesworth et al. (2001) state, "Despite near universal agreement concerning their responsibility to represent women, women legislators hold a variety of views about the nature of women's needs and interests and the best means to represent women in the policy-making process" (9). This would only be exacerbated by parties' cultural differences, as Freeman (1986) notes. She argues that the Republican ethos of individualism discourages women in their ranks from identifying with broad political identities such as gender or race.

Carroll (2003) also notes that fewer Republican women identify themselves as moderates in state houses than in 1988. The presence of those moderates proved important for those early women's caucuses that emerged in the late 1970s and early 1980s. If Republican women place themselves further to the right on the ideological spectrum from Democratic women, bipartisan caucus attempts may be more difficult. As Osborn (2012) finds, "Though women clearly differ from men in their parties on a number of items, they are . . . closer to the men in their parties than to women in the other party" (88). This difficulty would be expected, on the basis of the work of Shor and McCarty (2011), who report that polarization in state legislatures is increasing, though not uniformly, across states. Therefore, I expect the following:

H7: *Polarization constrains women's ability to organize a caucus.*

Proportion of Women in Their Respective Parties
Similarly, women's proportions within their political party may also influence their ability to organize with women across the aisle. Pressure to conform would be particularly strong for women in the Republican Party because of their smaller numbers (Crowder-Myers and Lauderdale 2014; Kanter 1977; Kanthak and Krause 2012) and the party's disdain for identity politics (Freeman 1986). Alternatively, the Democratic Party structure allows for identity politics, and so for this reason, I predict the following:

H8: *Larger proportions of women within both the Democratic and Republican parties facilitate the creation of a caucus.*

Racial Diversity among Women Legislators
Similarly, I consider a larger proportion of women-of-color legislators to be a positive political opportunity for women's caucuses. Their experience of bias within legislative institutions may be a motivator to create institutions that would address issues of inequality (Barrett 1997; Hawkesworth 2003; Smooth 2008). Latina legislators may be proponents of women's caucuses, based on findings by Luis Ricardo

Fraga and colleagues (2008). Their analysis of Latina legislators finds that they are more likely to support legislation advocated by women's caucuses even when their constituents oppose the measure. Further, they are more likely to support a measure supported by the women's caucus and opposed by the Latino caucus when a measure divides them (173). Combined with the strong Democratic political affinity of both African American and Latina legislators, larger proportions of women of color in a legislature seem to create a positive political opportunity for a women's caucus (CAWP 2017b).[17] In particular, African American and Latina legislators are likely to be participants in black and Hispanic caucuses, giving them the experience necessary to create a women's caucus. Therefore, I predict the following:

H9: *Larger proportions of women legislators of color facilitate the creation of women's caucuses.*

Proportion of Freshman Women Legislators

Beckwith (2007) posits that change within institutions cannot be attributed to women simply as a result of their proportion of the legislature. She adds that factoring in the relative newness of women holding office is a better indicator of women substantively representing other women. She argues that women who are newer to office are less likely to defy party and institutional norms than their incumbent women counterparts. For this hypothesis, a larger proportion of new women to the legislature is considered a negative demographic political opportunity because of the expected disinterest by newly elected women who are motivated to conform rather than distinguish themselves by gender. Therefore, I predict the following:

H10: *Larger proportions of newly elected women legislators constrain women's organizing.*

Resources to Get the Job Done

Resources are vital to the establishment of organizations. In order to carry out activities, members must be able to draw upon time, money, and expertise to accomplish their goals. In the case of women's caucuses, some resources may be internal to legislatures (discussed above: staff, time) or come from advocates outside who might benefit from the establishment of a caucus.

External Organizations

Political demands made by women's organizations in the 1970s—for protection from sexual violence, access to healthcare, for example—outside of Congress created the context for the development of the CCWI (Hammond 1998; Gertzog 2004). Members of Congress felt pressure to respond to newly salient women's issues to which outside groups were calling their attention. CAWP (2001) also reports a close relationship between women state legislators and these groups, and Anthony J. Nownes and Grant Neeley (1996) argue that such groups emerge when entrepreneurs' (insiders) and patrons' (outsiders) interests coincide. For this reason, a women's caucus may emerge with the encouragement of women's organizations (outsiders) that feel that a women's caucus is more effective in dealing with the issues most salient to them than action taken by individual legislators (insiders). These resources may supplement those associated with more professional legislatures. Therefore, I hypothesize the following:

> H11: *Encouragement and support from external women's groups facilitate caucus creation.*

Framing the Task at Hand

In establishing a women's caucus, caucus entrepreneurs are required to recruit potential members and, in some cases, defend themselves against opposition. McAdam, McCarthy, and Zald (1996) refer to this as "strategic efforts by groups of people to fashion shared understandings of the world and of themselves that legitimate and motivate collective action" (6). Specifically, in forming a caucus, legislators are creating what is referred to in social movement theory as a mobilizing structure that addresses "adherents and activists in the movement itself—as well as . . . bystanders, opponents, and authorities" (149).

Caucus entrepreneurs argue for a caucus by framing it as providing certain benefits to potential participants (Salisbury 1969). So in evaluating the frames that would affect the creation of a women's caucus, I consider the justifications legislators put forth legitimizing collective organizing. I hypothesize below that some caucus purposes are more likely to result in successful caucus launches than others. Finally, I hypothesize that the existence of counter-frames, opposition from party leaders or male colleagues, are likely to hurt the chances of a successful caucus launch.

Gender Consciousness

Women legislators must first share the belief that women are a relevant political category in order for a women's caucus attempt to be successful. I refer to this frame as gender consciousness. Without a shared belief in women's different experiences and political cause to act on those differences, why create a women's caucus? I hypothesize that gender consciousness, as a shared belief among women legislators, is crucial to both a caucus attempt and the success of that attempt. Components of group consciousness are identified by Roberta Sigel (1996) as

> identification with the group, attachment to it, and commitment to action on its behalf. A vital fourth component of consciousness . . . involves assigning priority (or at least high priority) to membership in the disadvantaged group over memberships in other groups to which one belongs. (127)

For Sigel, this priority is an important element because it explains why gender consciousness is so difficult to develop. She argues that women's membership in other identity groups often inhibits their development of gender consciousness. This split loyalty is an important observation in particular for women legislators for whom party identity is particularly strong. Institutional norms demand party loyalty above other identities, which complicates women's participation in a caucus, especially for Republican women.[18]

By signifying gender as important and initiating an organization centered on their gendered identity rather than party, women legislators are overcoming an important hurdle in gender consciousness development.[19] Whether or not women are able to create and maintain a bipartisan caucus depends on their ability to work across party lines. I therefore hypothesize the following:

> H12: *Caucus attempts are more likely to be successful when women legislators (both organizers and participants) identify solidarity (common interests and challenges) with other women and acknowledge that collective action on behalf of their membership in that group is appropriate.*

Party Dissatisfaction

Caucuses emerge when the existing committee and party structures fail to adequately address new issues important to members (Hammond 1998). The institution's inadequacies may be a result of interested members not serving on the relevant committees, party leadership ignoring the new issue, or the committee structure not being able to address an issue that crosses traditional legislative boundaries. "Women's issues" are complicated and often cross multiple boundaries. Caucus attempts are more likely to succeed when the perceived unresponsiveness of political parties strains women's obligation to that party identity. Women legislators who acknowledge party or committee unresponsiveness have a sound argument for the necessity of a women's caucus to respond to a legitimate need. Therefore, I expect the following:

> H13: *When women legislators perceive political parties or the committee system as unresponsive to the issues important to them, caucus attempts are more successful.*

Similarly, if women are included at the highest levels of leadership within a legislature, they may not see a need to create a caucus as an alternative route to legislative power and influence. If party leaders exclude women from these ranks, that isolation may be a motivating factor for legislators who are looking for a way to influence legislative agendas and outcomes. For these reasons, I expect the following:

> H14: *In legislatures with few women in positions of leadership, caucus attempts are more likely to succeed.*

Caucus Type

The purpose of a proposed caucus is an important frame to consider when hypothesizing what results in successful caucus creation. Not all legislators may agree on what type of women's caucus to create, what strategies are appropriate to improve the lives of women legislators, or what type of membership is appropriate. I hypothesize that caucus attempts are more likely to succeed when the purpose is identified as primarily social in nature, in part because of the polarized context of the post-Obama era. As Shor and McCarty (2011) find, polarization in aggregate at the state level has increased since the early 2000s, rendering policy caucuses less desirable and therefore their attempts potentially less successful. This lack of common ground may strike women in particular, considering Carroll's (2003) evidence of fewer moderates among Republican women legislators. Therefore, I expect the following:

> H15: *Attempts at establishing policy caucuses are less likely to succeed.*

Opposition from Party Leaders or Male Colleagues

Once women legislators decide to attempt a caucus, they may have to contend with the opposition's competing narratives. Acknowledging a common identity (gender in this case) and successfully employing that discourse in competition with challenges to the validity of that claim are vital to the formation and maintenance of women's caucuses. It is possible that party leaders will challenge Republican women to identify as individuals rather than as members of special interest groups (Freeman 1986; Dodson 2006). Democratic leaders are likely to oppose a bipartisan women's caucus in highly competitive and polarized chambers as well. Most likely, challenges to women forming their own group will come from party leaders (men or women) who have an interest in women identifying first as party members, requiring loyalty to that caucus before others. Challenges by party leadership are particularly detrimental because they threaten women's political future and effectiveness. It is also possible, however, that opposition expressed by male colleagues more generally would be detrimental to caucus attempts. Therefore, I hypothesize the following:

H16: *When party leaders or male colleagues express opposition to the creation of a women's caucus, that attempt is less likely to succeed.*

The following four case studies include examinations of attempts at creating a women's legislative caucus within the years 2006–2010. For my purposes, I define a caucus attempt as an instance in which an actor or group (either within the legislature or from outside) contacts state legislators and asks them to participate in a bipartisan women's group. This contact may be made informally through conversation or more formally through an email or letter. It is this contact only, not attendance at any group meeting, that constitutes an attempt. By beginning with initial recruitment, I am able to establish those opportunities, resources, and frames associated with a successful caucus attempt, as well as those that do not succeed. For my purposes, I define a successful caucus attempt as the establishment of a group that continues to meet one year after the original founding. A failed attempt is any group that fails to meet for one year.

Like Mueller (1984), I demonstrate that many of the factors affecting women's organizing in the 1970s and 1980s—men's perceptions, party differences, issue disagreements—remain important. For this purpose, I turn to these case studies to evaluate the role of caucus entrepreneurs in leveraging political opportunities, resources, and frames in the establishment of women's caucuses. Through this analysis, I elucidate how gender influences women's decisions to caucus, men's reactions to those decisions, and how formal and informal rules inhibit or facilitate the creation of women's caucuses.

4

THE NEW JERSEY WOMEN'S LEGISLATIVE CAUCUS

TIMELINE

Early 1990s: Informal caucus.

Late 2008, early 2009: Discussions held at the Center for American Women and Politics, Eagleton Institute of Politics, among women legislators interested in forming a women's caucus.

February 26, 2009: Formal leadership selected.

September 30, 2009: A forum at the Center for American Women and Politics was held to honor retiring legislative staffer Kathy Crotty, who transitioned to become the caucus volunteer staffer.

October 2, 2009: Party Democracy Act signed into law.

April 29, 2010: First official event, a reception that brought together women serving in the legislative and executive branches.

June 7, 2010: Last official event, legislative hearing on women's health at the state house organized and managed by women of the caucus.

June 21, 2010: Family Planning Grant bill introduced in the Senate.

July 23, 2010: Family Planning Grant bill vetoed by Governor Chris Christie.

September 20, 2010: Family Planning Grant bill veto override vote fails.

In the 2007 New Jersey state legislative election, a surge of women took office following a corruption purge. Seasoned legislative veterans, such as Senators Loretta Weinberg (D) and Diane Allen (R), were poised to formalize existing social ties with the help of an available and capable volunteer staffer, Kathy Crotty. The political experience these women brought to the table at a time when women were taking their place in the New Jersey State Legislature enabled them to organize a women's policy caucus. These entrepreneurs unified women around three frames in particular—gender consciousness (that women shared life experiences that distinguished them from their male colleagues), party dissatisfaction, and public policy as a priority. (For additional demographic details about the interview subjects cited in this chapter, see Table 4.1.)

Women legislators in New Jersey believed they could find common ground and bring issues to the larger legislative agenda despite belonging to different parties. The public policy frame, however, proved to be the demise of the caucus; it ceased to meet beyond 2010, when Republican women, including Senator Allen, failed to support a women's health bill, which was seen as a betrayal by their Democratic female colleagues, especially Senator Weinberg. The New Jersey case illustrates the benefits of a powerful entrepreneur, like Senator Weinberg, for caucus creation, but also the costs of relying too heavily on one person to maintain the alliance.

As I have argued, women legislators make the decision to caucus on the basis of their perceptions of the political environment and balance their own objectives with what is possible. They make these decisions within a gendered and partisan landscape while maintaining

TABLE 4.1. NEW JERSEY INTERVIEW SUBJECTS (12) DEMOGRAPHICS		
Party affiliation	Legislative leaders	Gender
6 Republicans, 5 Democrats, 1 nonpartisan staffer	2	2 male, 10 female

both gendered and partisan identities. The New Jersey political culture primed women to organize in reaction to perceived gender marginalization by party leaders, while at the same time the increasingly polarized parties presented challenges the fledgling caucus could not ultimately overcome.

A POWERFUL LEADER SEIZES OPPORTUNITY

Structural opportunity plays an important role in the emergence of social movements, which creates space within institutions for claims to take hold (McAdam, McCarthy, and Zald 1996). In any state legislature, political opportunities can arise from shifts in power or perception. One structural opportunity present in New Jersey at the time of caucus formation was the legislative leadership's concerns about partisanship. Crotty noted a desire among the legislative leadership to minimize the harsh partisanship that has been present since the 1990s in the legislature in general. She suggested that the leadership may have been looking for something like a bipartisan caucus as another way to achieve their own goal. In reality, Democrats, who controlled both houses and the governorship, were looking to run the table with moderate Republican support. Women did not report any backlash, nor did male leaders admit to opposing the caucus.[1] However, party differences intensified under divided government when Republican governor Chris Christie was elected, complicating caucus maintenance for both Democratic and Republican organizers.

The most important political opportunity available to the women legislators of New Jersey from 2007 to 2009 was an influx of women legislators with a gender consciousness that had been raised by their marginalization within the political parties. Experienced entrepreneurs recognized and capitalized on this opportunity. The women interviewed mentioned friendship across party lines as a consequence of proximity. The ladies' room in the Capitol came up in several interviews as a place where women spoke informally and got to know each other. Women frequently noted the role of Senator Weinberg as a uniter, an influential member of the legislature who ran as Governor Jon Corzine's (D) lieutenant gubernatorial candidate in 2009.

Senator Weinberg's efforts to welcome women—even those across the aisle—were particularly important. As one Republican assembly-woman noted:

> I can remember on my first day or second day, after I was sworn in, that Loretta Weinberg approached me and welcomed me to the assembly and she said, "We would like to get you involved—we have this little women's caucus, unofficial, and we would like to have you." And I said, "Oh, great." So no hesitation on my part for it.[2]

Many stated that, because women are a minority in the legislature, a bond was inevitable. Senator Jennifer Beck (R) cited a natural bond between women several times throughout her interview:

> I think that there is a natural camaraderie, maybe being a minor-ity we sort of naturally have a camaraderie. . . . I think it is im-portant that women come together and share what is I believe a natural bond and that we do address policy issues a little bit differently.[3]

Assemblywoman Amy Handlin (R) also notes that similar interests led to friendships and sometimes legislation:

> I guess, at all kinds of events of all different sorts, we, some of us at least, would kind of just strike up conversations with each other in an informal way. And sometimes we tried to do leg-islation together that we had particular interests in and things like that. So one thing led to another. . . . These are the people who I tend to socialize with and spend more time around on an informal basis. . . . [They] tend to be the other women.[4]

The need for a caucus—and recognition of women's work in the legislature—was highlighted at a forum at the Center for American Women and Politics in September 2009. From this point, women in both houses and parties in New Jersey worked on caucus formatting, holding the first official event in April 2010, which was a reception that brought together women serving in the legislative and executive branches.

The women chose the caucus leadership informally, with a consensus that there should be women from each house and each party included. The party caucuses in both houses then decided which woman would represent them as cochair. This is the only instance of intraparty decision making within my four case studies—within a bipartisan organization, the leadership was still selected within party caucuses. This particular selection process highlights the strength of institutional norms influencing the practices of even nontraditional organizations such as women's caucuses, particularly the institutional norm of partisan decision making. On the senate side, the obvious choices were Senator Allen because of her seniority (having served in the legislature since 1996) and Senator Weinberg, who was widely perceived as the caucus entrepreneur in this case. The women in the assembly also informally selected Amy Handlin and L. Grace Spencer (D) as leaders. Handlin's selection was largely out of default—no other Republican women stepped forward as potential candidates, indicating weaker support for the caucus among House Republican women. Spencer's youth and race (as the only African American or woman of color in caucus leadership) were noted as assets by members. Although all four women were the public leaders of the group, Senator Allen was dealing with her mother's ill health at the time and Senator Weinberg was widely perceived to be the real force behind the initiative. This perception would prove important for the survival of the caucus because of Weinberg's capacity to build and maintain relationships—currency in any legislature but particularly important in New Jersey.

Political Culture

New Jersey political culture has a reputation for corruption, and while some public officials may serve with integrity, "others believe that an officeholder's primary responsibility is to serve himself and those who have supported him directly, favoring them even at the expense of the public" (Elazar 1984, 117). The emphasis on relationships and quid pro quo means that organizing—including for the women's caucus—is a function of who is close to whom and how relationships can be leveraged. In any similar political climate, when powerful players oppose a women's caucus, we might expect political loyalties to be tested.

Historically, New Jersey's political power has rested in the executive branch with a less powerful legislature. In the modern era, however, legislators have gained more experience, focused on policy, and raised independent campaign funds, which has led to political independence from the power of the governor. Increased professionalization, and the staff that came with it, has given legislators the policy information they needed to challenge powerful governors (Salmore and Salmore 2008). As the New Jersey legislature increased its institutionalization in the 1980s and 1990s and legislators increased their knowledge and time in office, political practices also changed. Political corruption flourished, as "lawmakers implicitly agreed to turn a blind eye to practices that served their careers" (Salmore and Salmore 2008, 187). When this level of corruption became unacceptable to the public, many legislators left office as a result of investigations. This attention to corruption played a role in the creation of the women's caucus in New Jersey as women filled many of the open seats left vacant by male legislators prosecuted for political crimes. The majority of investigations in New Jersey that targeted men politicians and women's presence in international legislative bodies have been associated with lower rates of corruption (Dollar, Fisman, and Gatti 2001; Swamy et al. 2001). While seemingly gender-neutral, investigations into political corruption had the gendered effect of opening the door for an influx of women candidates, which subsequently resulted in the creation of a women's caucus set to further change the gendered political landscape. These newly elected women were eager to leverage their power, and women legislators with seniority were ready to act.

Women's Presence and Political Parties

New Jersey's record on electing women has been described as "mediocre at best" (Carroll and Dittmar 2012, 2). Party leaders who acted as gatekeepers did little to recruit women to run for office; thus, any woman elected to the legislature needed to be a self-starter (McCormick and McCormick 1994). Women were prepared to take advantage of unique political opportunities presented by corruption investigations, which led to the doubling of the number of women in the state legislature in New Jersey between 2004 and 2011 (Carroll and Dittmar 2012). Concurrently, women's organizations had drawn attention to the lack of women's representation and began training and recruiting women to run. As a consequence, an unusual number of open seats and the work of critical actors who directly advocated for more women candidates contributed to the surge of women officeholders after 2004 (Carroll and Dittmar 2012). A similar surge in 2007 swept into office women who were cognizant of the role gender had played in their political careers and who were open to the idea of organizing around that identity, particularly when cued by powerful senior women legislators.

New Jersey represents an ideal test case to evaluate whether the proportion of women in a legislative body influences the formation of the caucus. Prior to the 2009 attempt to create a women's caucus, women in the New Jersey legislature had participated in informal social groups. Attempts at making this arrangement more formal occurred, but a lack of numbers was cited by the women as one reason for failure. The number of women was particularly relevant in the senate, where there were only recently enough women on both sides of the aisle to make a caucus reasonable, according to interviewees.[5] When the caucus emerged, New Jersey was ranked twelfth in the country in gender proportions, with women making up 30 percent of the legislature. (For additional demographic details about the state, see Table 4.2.)

Parties are responsible for candidate recruitment, organization of the legislature, and setting the political agenda. In New Jersey, particularly strong parties have been described as "the bone and sinew of our political system, active and competitive in their drives for voter allegiance and government power" (Connors and Dunham 1993, 99). Powerful county chairs largely determined the candidates and leadership positions for the legislature and excluded women (Carroll and Dittmar 2012; McCormick and McCormick 1994). The control of political power in New Jersey by party organizations contributed to

TABLE 4.2. NEW JERSEY DEMOGRAPHICS (NCSL 2010; U.S. CENSUS BUREAU 2011)	
2010 population	8,791,894
Population density	Ranked 1st in the nation
Political culture (Elazar 1984)	Individualistic
Party control—assembly (2009)	Democrat
Party control—senate (2009)	Democrat
Party of the governor (2009)	Democrat
Proportion of women—legislature (2009)	30% Ranked 12th in the nation
Proportion of women—legislative leadership (2009)	25% Ranked 24th in the nation
Party competition—assembly (2009)	16-seat difference
Party competition—senate (2009)	6-seat difference
Professionalization (Squire 2007)	Ranked 11th in the nation

the frustrations of women who had been elected to office, as they often felt stymied by party bosses.

In contradiction to Beckwith's (2007) hypothesis that new women would be averse to a caucus, interview subjects here cite the election of a surge of new women legislators as a primary reason for the development of a formal organization. New Jersey saw a surge in women elected to the legislature between 2004 and 2010. In 2007, in particular, a large number of women were elected to the legislature, dramatically increasing the number from twenty-six to thirty-five.[6] This change took them from twenty-seventh in the nation, in terms of women's representation, to fourteenth. All interviewees cited this increase as the reason for the emergence of a women's caucus at this particular time in history. Two women remember Senator Shirley Turner's (D) role in reviving an attempt to create a women's caucus:

> This time, when we finally got together, I believe it was Shirley who took the initiative . . . to again say, "Let's try it again." And we all said, "Yeah, let's try it again." And then we came together, and it was a large group of women that came together, whereas

other times, the large group wasn't there because women weren't elected in force, but this seemed to be a more activist group. Perhaps many new members, younger members . . .[7]

Allen's comments point to the importance of not only a threshold of women but also women who are willing to challenge the status quo— women with a shared gender consciousness. It appears, in this case, that the combination of senior women leaders and new women not afraid to signal their gender as politically salient allowed for the possibility of a caucus to emerge.

Women made up 28 percent of the Republican Party in New Jersey's State Assembly in 2009, which is the highest out of my four case studies (CAWP 2009b; NCSL 2009). In this case, a larger proportion of Republican women correlated with a successful caucus attempt. Having more women within the party may enable women to take more risks—including working across the aisle—whereas a smaller proportion might constrain women's choices, as to engage in bipartisan work with other women could be perceived by the party as disloyal. Republican and Democratic women face different challenges when deciding whether to caucus or not because they are weighing different costs.

Party Democracy Act

In reaction to this exclusion by political party leaders, the women's caucus chose party reform as their first policy area rallying them together against a common enemy. The first legislative priority for the New Jersey Women's Legislative Caucus was the Party Democracy Act, which was signed into law on October 2, 2009. The bill required county political party committees to adopt constitutions and bylaws and provide lists of committee members to the county clerk. It also eliminated fixed terms for committee members and chairs (New Jersey State Legislature Assembly 2008–2009).

Many women noted that early successes were important for the women moving forward because they "showed that women could get together across the aisle, and we had people, women from both houses, and I would say that, probably, is what gave us the energy to think that this might be the time."[8] While the ethics reform at the center of this legislation was not a traditional "women's issue," like reproductive health or domestic violence, women's status as outsiders in the political process led to bipartisan efforts by female leaders on the issue.[9] The women legislators did not initiate this legislation, which was brought to the legislature by an outside advocacy group, but rallied around it early in the legislative process. It was an issue they all agreed was important because of their experience in political parties across the state. For example, Assemblywomen Mary Pat Angelini (R) retold this story:

> I heard rumors for years that he (Monmouth Republican Party Chair Bill Dowd) sat in the living room of a very prominent Republican in that county and they decided who was going to run for what and that was it. That was the way it was done and has always been done. A little sunshine on that process would have disinfected a lot of stuff that was going on there.[10]

Many women legislators felt that party leaders discouraged their participation in elective office, and this exclusion united women on both sides of the aisle in supporting legislation that would make the process of nomination more transparent.

What type of legislation the caucus would prioritize would emerge from the shared interests and values of the women. Women legislators, especially Republican women, did not want the emphasis of the caucus to narrow their impact to traditional "women's issues." Senator Beck put it this way:

> Diane Allen and Loretta Weinberg felt that it was sensible for us to come together and find common ground and become advocates for certain policy issues and that we should not be limited simply to women's and children's issues. We obviously have a lot to say about fiscal issues, and the challenges of the budget and ethics etc. so that we could find other policy topics, not that we are not involved in women's [issues]. Those are natural, and we are all involved in them, but there are other topics too to draw on. . . . I think it is interesting that our first topic that we

addressed was not an issue of health care for children or domestic violence, etc. but . . . an issue of ethics.[11]

Party differences did emerge, however, on the next policy issue that the caucus faced.

Party Polarization and Women's Differences

Party polarization within a legislature can negatively affect the launch of a women's caucus by preventing women from trusting each other and finding common interests. In the New Jersey case, legislators cited a natural bond between women as the explanation for why a bipartisan caucus emerged. Gender consciousness among the women legislators enabled them to overcome party differences initially. When asked why they chose a bipartisan model rather than organizing within their respective parties, several women noted that, because of life experiences, women have interests in common that can be dealt with across party lines. They felt that other women understood these issues better than men and that, if a consensus existed among women across party lines, more attention would be paid to those issues and that their collective voice would carry more weight than any individual efforts. As Assemblywoman Joan Voss (D) explains, "There was a strong sentiment that women have a reason to coalesce even across party and that they do so differently than men. And because there are so few, both Republicans and Democrats have to work together, I mean, if we're going to get anything accomplished."[12] Kathy Crotty also noted that women legislate differently:

> I think they [women] still recognize that they have more in common with each other. . . . They [men] like to fight. I think the difference is, I think women are much more result oriented. They want an outcome rather than winning. I think that is one of the things that they would talk to you about. Going back to their life experiences, raising a family, that is what you have to do. . . . [Y]ou have children who have differences, you have a spouse that has differences, [so] that is one of the things you do.

> You facilitate consensus in your family. It [is] natural to them, and they don't have time to fool around with process.[13]

During the time of the initial founding of the New Jersey caucus, most of the women agreed that, generally speaking, women are more bipartisan than men. It was this commonality across party lines that enabled the caucus to emerge.

The Party Democracy bill passed and the early success of this legislative win generated additional enthusiasm for public policy action from the caucus. All of the women noted that education and healthcare were likely issues to be addressed by the caucus. Indeed, in early June 2010, women from the caucus engaged in bipartisan action that concerned access to medical care for New Jersey women. Sixteen women from both parties and both houses heard testimony for more than three hours from physicians, medical school administrators, and midwives about the availability of quality health care for women. However, while it appeared that the women's caucus would be a viable vehicle for bipartisan action on women's issues in the New Jersey legislature, this testimony did not produce any formal legislation.

THE RESOURCES TO GET THE JOB DONE

The mobilization of resources that include not only financial contributions but also time and energy is a crucial factor in organizing (McAdam, McCarthy, and Zald 1996). Without the time and space to meet, a caucus cannot function. Further, staff is necessary in order to coordinate meetings and research for the organization to accomplish its goals. This dependence on staffing is particularly true for a policy caucus such as the one in New Jersey. The resources I expected to facilitate the creation of a women's caucus included support from external women's groups, staff, and time. Further, entrepreneurs are vital resources enabling the caucus to get off the ground.

External Organizations

Women's organizations outside the legislature can be resources for women legislators in their attempt to caucus. Organizations can provide legitimacy to caucus entrepreneurs' claims that a caucus is necessary. They can also provide information and policy research for policy-oriented groups. In New Jersey, for example, several women's organizations like CAWP worked to ameliorate the party bias limiting the number of women in office. While Assemblywoman Angelini did not feel that her party had discriminated against her as a woman in any specific way, she cited apathy when she first stepped out into the political arena, which was overcome only by her participation in a Republican women's organization dedicated to mobilizing potential women candidates:

> I was a member of the Christie Todd Whitman Excellence in Public Service Series [an organization designed to encourage women candidates], and as I was going through that, I wrote a letter with my resume and sent it to our party chairperson, the Republican chair in Monmouth County. His name was Bill Dowd. . . . He never even responded to me. I didn't even know, I didn't know about county committees. I mean I learned that through the Whitman series.[14]

This type of preparation provided by external women's groups, such as CAWP, is credited with the surge of women into the legislature enabling a caucus to form.

In some states, in addition to candidate recruitment and training external women's organizations host events to bring the women legislators together. New Jersey had the assistance of a few outside groups when they were starting out. CAWP at the Eagleton Institute of Politics at Rutgers University hosted some of the informal meetings during which women discussed the idea of a caucus and potential formalization. It was important, as noted by volunteer caucus staffer Kathy Crotty, for there to be a neutral site for coming together, where women of both parties felt comfortable. External organizations provided a nonpartisan space for organizing, indicating how influential party is and how difficult it would be to ignore within the physical space of the legislature. The Woodrow Wilson School of Public and International Affairs also hosted an initial meeting for the women. When pressed, however, the interviewees all stated that the impetus for organizing was internal to the women legislators themselves, not driven by outside influences.

Professionalism

Professionalism may also positively affect a women's caucus attempt by providing women legislators with staff and time. In the New Jersey case, the importance of the availability of a newly retired senate staffer was often repeated. Kathy Crotty, who served as executive director of the Senate Majority Office for twenty-three years, volunteered her time to staff the Women's Legislative Caucus. According to Assemblywoman Nellie Pou (D), Crotty's experience and respected reputation on both sides of the aisle made her an ideal organizer:

> I think the fact that we were able to get someone, Kathy Crotty . . . the timing of that, the fact that she had retired, her interest in women's issues—she is a giant in itself—her personality her ability to get things done, her wealth of knowledge in terms of how the legislature works because she worked for so many years in such an important position allowed for the ongoing coordination and communication of the women's caucus. The resources were available and the timing; it was a good marriage for all of us.[15]

Crotty worked closely with the caucus cochairs to plan and organize events. She was responsible for finding meeting locations, dates and times that worked for all the members, and for promoting the caucus to a broader public. Because Crotty was doing this work, the caucus cochairs did not have to take time away from their other legislative responsibilities. She also would keep the cochairs motivated and on task. She was, however, a retired legislative staffer and not paid by the legislature for this work. In this case, staffing was crucial, according to caucus members, but not a function of the level of New Jersey's professionalization.

Time

Because gender roles outside the legislature influence legislators' experience within the institution, it may be difficult for women legislators to build the relationships necessary for a bipartisan caucus. Opportunities during session for socializing may be few and far between. Women's societal roles have been an impediment to a woman's desire for both a family and a political career (Blair and Henry 1981; Carroll 1989; Dodson 1997; Fulton et al. 2006; Kirkpatrick 1974; Lawless and Fox 2005; Stoper 1977; Thomas 2002). Today, the balance between serving both the legislature and the family pose particular challenges for women, especially those wanting to do something beyond their own district concerns. In all these cases, including New Jersey, the ability to get to know one another was challenged by gender norms because of women legislators' disproportionate responsibility for family obligations. One woman legislator explained that it was difficult to socialize and get to know her colleagues because of her role in the family:

> I have three small children, okay, so literally it takes me two hours to drive down, two hours to drive back to Trenton. I don't have the ability in my life to hang out and just go have a drink or go to dinner or you know what I'm saying? That is just not my, that's not my life. But for some of the men who are at different points in their lives—and I'm not criticizing them, I'm just telling you a reality—that they have the ability to have this network of "Oh, let's go out and smoke a cigar" or "Let's go out and"—and I know this sounds sort of weird, but it's a different, they have it different.[16]

Participation in a caucus is an extra pull on a woman legislator's time and focus. She may consider it less important than her obligations to her family. On the other hand, this imbalance of responsibility is also something that draws women together in a common bond.

Time in office is another factor in the creation of women's caucuses. Conceivably, term limits could prevent women from organizing by restricting their time in office, which then limits their ability to develop relationships and hone the political skills necessary to organize. They may shorten women's policy horizons, requiring a triage attitude toward what is possible in a limited time frame. New Jersey does not have term limits and therefore these potential obstacles were not present in this case. However, the cocreators of that caucus, Senator Weinberg and Senator Allen, were very senior members among the women, indicating that experience gained over many terms in office develops caucus entrepreneurs' repertoire of political skills.

Senator Weinberg was first elected to the New Jersey State Assembly in 1992 and the state senate in 2006. Senator Allen was first elected to the New Jersey State Assembly in 1996 and moved to the state senate in 1998. Their experience very likely influenced their success. When this experience met with the exuberance of newly elected women, Senators Allen and Weinberg recognized and seized a political opportunity. It would be reasonable to then expect that term limits in other states may hurt those women's ability to organize by limiting women legislators' experience in office.[17]

Entrepreneurs

When asked if a caucus would have been formed were it not for Senator Weinberg's initiative, Crotty, caucus volunteer staffer, said:

> Maybe. Less likely. . . . These things are so much a function of those who assume the leadership positions. So if Loretta maintains her position and her interest, which I am sure she would if she stays, then I think it would remain viable. And if the other women recognize that this is a way to advance their own agenda and have influence, then they will too—if they are smart.[18]

Some precedent for organizing among women in New Jersey existed prior to the influx of women into the legislature. In the 1990s, women (including then assemblywomen Weinberg and Allen) had built relationships with one another across party lines. These preexisting relationships laid the foundation of trust between them. Through these informal ties, women legislators shared stories of party bias and family obligations, establishing common ground.

FRAMING THE TASK AT HAND

For a caucus launch to succeed, entrepreneurs must recruit participants. The message they send about why women would want to spend their limited time and attention on this organization is crucial to the creation of a caucus. Caucus entrepreneurs can emphasize women's common experiences in order to unite the women and highlight their need for a place to support one another in a male-dominated space. They may respond to messages that acknowledge their marginalization by party leaders. They may also choose to argue that their unique voices are necessary to shape policy in the state. In the case of New Jersey, caucus entrepreneurs argued strongly that they could and should pursue a joint policy agenda.

Gender Consciousness

In Chapter 3, I hypothesized that gender consciousness was likely a frame employed in states where caucus attempts were successful. My research reveals that recognition of common interests among women legislators corresponds to successful attempts to create a women's caucus because common interests can be a useful argument for why a women's caucus are necessary. In the case of New Jersey, women legislators there often cited a "natural bond" among women, common interests and experiences that linked them to one another despite party labels.

Caucus members cited shared life experience as something that set them apart from their male colleagues and brought them together as a caucus. For example, all of the interviewed women stated they believed that men and women bring something different to the legislature. While the legislators did not like categorizing issues as "women's issues," they noted that women do not have the same reputation for corruption as their male counterparts and that it is important that women be represented in the body. Crotty noted that different life experience brings different perspectives on policy:

> I think in part it has something to do with the issues they [men] may be insensitive to . . . which are a function of the fact that women have a unique life experience. The forty-eight-hour rule is a good example of that. . . . None of these people have ever been in a hospital and delivered a baby, and so they are not very well equipped to answer whether you are supposed to kick

someone out after they have the baby. . . . [T]he same thing [is true] with the mastectomies and all that. They may have had wives who have [had these experiences], but that is still not the same.[19]

Senator Beck similarly reflects, "I think it is important that women come together and share what is, I believe, a natural bond and that we do address policy issues a little bit differently."[20] It appears that without this recognition of common experiences and interests, a caucus would not have emerged.

Party Dissatisfaction

Women may be motivated to caucus if they are dissatisfied with party structures and party responses to policy issues as previously demonstrated at the federal level (Gertzog 2004; Hammond 1998). Therefore, I hypothesized that it may be possible to correlate the use of party dissatisfaction as a frame to successful caucus attempts.

Political parties in New Jersey do not have a strong record of nurturing and promoting women in state politics. With power concentrated at the county party-chair level, many women reported negative experiences within their own political parties. It is no surprise then that a bill that demanded more transparency for political party committees motivated women legislators to act. Senator Weinberg said, "I thought my experiences were unique to me, but then I brought it up at a women's legislative meeting, and we all had a war story to tell, on both sides of the aisle."[21]

Senator Weinberg had been an assemblywoman in District 37 in Bergen County from 1992 to 2005. When the sitting state senator in her district died, and Weinberg was chosen to fill the vacancy, she pursued her party's nomination when it was time to run for the seat, despite the Democratic Party chair's preference for another candidate. She alleged that the party chair had removed and added members to the party committee (who would nominate the candidate) throughout the process. Ultimately, Weinberg went to court in order to validate her nomination to the ballot. She won that battle as well as the senate seat. Crotty explained how this experience led to women's support of the Party Democracy Act legislation:

> That drove her [Senator Weinberg] to recognize that without the county committee list being published she didn't really know or understand what the rules and the bylaws of the convention were and how it is conducted, who can vote and how is it a secret ballot, machine vote, voice vote? She didn't really know that.[22]

The lack of transparency in the process disadvantaged Senator Weinberg politically just as it had her colleague Assemblywoman Angelini. However, she was not cowed by powerful party interests as an individual candidate and she encouraged other women legislators to support the Party Democracy Act (PDA) to reform a system that had wronged her and her colleagues. Crotty continued:

> She [Weinberg] talked to a lot of the women: Senator Diane Allen, who had conflicts with her county party leadership, as well as other women, who had very similar experiences where they had been disadvantaged in terms of the way the political apparatus operated. She got all of them to cosponsor it, and the changes were not dramatic, but these are the kinds of things that entrench political interests; they were very threatened.[23]

Not all legislators, however, saw the PDA as a gender issue. In particular, two Republican women cited it as a general, but nongendered issue. Assemblywoman Handlin described it as an "everybody issue."[24] Assemblywoman Angelini described it similarly.[25] When asked why the PDA legislation was the first issue item for the caucus, Crotty responded:

> I think from the discussions we had very early on, they [the women's caucus] are very sensitive to the idea that they probably need to stay away from some of the socially sensitive issues, because there are diverse viewpoints and if the discussions break

down over issues like abortion, they are going to get nowhere. So they would really forfeit an opportunity to work on the Democracy Act or this access-to-physicians issue.[26]

Senator Jennifer Beck was asked if the PDA legislation could be considered a "women's issue," and responded: "I do think it is a women's issue, because by and large women aren't heading up the political organizations that are nominating candidates . . . and in this case, these two elected officials [Senator Weinberg and Senator Allen] faced significant challenges from those organizational structures."[27]

Most women admitted that New Jersey does not have a particularly women-friendly history. Until 2007, New Jersey ranked low among states in number of women in public office (CAWP 2018). Women legislators who reported that they themselves had not faced opposition from party leaders when running for public office nonetheless cited examples of other sitting women legislators who had faced such opposition. Few told their own stories and many were hesitant to describe experiences as negative. Some accounts described being excluded from decision making. Assemblywoman Alison McHose (R) noted, "There was a situation where, I was not privy to some information, and I kind of felt like if I were a man, that I would not have been treated the same way."[28] She went on to note that, in her assessment "it was almost as if they didn't want to tell me because they thought that my response would be emotional. You know what I'm saying?" Others talked about gendered behavior that diminished their contribution: "New Jersey had very few women in the legislature when I first got down there. . . . And so you kind of get patted on the head and tolerated. Having been a teacher for over forty years, I have a very big mouth and so I don't get patted on the head very long."[29]

When asked if women experience the legislature differently because of their gender, Senator Diane Allen recounted this incident that she observed with another woman legislator and former Senate majority leader Richard Codey (D):

Oh, my gosh. She stood up to say something, and he just went after her, and it was so inappropriate. And I remember it's happened a couple of times where people have treated her inappropriately. She's a young, good-looking woman, and that's—it's tough. It's harder to do. I've just been around long enough to have given as good as I've gotten, perhaps.[30]

Allen went on to describe that, beyond explicit bias, there are different standards for women and men in the legislature. The acknowledgment of the experiences of women and men in the legislature as different is a signal of gender consciousness, another motivating factor for a women's caucus. Dissatisfaction with the treatment one receives from political party leadership may trigger gender consciousness, indicating that these frames can intersect and mutually reinforce each other. If women know they are being held to different standards, then organizing a space for support and action is a legitimate step toward ameliorating gender inequality within the legislature. This atmosphere was present in New Jersey as Allen explains:

> I will tell you that if you have had a male member with—I'll use this gingerly—with less intelligence and a female member with less intelligence, the male member would probably skate through, and the female would be picked on and shown up and . . . [t]here are different standards.[31]

Others' stories were specific to their candidacy and lack of party support.

> I mean, there were just many years of finding it very difficult to make any headway against a very, very entrenched group of people who didn't want any change and didn't want any new ideas, and a lot of them ended up going to jail, so . . .[32]

> Every county has a Republican and Democrat chairman, and they're the ones that really call the shots, okay.[33]

Some legislators cited this bias as an explanation for the caucus:

> I think it was solely just there were enough of us who wanted to at least try it. I mean, none of us knew and we still don't know

what kind of results it will actually produce. But, again, there were enough of us who were frustrated with business as usual.[34]

Women represent 50 percent of the voters in the state of New Jersey. And I think that we are an important voting bloc, and we should be heard. There are some, as I alluded to before, that get frustrated that the party chairmen, who are often involved with selecting candidates to run at different levels, are primarily all men. I'm proud on the Republican side that my home county of Sussex has a female chair right now, so, but I think she's the only one in the whole Republican Party statewide. So we definitely, as I said, just wanted—it's one more way that we can express our strength, and I think it's important.[35]

Bias within the party system appears to have been the impetus for the first major piece of legislation that the New Jersey caucus took on as a group—the PDA—as well as the frame used to unite the women in their cause. Women's experience with intraparty bias spoke to their shared life experience as excluded from the traditional path to power reserved for men.

Women in New Jersey have fought their way into the legislature, sometimes in opposition to traditional party leadership. They feel they have been through something similar as a consequence of their gender and therefore, once inside the institution, their common experience produced a shared belief that women deserved respect from their political parties. A bipartisan caucus, then, is not surprising under conditions in which women felt slighted or discriminated against by political parties.

Caucus Type

In New Jersey, policy was definitely a priority for the caucus. These women were committed to influencing the policy agenda from the beginning. As Assemblywoman McHose noted:

Many of us felt that we might have an opportunity to work on issues as a whole, as I said, from both parties and we thought that this would be an effective way to do it and to have an official caucus rather than an informal caucus, which we had had in the past. We decided to really make it a legitimate organization—not legitimate, like formal, and organize it—so that people would recognize us, we would like to be looked at as a force to be reckoned with.[36]

The women agreed that they did not want the caucus to be constrained by a preoccupation with traditional "women's issues." All had hopes that this caucus, while it was an organization for women, would be a mechanism by which women could have an impact more broadly within the legislature. At the one organizational meeting I attended, the focus was a discussion of legislation that had already passed but that many of the women had problems with and wanted to improve in future actions. For example, they talked about ways to improve divorce laws in the state so that women would not suffer as much financial strain when a marriage ended. They discussed the sharing of information surrounding the bill and planned a discussion of further action by the group once all had a chance to look over the new information.

How caucus entrepreneurs frame the actions of the caucus determines their ability to mobilize members. When Assemblywoman Handlin was asked, "Do you think that the women's caucus will focus specifically on women's issues bills or do you expect them to expand beyond?" she noted the importance of consensus and framing and the long-term success of the caucus: "I think it depends how successful we are with this health care stuff."[37] In this case, policy did not affect the success of the attempt to create a women's caucus and even aided in the attempt by uniting the women around the successful Party Democracy Act; however, it may hurt the long-term maintenance of the group.

Family Planning Grant

The first (and final) test of the unity of the New Jersey caucus would be the Family Planning Grant bill sponsored by Senator Loretta Weinberg and a handful of Democratic (men and women) legislators in late June 2010. The bill appropriated funds to family planning centers for preventative health care for citizens in the community. Eighteen women sponsored or cosponsored the bill; all were Democrats. Initially, the two Republican senators, Diane Allen and Jennifer Beck, voted yes for the bill, but in a later round of voting, Senator Allen rescinded her support of the bill, stating on her website:

> Initially, we supported S-2139, which rededicates $7.5 million from the State Employees' Prescription Drug Program toward further women's health initiatives. However, upon further review by the State Treasurer, it is now clear that this transfer would place the state prescription fund into a $5.6 million deficit and risk access to needed medicines for women and children. Therefore, if Senator President Sweeney (D) calls for a veto override of S-2139, we will vote to support maintaining a balanced budget and ensure there is continued access to prescription medicines for families. (D. Allen 2010)

In the assembly, six Republican women voted no on the bill; three abstained. While Assemblywoman Nellie Pou (D) was recorded as "not voting," she had this to say about the split among the women:

> I would say, though, that while it is important that we have that [a women's caucus], it really needs to have the ability to work and advocate on women's issues. We cannot pick and choose and separate what those issues are. . . . It was important to see that both the Democrats and Republican women and members of the women's legislative caucus stood behind this issue [Family Planning Bill]. I find it very difficult to believe that not one Republican woman would . . . be in support of this. I am sure that is not the case. So we have to really assess are we really, really going to be there on issues that affect women, or are we going to pick issues along party lines from a philosophical view?[38]

Since this vote, the Women's Legislative Caucus of New Jersey has not held a bipartisan meeting. Senator Weinberg described the impact of this controversy on the caucus in this way:

We had a kind of big setback and a little disappointment, which I have sort of not yet worked through in my own head, as well as dealing with some of the women in the caucus. . . . I was very disappointed that not one woman, some of them abstained . . . so I have not talked to some of my counterparts on the other side of the aisle, because first of all, I was too hot under the collar. If you couldn't stand up on this, then what is the object of us even having a women's caucus?[39]

In summary, eighteen women sponsored or cosponsored the bill—all Democrats. In the initial vote for passage in the senate, the two Republican senators, Allen and Beck, voted yes for the bill. In a later round of voting, Senator Allen rescinded her support of the bill. Democratic women legislators attribute this lack of support to pressure from the newly elected Republican governor Chris Christie. Allen and other Republican legislators denied this as the primary cause of the change in vote.[40]

Following the failure of the Family Planning Grant bill, the caucus held no further bipartisan meetings or hearings. Democratic women legislators expressed disappointment that the women were not able to vote together in support of a bill they felt was an obvious policy position for the caucus. In contrast, Senator Allen denied that her withdrawal of support for this bill reflected in any way an abdication of her support of women's health.[41] She saw this as a fiscal responsibility issue and argued that had the money been available in the budget she would have had no problem supporting it. In interviews, some Democratic and Republican women expressed hope that this disagreement would not prevent the group from working together in the next legislative session. However, as of this writing, the group has not met since June 2010.[42]

In Chapter 3, I hypothesized that caucuses that set socializing as the top priority for organizing a caucus were more likely to succeed than those who set public policy as their primary function. From the start, the caucus founders framed the New Jersey Women's Legislative Caucus as a policy caucus. Women were already socially connected to each other through informal caucuses in the House and senior women legislators who took the initiative to mentor newer members. The legislators then did not see networking as the primary function of the caucus. Nurturing a social network for women legislators was not a frame used in the New Jersey attempt to create a women's caucus.

LOOKING TO THE FUTURE

The interview data from the New Jersey case demonstrate the importance of caucus entrepreneurs and their ability to navigate their political circumstances to organize women within legislatures. The previous informal relationships among women in both houses served as a starting point that needed a catalyst in order to gain sufficient momentum for regeneration. The influx of women in the 2007 election provided that catalyst. Women recognized that their numbers meant that they would have to band together to have an impact. Entrepreneurs (the more senior women legislators) seized on this political opportunity by appealing to commonalities among women, including bias in the political structure and relying on a well-respected volunteer to bring participants together and manage the day-to-day organizing of group events. Newly elected women who believed that women brought a different voice to the legislature welcomed the initiative of more senior legislators.

The caucus entrepreneurs employed frames—gender consciousness, dissatisfaction with political parties, and policy as a priority— that were initially successful in motivating women to participate in the caucus. Women in this legislature were certainly dissatisfied with the existing political structures and the difficulties women faced in winning elective office. Women legislators cited the caucus as offering more weight to women's voices in the legislature as an agenda-altering mechanism. Women in the legislature had already brought attention, as individuals, to issues important to them; the caucus was seen as another way, among many, to accomplish those goals.

The question remains whether the caucus will be able to maintain this purpose over the long term. Issues affecting women's health, such as the Family Planning Grant bill, show that while partisan pressure was not present at the initial founding of the caucus, they have arisen, presenting a tough choice for both Democratic and Republican women. Despite the seemingly oppositional nature of their first piece of legislation, which challenged traditional party operations, all the women reported that the Party Democracy Act was so common sense that no one could be publically opposed to it. While the political infrastructure was not happy with the change, it was politically fatal to oppose transparency in the process. The Family Planning Grant bill, which received negative attention from the Republican governor, proved to be divisive.

Although New Jersey is a successful case in that they met for one year after an initial attempt by women legislators, whether or not it will successfully maintain itself remains to be seen. The New Jersey Women's Legislative Caucus has not met since their June 2010 hearing on women's health disparities. No cochairs have called for meetings nor have they communicated with each other specifically about the caucus. Whether or not the caucus will continue to exist is a question answered differently by each interview subject. Assemblywoman Spencer seemed hopeful that the caucus will take up new topics in the next session, including funding for domestic violence centers, reproductive issues, funding of family health care centers, and human trafficking. She said, "Next year we will probably get started back up again because there are some issues that will be coming up that we will have to tackle together" although she admits that with the new governor, "the dynamics changed."[43] Assemblywoman Nellie Pou expressed her regret:

> We wanted to serve as a strong force on women's issues. . . . But my disappointment is that when we are tested and given the opportunity to do that, we do good in one but then once it becomes a party label issue, we retreat. That should not be the case on both sides. It just so happened that this happened to the Republican women. I hope that we never come upon an issue [where] the Democratic women will be in a position to pull the same reaction that just happened [on the Family Planning Grant bill].[44]

Senator Allen was more vague but hopeful, stating that she believed women would get past the setback that the Family Planning Grant bill presented and find common ground where they could work together:

I think that a lot of politics got involved, unfortunately . . . [and] made it a little difficult to bring everybody together. My sense is that in the coming year, as we move into new areas and perhaps have the luxury of a year without political pressure—although it being a presidential year, who knows? (it is never easy)—my hope is, and I can't speak for everybody, but most of the women who were involved or who I have spoken to all want to see this kind of thing work.[45]

Allen's prognosis for the future effect of this issue on the caucus was this: "I am not happy with the way politics gets involved in important issues, but sometimes it does, but now hopefully the other side will just drop it, and let's actually find some money and move forward."[46] Here, from her perspective, the politics is partisanship and the important issue is women's health. She sees Democrats, not men, as "the other side." Assemblywoman Amy Handlin attributed the lack of communication and meetings to partisanship, which she too felt could be overcome. But she was not aware of any plans to meet or work together in the immediate future.[47] Finally, Senator Weinberg was the least optimistic stating that it was doubtful that women legislators would have a productive working relationship until a new governor (presumably a Democrat) was elected.[48] She continues to work across partisan lines with individual women but does not believe that collective action can be successful in the current political climate. For instance, she and Senator Beck put forward S-2665 (2010–2011), which called for the repeal of several New Jersey state laws that included sexist language. Governor Christie signed this bill into law August 19, 2011.

Finally, Crotty, volunteer staffer, is the only one involved to admit that the effort at a women's caucus is unlikely to continue in New Jersey:

The efforts to have a bipartisan women's caucus pretty much fell apart in June of 2010, when the women on the Republican side refused to support the health funding for the family planning program. There was a sort of pause in the activity. . . . There was a discussion to try to get it going again, but there were subsequent attempts to restore the money, and again it was done on a completely partisan basis. I think folks just concluded, at least Senator Weinberg concluded, that if they wouldn't stand up for that issue, then what was the point?[49]

Crotty implied that without Senator Weinberg to instigate a meeting, any caucus is unlikely to succeed. Her prediction seems to hold, considering that in 2012, no other cochair called a meeting or organized an event. While the caucus has not met since 2010, Senators Weinberg and Allen made another attempt in 2017 at working together—this time on equal pay legislation. Their bill would increase the size of damages that victims of discrimination can seek, and includes other measures, such as strict reporting requirements for companies doing business with the state. Then-governor Christie, however, reemerged as a spoiler, and, as of June 2017, Senator Allen moved forward with her own bill following Christie's conditional veto of the Weinberg-Allen cosponsored bill (Reitmeyer 2017). In April 2018, with a newly elected Democratic governor Phil Murphy in place, Senator Weinberg saw her bill S104, the Diane B. Allen Equal Pay Act, signed into law (Arco 2018).

In New Jersey, women reinvigorated an on-again, off-again social network after a game-changing election in 2007 ushered in women to fill spots vacated by men under indictment. These women, encouraged by respected leadership, took on the issue of ethics by supporting a bill that will open doors for future women candidates and help them avoid the discrimination that has been so pervasive. Whether or not the women continue to see collective action as an effective way to accomplish their goals will be a function of participants' cost-and-benefit analysis. If women continue to disagree on issues, they may decide to avoid policy and focus the caucus on mentoring and support for members instead. They may decide to caucus only within their political parties. The motivation to form a women's caucus, a shared-issue priority as a consequence of similar life experience, is challenged by one of the most fundamental identities of a legislator, political party. How the women of the New Jersey State legislature choose to balance both their gender and party identity will determine the success or failure of the women's caucus. Despite negative experiences as party members, the women legislators here are still constrained by that identity in their advocacy on behalf of women. Institutionally, open seats created by corruption investigations allowed for an influx of mo-tivated women legislators that senior women recognized as a political opportunity. These caucus entrepreneurs seized this opportunity and mobilized frames around longtime discrimination by political parties in candidate recruitment and support. Unfortunately, an electoral shift in which a Republican took control of the governorship in 2010 disrupted the alliance between Democratic and Republican women putting the caucus at risk and demonstrating that elections can serve as both political opportunities and obstacles to women's organizing.

In the next chapter, I consider the Colorado Women's Legislative Caucus, which was also formed in 2009. It is the second successful case of the creation of a women's caucus and, unlike its New Jersey counterpart, has flourished since its founding. By comparing New Jersey and Colorado, I identify which factors are common to both and therefore influential in determining the success of a caucus launch and how their two approaches diverged, leading to very different long-term outcomes.

5

THE COLORADO WOMEN'S LEGISLATIVE CAUCUS

TIMELINE

1980s: Initial caucus attempt is thwarted by legislative leadership.

1995: 100th-anniversary celebration of first women to serve in the legislature.

December 2009: Representative Karen Middleton secures grant from the Women's Foundation of Colorado.

February 17, 2009: First official event, a social happy hour.

Beginning of 2010 session: NCSL meeting to learn about best practices of women's caucuses.

March 2010: Women's History Month floor recognition of women in legislature.

April 2010: Event at Governor's Mansion that brought together former and current women officeholders.

August 2010: Ethics Commission grants permission for 501(c)3 with Metropolitan State College of Denver.

End of 2010 session: Representative Karen Middleton leaves the legislature and Representative Jeanne Labuda (D) takes her place on the executive board.

In Colorado, Democratic representative Karen Middleton, a motivated entrepreneur, sought to take advantage of the large number of women in office by initiating a women's caucus. Envisioning the long-term impact of this number, she and her fellow early adopters compromised on their own expectations for its impact on policy and instead sought to establish a social caucus with bipartisan participation. These women, supported by the Women's Foundation of Colorado, prioritized women's history and relationship building, rather than policy, which allowed the caucus to succeed, as Republican women would likely not have participated otherwise.[1] The external support from the Women's Foundation was vital to the logistical launch of this caucus, enabling a staffer outside of the legislative structure to organize events and accomplish its research goals. While women and men legislators in Colorado acknowledged women's different styles and contributions to the legislature, this perceived difference was not necessarily connected to caucus creation. The important mobilizing frames in Colorado included a shared interest in women's historical contribution to politics in the state, a noncontroversial theme that attracted even reluctant legislators to the caucus. The Colorado case demonstrates the importance of caucus entrepreneurs tempering their own ambitions for the group with political reality. By establishing what was possible at the time—a social caucus—Representative Middleton built a foundation from which a policy agenda could emerge at some point in the future. (For additional demographic details about the interview subjects cited in this chapter, see Table 5.1.)

TABLE 5.1. COLORADO INTERVIEW SUBJECTS (13) DEMOGRAPHICS		
Party affiliation	Legislative leaders	Gender
2 Republicans, 10 Democrats, 1 nonpartisan staffer	2	2 male, 11 female

A SAVVY NEWCOMER SEIZES OPPORTUNITY

In December 2009, Representative Middleton, having assumed office in 2008, secured an $8,500 grant from the Women's Foundation of Colorado (WFC) to assist with historical research on women in the legislature and support staff and events for a women's caucus she intended to create. She discussed her plan informally with her own mentor, Senator Suzanne Williams (D), and Speaker of the House Terrance Carroll (D). The Colorado Women's Legislative Caucus held its first official event on February 17, 2009—an informal happy hour for all women legislators. At this meeting, the women legislators decided among themselves that policy consensus would not be sought among the members. They determined three goals for the caucus: (1) connect women legislators, (2) draw from history, and (3) build camaraderie by listening to and sharing life experiences with one another. The first four board members of the caucus were Representative Middleton, the founder of the caucus, Senator Williams, Representative Marsha Looper (R), and Senator Nancy Spence (R). Representative Middleton approached the other three women informally, asking them to serve as contacts for the group until it could be formalized and elections could select the official leaders. These four board members came up with a preliminary plan for the caucus.

The activities prioritized by the leadership focused on the theme agreed on for the caucus, which was primarily social in nature, relying on a shared interest in women's contributions to the state's political history. In March 2010, the women legislators celebrated Women's History Month by speaking each morning of session in the public comments. Every day a different woman legislator would speak on the floor, honoring a woman who had served previously in the legislature. The women featured were selected from the 115 years since the first woman was elected to the state legislature in 1894. The following month, women legislators held an event at the governor's residence and invited all women who had previously served to attend and share their stories. This event was very popular with current women officeholders, who spoke fondly of the opportunity to hear from other women who had faced similar experiences.

The example of the Colorado Women's Legislative Caucus illustrates the importance of a caucus entrepreneur correctly reading the political environment. The political opportunities that played the biggest role in Colorado's establishment of a women's caucus were the increase in the number of women elected to office and the recent drift toward partisanship in the state. Representative Middleton wanted to harness the collective power of women whose presence was significant at 37 percent. With partisanship on the rise in a state that had been historically divided more along issues than party, many members were inclined to support a bipartisan social group in order to stave off increasingly divisive politics. Similarly, a political opportunity was created by new institutional rules restricting socializing among members, positioning a social caucus as an ideal pitch to legislators who were feeling increasingly isolated.

Political Culture

There are three components of political culture that mattered for the establishment of the women's caucus in Colorado, which created political opportunities specific to its political history. First, the long history of women's political participation resulted in their inclusion in government for far longer than in other states. Second, Colorado also has institutionalized direct democracy that led, in 2006, to Amendment 41, which left legislators looking for opportunities to connect.[2] This perceived need facilitated the establishment of a women's caucus. More women in office, a desire to connect, and a lack of strong opposition enabled Middleton and her colleagues to create a women's caucus even in an increasingly partisan environment.

Colorado's geopolitical history as a western territory has a particular relevance for women's political organizing. Many women legislators describe Colorado's political history as one friendly to women's political participation and open to women's influence. Cindy Rosenthal (1998, 138) describes Colorado as a place where "women are setting the standards of leadership" and attributes this role to their proportion in the legislature and a general political culture in Colorado supportive of what she calls integrative leadership. Colorado in recent history has been among the top states for women's proportions in the legislature (C. Rosenthal 1998; CAWP 2016a). Ehrenhalt (1992, 203–205) characterizes the Republican women of Colorado as moderate, quietly feminist, and pro-choice.[3] These feelings that the electorate was open to women's participation and the acceptance of gender as a valid political identity made women legislators feel comfortable creating a women's group.

In 2009, Colorado ranked third in the country according to gender proportions, with women making up 37 percent of the legislature. Twelve women were serving in the state senate and twenty-five in the state assembly (CAWP 2009b). There were nineteen Democratic women serving in the assembly and eleven serving in the senate, as well as six Republican women serving in the assembly and one serving in the senate. Women in the Democratic Party have been more successful in attaining leadership positions than women in the Republican Party, but Cindy Rosenthal (1998) does report episodes of gender bias in leadership races for women of both parties. The state ranked fifth in the nation in terms of the proportion of women serving in legislative leadership positions, with 25 percent held by women (2/8 positions). Senator Betty Boyd (D) was Senate President Pro Tempore, and Representative Kathleen Curry (D) was serving as Speaker Pro Tempore. Colorado ranked first in the nation, with women holding 50 percent of committee chairmanships (10/20 chairmanships) (CAWP 2009a).[4] (For additional demographic details about the state, see Table 5.2.) Colorado is a state with a moralistic dominant political culture (Elazar 1984) that is noted for the "commonwealth conception" and "its search for the good society" and where "the general public and the politicians conceive of politics as a public activity centered on some notion of the public good." In this culture, it is appropriate for government to intrude on private affairs if necessary for the "well-being of the community" (117). This notion of the public good as the primary objective of government contributes to a political culture that emphasizes good government and disdains corruption.

Colorado's recent political history "has experienced a great deal of anti-tax fervor" (Daum, Duffy, and Straayer 2011, 3), which makes it difficult for the state to raise funds for services like education. It

TABLE 5.2. COLORADO DEMOGRAPHICS (NCSL 2010; U.S. CENSUS BUREAU 2011)	
2010 population	5,029,196
Population ranking	Ranked 22nd in the nation
Political culture (Elazar 1984)	Moralistic dominant
Party control—assembly (2009)	Democrat
Party control—senate (2009)	Democrat
Party of the governor (2009)	Democrat
Proportion of women—legislature (2009)	37% Ranked 3rd in the nation
Proportion of women—legislative leadership (2009)	25% Ranked 5th in the nation
Party competition—assembly (2009)	11-seat difference
Party competition—senate (2009)	7-seat difference
Professionalization (Squire 2007)	Ranked 15th in the nation

has high local and sales taxes as a result of its decentralized tax structure (Daum, Duffy, and Straayer 2011) that, in part, is a consequence of its political landscape, notably its strong direct democracy, with frequent use of the citizen initiative that limits the power of elected officials in favor of individual citizens (Daum, Duffy, and Straayer 2011, 89). An example of such an initiative is Amendment 41, which greatly restricted public officials' conduct in an effort to bolster public confidence in government and reduced any perceived special favors for those holding public office. This seemingly benign initiative had significant consequences for legislators and played an important role in the development of the women's caucus in Colorado (Colorado Legislature Assembly 2006).

Colorado has a history of direct democracy and aspires to transparent good government. As a consequence, many legislators there cited strict ethics laws as constraining their activities and complicating the policy process. Restrictions on lobbyists have curtailed most social functions and receptions. Because many legislators perceived the legislature as damaged by deteriorating relationships and obstacles to socializing, a political opportunity was available to Representative Middleton, who set out to create a social caucus that would create a network for women to get to know each other on a personal level. However, concern over the WFC grant secured by Representative Middleton caused other women legislators to "raise a red flag" about the strict ethics laws in the state. Specifically, they were concerned that any financial support from an outside group may violate Amendment 41. As a result, the caucus remained informal until the Independent Ethics Commission of Colorado issued an advisory opinion in August 2010.

Many legislators pointed out the need for a social caucus because of a restriction on lobbying in Amendment 41 that was widely perceived as limiting legislators' ability to get to know one another. Representative Susan Ryden (D) explained it in this way:

> It's not that there aren't a lot of events now, but they're all just very, like, brief little one-hour cocktail parties and things like that. And usually with a focus of whatever that group that's sponsoring it wants to talk to you about. So they talk to you, and we don't talk to each other that much, so I understand that there was a lot more talking together back in the old days and that has pretty much gone away.[5]

Ryden connected this institutional change to an increase in partisanship: "I think that may also have led to this more partisan atmosphere. When people aren't talking to each other, they can conjure up all kinds of fear and loathing about the other people when they don't talk directly to them."[6] The founder of the caucus, Representative Middleton, agreed:

> These campaign finance laws have removed the ability to be social—cocktail receptions and luncheons and all the ways you build relationships in normal society and, in fact, any other area you do business ha[ve] been regulated out of the legislative structure. . . . [T]hat really cut into the ability to build relationships. . . . My sense is that a lot of the work of being a statesman or statesperson involves knowing people and asking them to do things based on a personal relationship, and you don't have that in the way that legislatures are being operated right now

without some additional support, and that's what the caucus was really set up to try to support.[7]

Other legislators agreed that getting to know other legislators in social settings was beneficial to the legislative process, indicating that having a personal relationship can facilitate teamwork. Representative Carole Murray (R) agreed:

> When we're on the floor, people that you don't necessarily share time with in committee or have any reason to be around because maybe you're in a different party, you just get to know them as a person rather than just a seat on the floor who votes against everything you believe in. . . . The more that you can relate to people as people, they'll at least be open to you talking to them, and that's all you can ask. . . . [O]ccasionally they may vote for one of your bills that they're not really crazy about, but they say, "Well, Carole's a good gal. I'll vote for her bill on this one."[8]

In fact, several legislators on both sides of the aisle referred to Amendment 41, which reads in part:

> The people of the state of Colorado hereby find and declare that the conduct of public officers, members of the general assembly, local government officials, and government employees must hold the respect and confidence of the people; [t]hey shall carry out their duties for the benefit of the people of the state; they shall, therefore, avoid conduct that is in violation of their public trust or that creates a justifiable impression among members of the public that such trust is being violated; any effort to realize personal financial gain through public office other than compensation provided by law is a violation of that trust. (Colorado Legislature Assembly 2006)

This initiative, however, was cited by John A. Straayer in "Direct Democracy's Disaster" as having a series of unintended consequences that hurt the legislative process:

Its consequences to date include issuance of official opinions to the effect that scholarships for children of public employees and performance awards for employees are probably illegal; the resignation of more than a half-dozen legislators; questions as to whether the newly elected governor may legally recruit legislators for positions in his cabinet; and the curtailment of Capitol breakfasts, which had been enjoyed by legislators, staffers and student interns for decades. (Straayer 2007, 30)

Despite the delay in formalization, the women's caucus continued to participate in a range of activities, wanting to move the organization forward while awaiting the ethics inquiry that Middleton sought in order to confirm that establishing the women's caucus in conjunction with the WFC grant would not violate Amendment 41. A breakfast meeting was held during the beginning of the 2010 session during which Katie Ziegler, coordinator of the Women's Network of the NCSL, presented the group with best practices from women's caucuses across the country. In August 2010, Representative Middleton secured permission from the Ethics Commission to partner with a 501(c)3 (nonprofit) organization, the Metropolitan State College of Denver, to manage and dispense the WFC grant. This decision alleviated any concern the legislators had about participating in a caucus with outside financial support. Once the advisory opinion was issued, the original four board members stayed on in leadership positions. To garner participation, Middleton and her staffer, Laura Hoeppner, focused activities on something all the women in Colorado did share—a common political history. Celebrating the long tradition of women in the legislature was something they could all partake in without alienating anyone with policy demands. Representative Middleton left office at the end of her term in 2010 to work for Emerge America, an organization that recruits and supports women candidates for public office. She was replaced on the board by Representative Jeanne Labuda.

Gender and Political Party

The political culture in Colorado experienced a jolt in 2004 that affected the political calculus of both Democrats and Republicans. This disruption in Republican control was a consequence of changing demographics. Of state residents in 2007, 58 percent were non-natives attracted to the state for its natural resources and the accompanying economic opportunities, including tourism, the oil and gas industry, and most recently technology. These waves of immigration affected Colorado politics, with the state looking more purple than clearly blue or red during the 2008 election season (National Journal Almanac 2011). This shift in party dynamics created a political opportunity structure in Colorado, with incoming Democratic women seeking alliances with Republican women now finding themselves in the minority.

Despite the increase in partisanship observed by former and current members following the 2008 election, the legislative environment was largely perceived by those I interviewed as a collegial one, in which the issue determined the level of resistance by party-line voters and committee chairmen. Institutional rules and a tone set by leadership contributed to this collegial atmosphere, where issue rather than party identity regulates all behavior and choices of association. Regardless, women legislators are not ready to have policy discussions as a part of the caucus. The perception of partisanship in Colorado was colored by whether or not a legislator was a member of the majority party or not. When current women legislators held events at which former women legislators attended, there was a marked difference in experiences. Former members noted the increase in partisanship from the environment in which they served. As Representative Ryden explained, "When we had the union of the former representatives and senators, several of them were just appalled at the behavior today and the partisan stuff that's going on."[9]

When asked if this partisanship would prove to be a problem for a women's caucus, Former Democratic House majority leader Paul Weissmann asserted quite emphatically, "Yeah. Party trumps sex."[10] When asked about male reaction to the caucus, Hoeppner reported, "The guys at the beginning said silly things like 'Here comes the women's caucus.' And when we announce events, they'll say things like 'And the men's caucus will be meeting at such-and-such bar.' And that's fine. I think that focusing on the histories last year was a big part of the reason that we didn't end up with a lot of negative energy."[11]

Here, she indicates that the focus on women's history rather than policy was a protection for the caucus, isolating it from opposition from party leadership or male colleagues. On the one hand, by limiting their own purposes, the women's caucus encouraged bipartisan participation; on the other hand it limited caucus potential for influence and risked women not being taken seriously by their male colleagues. Representative Beth McCann (D) said, "I don't think it's seen as a threat or as real powerful, so what do they care, you know? Women want to get together and have a drink, that kind of thing."[12]

However, former Democratic leader Paul Weissmann said, "I just don't believe [a women's caucus] is productive for the institution. I think that people have more power and ability if they are a legislator and they work with other legislators. I don't know you have any more power and authority if you team up."[13] This view contradicts an earlier statement he made that indicated that the reason non-party caucuses were not influential was due to their lack of vote cohesion on issues. When pressed, Weissmann noted that, historically, Republican women were particularly successful policy-wise when they worked across the aisle. "They played issue by issue; they didn't play partisan. . . . They were a key to anything you wanted to get done. This handful of women Republicans were key. You couldn't do anything without them."[14]

Additionally, not all legislators saw party as the dividing line. Senator Ellen Roberts (R), for example, said (and Representative Ryden agreed), "There's definitely partisan politics, but I think in Colorado, particularly in my area, we will—on the western slope—we will band together more based on regional common interests and not necessarily partisan, but it's kind of up to each individual legislator because there are some who work that way and then there's others whose comfort zone is kind of only in their party caucus."[15] Other legislators noted that it was not Republican women who were reluctant to join but rather Tea Party Republican women, indicating that ideology more than party in isolation was influencing the caucus's ability to recruit women from both parties.

Democrats controlled both houses of the Colorado legislature in 2009, when the caucus was first launched. One Democratic legislator indicated that Republican women may have received some pressure not to consort with the other party, but that it was the consequence of who was in the majority. She said, "When we were in the majority, I think there was much more pressure against them getting involved with us in anything. Now that they're in the majority, in the House anyway, I'm sensing that they're not as worried about that."[16] No Republican women reported any such pressure to disassociate with Democrats either while they were in the minority in 2009 or when in the majority in 2011, when some interviews took place.

The caucus founder Representative Middleton did not indicate that a Democratic majority was at all considered in her decision to create a caucus. She discussed her decision with the speaker of the house, not to seek his permission, but simply to inform him. Middleton admitted that she and the speaker had a good relationship, but there was no indication she would have changed her strategy in a Republican majority, as she was not seeking any support from the legislature for the caucus. In Colorado, there is no history of institutional support for caucuses of any type other than party caucuses. As in New Jersey, in Colorado there had been informal women's caucuses in the past but not recently. Of particular note, a speaker of the house concerned about party loyalty disrupted an attempt to create a formal women's caucus in the 1980s (Sanbonmatsu 2008). The last memory legislators or staff had of any organization by women was an event in 1995 that had honored the one-hundred-year history of women in the Colorado legislature, where women legislators gathered information on former women serving in the legislature and held an event during which women wore nineteenth-century costumes.

Caucuses other than party caucuses have not been common in Colorado. During my interviews, legislators mentioned pro-choice, labor, sportsman, and small business caucuses— even a newly emerging green caucus—but legislators did not identify any of these caucuses as influential or having very formal leadership structures or meeting schedules. In fact, the Green Caucus emerged during my interview phase, and the leaders of that group had contacted members of the women's caucus for advice about how to get started. There was no Black or Hispanic Caucus in Colorado in 2009.

Legislative leadership perceived non-party caucuses as non-essential, non-threatening, and not influential. This perception was in part due to their informal structure, as well as their reluctance or inability to command uniform votes from their members. When asked why groups emerged, one legislative leader hypothesized that it gave groups with shared interests legitimacy to organize information meetings and bring players to the table for discussion. One woman legislator, in discussing her participation in these groups, explained that building relationships through these groups was the first step to creating and working to pass legislation. Because legislators did not perceive nonparty caucuses as particularly influential in this legislature, they were not referenced as important in the creation of a women's caucus. Representative Middleton did not look to other groups for modeling or validation. Positively, other caucuses did not act in competition with the women's caucus for time or loyalty.

As was the case in New Jersey, in Colorado some Democratic women legislators suspected that Republican women were pressured not to participate in a bipartisan women's caucus. Founder Representative Karen Middleton said:

> We had a few Republican women who were sort of tough to engage, and so we—there's only one woman in the Senate who's a Republican or was at the time, but there are a handful of women in the House and some of them actually sort of shied away from it because they didn't want to be labeled by their Republican colleagues, so it sounded like they were getting a bit more pressure about whether they were engaged or not.[17]

Women's Presence and Political Parties

In 2009, Colorado's State Legislature was 37 percent women. This proportion ranked them third in the country. Their numbers would place them on the high end of the spectrum where perhaps women would feel that a women's caucus was unnecessary. In fact, however, many women legislators acknowledged that it was wanting to take advantage of their numbers that mattered: "What I saw was with that number of women overall . . . I didn't think there was a sense of collaborating as women [that was] . . . nearly as strong as it could have been, which was part of my motivation for forming the caucus."[18] It was for Representative Middleton more than women's proportion that mattered. She wanted to mobilize those numbers for influence, triggering the creation of a caucus. The male legislative leadership recognized the impetus provided by their numbers in office as well: "I think when you look around the room and think, 'Oh my god, look how many of us are here; we need to start working together on things,' I think it was just the sheer number in the positions that they were in that brought them together."[19]

Women in Colorado hold more seats in the legislature than in other states due in part to a political history that allowed for women to enter politics earlier than the rest of the country. The presence of many women was a political opportunity seized by the caucus entrepreneurs in this case. Further, strict ethics rules, perceived by legislators as impeding the legislative process by isolating them from each other, created a problem for which Middleton's caucus was a solution. Political leaders in Colorado did not see caucuses as credible threats and therefore no real opposition emerged. The case of the Colorado Women's Legislative Caucus clearly illustrates the role of political context in the creation of a caucus and how it can be leveraged by savvy entrepreneurs.

THE RESOURCES TO GET THE JOB DONE

The acquisition of resources was crucial to the success of the Colorado Women's Legislative Caucus. In particular, like New Jersey, the selection of a volunteer staffer who was perceived to be bipartisan and able to do the logistical and research work prioritized by the caucus was determinative of whether or not the caucus launch occurred. In Colorado, due to institutional rules, the partnership with an outside entity enabled the caucus to manage funds to support their projects that would have otherwise lacked financing. Entrepreneurs and their political interests are vital to the process of group formation as both must align with the political environment in order for a group to form (Salisbury 1969; Nownes and Neely 1996), and Middleton's skillfulness was certainly crucial in this case. The political context specific to Colorado indicates that different resources may be necessary for women's caucuses, depending on the institutional arrangements of the legislature and entrepreneurs' ability to exploit them.

External Organizations

In the case of Colorado, the initiative for the women's caucus was internal. There was not external pressure from women's groups to create a women's caucus. Instead, a sitting representative was motivated to form a group and sought out support to fund this caucus from external organizations. The Women's Foundation and the Metropolitan State College of Denver were integral to the success of the caucus in this case particularly because of the ethics inquiry and Amendment 41. Without an external organization to manage the funding, it is unlikely the caucus would have gone forward. Ethics laws, such as that propagated by Amendment 41, greatly affected Colorado legislators' abilities to raise and spend funds for any purpose, even legitimate political purposes (Colorado State Legislature 2006). Many women legislators expressed concern about the funding for the group and would not have felt comfortable moving forward without the decision from the Commission and the management by the Metropolitan State College of Denver. Like CAWP and the Woodrow Wilson School of Public and International Affairs in New Jersey, this external organization was crucial to the Colorado launch. Amendment 41 is an example of a specific institutional feature that both created a political opportunity—a sense that restricting socializing was bad for the legislature—and an initial hurdle for Middleton. This obstacle could have sunk the caucus were it not for a dedicated entrepreneur who persisted. Representative Ryden put it this way: "She [Middleton] worked really hard to get some sponsoring organizations and to get our bylaws and all of that set up. She did all of that work, so we just basically walked in and had a good time."[20] Additionally, the Women's Network of the National Conference of State Legislators assisted the group by sharing best practices from women's caucuses across the country at the meeting held during the 2010 session. This external organization provided research garnered from women's caucuses across the country, indicating that such monitoring is helpful to the proliferation of women's caucuses.

Professionalism

Colorado was ranked fifteenth in the nation in terms of professionalism, making its legislature highly professional (Squire 2007). This means that they are in session longer and have greater access to resources like staff, alleviating the concerns about the costs of caucus creation. Representative Beth McCann (D) stated that access to these resources weighs in the decision about caucus type:

> I personally would like to see it be more substantive, but whether anybody or even myself has the time to even do that is another question. We just, we don't have staff, and it's just ridiculous. So you really, like, every night I go home and I do an hour and a half or so or two hours of e-mail. It's just ridiculous. And, you can't keep up with all that, and then you've got your bills, and then you've got trying to, I mean stacks of materials to read. Yeah, everything is very labor-intensive for the legislator. We just . . . it's frustrating.[21]

More professional legislatures may provide more staff, who could take on some of the labor involved in managing a caucus. Volunteer caucus staffer Laura Hoeppner explains:

> You know, our state government budget is so tight. Staffing is so low on anything. People who would normally have an interest in this and would be doing it on the side in their lunch hours, like clerks or secretaries, don't have the bandwidth for it, I don't think. And the state is not going to come up with funding for this in my lifetime. This is just beyond the scope of what Coloradans think the government should be doing.[22]

Here, Hoeppner is pointing out the importance of the outside funding that makes her position possible. Because Representative Middleton was motivated to and able to secure outside funding, this caucus launch was possible. These funds financed the initial social activities and the staffer whose time and work were crucial to the launch. The amount of time and work necessary to launch a new group was beyond what the part-time legislative staffers would have been able to accomplish even in this highly professional legislature.

Time

Colorado's legislature is the only one of my four case studies that has term limits. I hypothesized in Chapter 3 that term-limited states are less likely to have successful attempts at creating a women's caucus because of the pressures of time in office affecting their decision to organize or participate in a caucus. Similarly, as in the New Jersey case, experience as a result of a long tenure in the legislature was important for the launching of a caucus in Colorado. No subjects mentioned term limits as positively or negatively affecting the decision to caucus, although Representative Middleton noted that term limits hurt legislators' ability to get to know one another. A caucus, in her view, was a way to resolve that challenge.[23] In this case, Representative Middleton began organizing the women's caucus almost immediately after assuming office in 2008. However, in recruiting early board members, she tapped those with longer tenures. Senator Williams had served eight years in the House before serving in the senate, Representative Looper had served since 2006, and Senator Spence had served in the State House of Representatives since 1999.

Another legislator, Beth McCann cited term limits as a positive for women more generally in Colorado as it limited "white male control" of the legislature and allowed for greater incorporation of women legislators more broadly:

> We also have term limits, so you don't have this buildup of power that stays with some old white guy, that's been there forever. . . . I think that an institution where people have been there a long time and they've built up their coalitions and you're trying to break into that—it's just much easier here to get your bills passed, to get to become in leadership because you don't have much time and nobody has much time and you have to do it. So I think that has a huge impact.[24]

Legislators cited term limits as a concern for caucus maintenance; however, Middleton and Hoeppner were careful to plan for succession. While the legislators point to the initial importance of these entrepreneurs, Representative Middleton and Senator Spence both recognized the risks of the caucus being personality driven. Representative Middleton put in place a structure so that once she left office the group could continue, including her own replacement on the board and a long-term staff position that would not be affected by term limits. Senator Spence and the other original board members took steps to expand the board to ensure the maintenance of the group beyond their own term limits.

Entrepreneurs

The roles of Middleton and other early supporters of the group were important to the successful caucus outcome. Like Weinberg in New Jersey, Representative Middleton (D) was perceived by fellow legislators as a good facilitator and organizer. Participants mentioned the important role played by Representative Middleton. The perception among Colorado women legislators was that both Middleton and her objectives were well suited to the political times. When asked if the group would have launched successfully without her, Representative Ryden said, "Not at that time and that place, I don't think. I think it really took someone with a vision and a real desire to make it happen, and she was it."[25] Caucus staffer Hoeppner added, "I think she wanted to build a relationship with people. She's really big on relationships. She doesn't just sit back; she's a real leader. She maintains friendships all across the country. She's a great networker. I think she sees the value in that. She saw that we needed to nurture that and be conscious of it, not just let things happen."[26]

Middleton was not alone in her efforts to start the women's caucus, which is important for the long-term survival of the organization. Representative Labuda (D) also noted the importance of the original board members: "Senator Nancy Spence was a prime pusher of this. If, and it's because she told me she was sick and tired, she was the only Republican woman in the Senate for so long, she had caucuses of one. She said those men just don't understand, so she was a prime pusher of this."[27]

FRAMING THE TASK AT HAND

In Colorado, the frame employed by the caucus entrepreneur was perhaps the most important factor explaining why the launch was successful. Republican women legislators serving in 2009 were not going to engage in policy with their Democratic counterparts. If that had been the frame that Representative Middleton had used, she would not have been able to garner any bipartisan participation. In framing it as a social caucus, she was able to neutralize any opposition from Republicans or men who challenged the need for a women's group particularly using the dissatisfaction with Amendment 41 as a justification. Representative Ryden (D) stated, "Karen Middleton was really a great organizer. . . . [S]he just really has a great ability to envision something and then carry it out and get people on board to make it happen."[28]

Women have long served in the Colorado legislature. In 1894, the first women state legislators in the country were voted into office (Cox 1996): Representatives Carrie Clyde Holly (R), Frances S. Klock (R), and Clara Cressingham (R). Since 1975 (when CAWP began documenting women's presence in state legislatures), Colorado has never ranked below eighth in the country for the share of women in office and it has been ranked first in the country from 2014 to 2016 (CAWP 2016b). This history played an important role in the creation of the caucus in Colorado.

As 37 percent of the legislature in 2009, women were not tokens within the institution. Further, women held a number of leadership positions and committee chairmanships. None of this incorporation, however, translated into political power, according to caucus founder Middleton. She wanted women to leverage their presence in order to achieve policy goals, but recognized the reticence on the part of Republican women legislators. Many of them did not acknowledge their gendered identity as politically salient and some of them considered themselves to be Tea Party members. Accepting this challenge to collective action on behalf of women, Middleton chose to prioritize relationship-building first, knowing that she would need a strong foundation in order to accomplish her ultimate goal of influencing public policy. As caucus staffer Laura Hoeppner explained:

I definitely have political interests, but for issues and gender, this is not that space. This is a space for people to come to have conversations. I think there is inherent value in that: building relationships, seeing each other, not in black-and-white terms, good versus evil. I think too often when we separate these people and don't let them have those conversations, that's what ends up happening. Men used to do it on the golf course and in the bar. Women are now doing it in a formal structure called women's caucuses.[29]

Gender Consciousness

Women legislators in Colorado reported that women bring a different perspective to the legislature by acknowledging gender consciousness. Recognizing generational divides, Representative Ryden attested to an overarching gender identity for women:

I think we have a lot of similar issues or experiences, like having children, families, work issues, overcoming discrimination and I think, I guess, older women probably feel like they had a lot more issues than a lot of younger women do, and most women—it's mostly a generational thing because women that are closer to my age, we share a lot of things in common, college experiences, etc. because I don't think most of us were that politically active, even in our earlier days. But as the women get younger, their issues, I think, are different and, but they still get along because they have similar experiences that they can, that they have in common, even if they're in different parties.[30]

She went on to describe an example of a time in committee when the women from both sides of the aisle "stood together against the men" on an issue involving alcohol and children. She cited their experience as mothers as motivating the consensus. She noted, however, that it was never discussed or strategized—it just happened organically as a result of their life experience.

Some legislators explained women's difference by comparing their behaviors to male legislators. Representative Carole Murray (R) put it this way:

> My mom was a stay-at-home mom and she always railed, she said, "What we need is more women in government to clean house and to do the right thing and to do the work." Instead of just puffing their chests out and acting like they're big shots. And that's really true. I really think that for the most part women tend to get into the details of government maybe more than men do. They understand how to bring in stakeholders to the table; when you have a bill, you bring in various stakeholders and try to get them to work through the issues and I, just in a general way, men are not as good at that, I think.[31]

Senator Angela Giron (D) agreed: "All the males are just 'let's move on.' They don't like long meetings; they tire of the process and just want to make a decision. We will make a decision, but let's just talk about it so we don't have to come back to that same decision."[32] She tempered this, however, by adding, "Because a person is a particular gender, a female, doesn't mean they know or understand women's issues. To me, that doesn't mean anything at all."[33] Here, she is hinting at the partisan differences among women just under the surface in Colorado, especially with the addition of Tea Party women to the legislature.

Representative McCann identified the struggle for women seeking to represent women more broadly while adhering to their party identity as well. She said, "Traditionally, the leaders in the women['s] movement are Democratic because it's just sort of the way it is. But that said, there are certainly Republican women who feel strongly about women's issues, so it's probably a combination. We probably both have various reasons for doing it. . . . I think it just depends on the individual, what their experience has been."[34]

When asked if women bring a difference to the institution, even a legislator who expressed opposition to the caucus, feeling it was unnecessary and inappropriate, agreed that women make a difference. Senator Roberts (R) said:

I'm sure, and I—it could be a sweeping generalization, but I think by and large we are here for solution making and that's why we'd look forward to a day where we were more of the decision makers, not to the exclusion of the males, but I think we bring different skill sets to the table in terms of discussing issues, negotiating what's a win, . . . and again, I think it goes back to sort of innate differences but also environmental, that as we, if you raise children, you find yourself sort of repeatedly saying, "Well, you can't get everything you want" and so that again compromising isn't a dirty word. It means that we all can maybe try and get along a little better.[35]

Male legislative leadership acknowledged this gender difference as well. Paul Weissman notes: "You have a good percentage of the legislature who are women, and I believe that does affect public policy. . . . I think the outcome is affected because there are a lot of women in the legislature."[36]

The self-identified nonparticipant also expressed a problem with self-segregation as women: "Why is it okay for us to do this exclusive arrangement, but if you wanted, we would be totally up in arms about the men doing the same."[37] Representative Millie Hamner (D) disagreed: "I think there are times when it is okay to separate us by our differences, for the camaraderie that comes with that, the collegiality that comes with that opportunity. I think that women are more comfortable talking about our feelings when we are in groups of women, so we could actually get down to some issues that could help us emotionally."[38]

Party Dissatisfaction

Subjects in Colorado disagreed about whether or not women experienced discrimination by party leaders. Some had not experienced it themselves but had observed it happening to others. For example, Representative Millie Hamner (D) observed gender differences in behavior between legislators and nonlegislative coworkers: "I do believe that there are times when other women in the organization maybe aren't being treated as respectfully as they could be, or there are some gender stereotypes, maybe in the clerk positions, maybe in the lobbyist positions. The way a legislator might act with a female lobby-ist—there are probably some interesting dynamics going on there."[39]

Hamner had not seen this at all among her legislative colleagues, however: "I will tell you I feel like an equal here. I don't feel that I am being treated differently because I am a woman."[40] Others admitted to feeling left out of the real decision making despite the fact that women held leadership positions. For example, Representative Ryden said, "Yes, there's still the tree house syndrome going on. You know, where they get up in the tree and pull up the ladder behind them and try to hide."[41] A former Democratic male legislative leader recognized possible bias against women in the legislature but also saw their abil-ity to overcome it:

> I used to watch pretty carefully how the Republicans treated Nancy Spence. She was the only woman in the Republican cau-cus. At times it seemed they were being kind of, as a whole, dis-respectful or not including her in conversations. But when we were passing progressive education legislation, she was the one I'd go to to round up and keep in line all of the Republican cau-cus, because we needed every single one of their votes. When they wanted to offer amendments that I thought would damage the bill, she would shut that down, so they respected her on the one hand. And she would say things on occasion [like] "I'm going to have to get the boys in line."[42]

Representative Hamner explained that in certain circumstances she uses her gender to her advantage: "I have found that capitalizing on the typical relationship between a man and a woman can work for leg-islators. I try to use my charm when needed."[43] Senator Giron added, "There are sort of different standards in that way for guys, and it's the same thing in every work environment. 'Oh you're not smiling today.' I don't think they'd say that to a man. But the freedom, I tend to be a hugger, but a man?"[44] These comments regarding appropriate behav-iors and standards for men indicate both the policing of gendered be-haviors and the political exploitation of different expectations of men and women when women use traditionally feminine social moves to their advantage.

Democratic legislators reported feeling free to vote their conscience and not feeling that leadership was heavy handed in demanding party loyalty or exacting any kind of revenge. As far as recruitment of women in the Democratic Party to run for office, a former legislative leader explained that while gender-based decisions are not common, women's difference did distinguish them as good potential candidates.[45] Despite this, one legislator did identify problems in the party caucus:

> Within the caucus, it's pretty much the old boys stuff still. I mean, you look at our leadership—we have women, older women in most of the positions except the top. And so we have a young man, and then his chief of staff is a man and I can see that they're grooming—there are a couple of young men that they're grooming, you can kind of tell; they include them in things, and we don't necessarily get included. So it's still there.[46]

When asked if a women's caucus could help address this problem, Representative McCann said:

> That's a good question. You know, we haven't, we haven't talked about it at a caucus. . . . Last year Representative Middleton was head, and she was more into that part of it, and so we had some little bit of discussion. But, you know, I haven't really talked to the Republican women about how they feel about their leadership, and we just haven't had that opportunity. It would be interesting to do.[47]

As in New Jersey, Colorado women legislators felt that younger women were more susceptible to gender bias. One legislator stated that her age, over fifty, insulated her from any type of questionable interactions. This attitude is an example of how intersectionality complicates the effect of gender on institutional norms and behaviors. Some women may have different experiences of gender bias as a result of another identity, such as age or race. A women's caucus offers these women an opportunity to discover and discuss these problems with other women who may have strategies for dealing with these challenges. Alternatively, these other identities may make relating to other women more difficult if race or age become divisive for women.

As far as dissatisfaction with how parties motivate the creation of the women's caucus, there is no evidence supporting that hypothesis. Some women do feel bias in the institution or within their party but they did not explicitly connect that to the need for a caucus. Nor did any participants beyond one feel that a caucus would potentially affect women's status in the parties or institution at large. Addressing bias in the institution was not one of the three purposes originally agreed on by the initial participants. Although in this case there was no reported overt opposition by party leadership against Republican women themselves or any pressure on Democratic women not to organize or participate in a caucus, one of the former male leaders of the legislature had this to say about nonparty caucuses:

> I don't mind people that spend time and focus on issues and do all that kind of stuff. I don't know that you need to formally form a caucus to do that. I don't know if you need to give yourself a fake legitimacy that it does to do that. Quite frankly I think it brings more splinters than it does coalitions. I don't know if it's the healthiest way to go about it. I've never been a big fan of caucuses. I've never been a member of any caucuses except the party caucus, which you are in whether you want it or not.[48]

He went on to say:

> This is going to sound very sexist and I don't mean it this way but I don't know how to say it any other way. There are some women, leadership or not, who have a chip, just like there are some men who have a chip but it comes off differently. They think that some people don't perceive that they should be in that position. Everything they do will come from that "I'm going to prove that I belong in this position."[49]

When asked if there is an old boys' network that these women are coming up against, he said, "I think it's just in their minds."[50]

Caucus Type

In Colorado, the entrepreneur determined and participants confirmed early on that this caucus would not deal with policy. While Representative Middleton had hoped that once initial bonds were created among the women policy would become a part of the caucus's mission, she acknowledged that initially it hurt her ability to convince women to participate. Representative Jeanne Labuda explained the decision in this way:

> One thing we agreed on early on is that we probably would not take any stances on issues, everybody would be free to vote the way she wanted to because when we first started, there was a women's issue of some sort that was coming up, but one of the women legislators did not feel comfortable with it, and so we decided right then and there we might discuss different bills that are coming up, but we would never take a vote to say whether we would support or not because you know how that goes— even if all 41 percent of us were there and one person says, "No, I don't like it," that person automatically is labeled not a true woman or something like that. And so we want to avoid that, so we don't take issues on, we don't support any bills or oppose any bills.[51]

Republican representative Carole Murray explained:

> I think there was some talk of trying to create some kind of a common political agenda, and we really struggled with that as Republicans, because they didn't really get our philosophy. So all of the topics they would bring up, we'd look at one another and go, "We can't go there." . . . I don't know [whether] we're gonna do any kind of a political agenda or not. I think probably Republican women are probably pretty uncomfortable with that.[52]

More than one subject explained that the issue of domestic violence was put forth initially as one on which women could possibly agree.

It was quickly abandoned when a Republican legislator joked that a solution to domestic violence was to support her legislation on gun rights. Another controversial point that had to be quickly dispensed with was vaccinations for children. It was clear from the start that Democratic and Republican legislators were unlikely to find common ground policy-wise. One Republican legislator explained why a social networking focus was more appropriate for the group:

> I think it's best to stay away from policy because we don't understand where the other side is and that's the nature of belonging to a different party, there is an innate difference between us. And there's no way that you can force that. Now you can have personal relationships with people and on some issues that are not part of that ideological core, you can bring them in, but I can tell you that there are a lot of people, whether it's men or women, if their name's on a bill and it's a Democrat and I'm a Republican and they're a Democrat, it's like, "Oh, that person's name's on that bill, that's a no." You don't want that to ever happen to you as a legislator because that reduces your effectiveness, so anything that you can do to increase those positive relationships is good for you, for your political survival in terms of passing a few bills occasionally. Not to mention, like I say, just the joy of sharing time with sharp women.[53]

The decision to prioritize the social-networking function of the caucus was frustrating for some Democratic women who felt if a caucus was not going to deal with issues, what was the point? For example, one Democratic legislator put it this way, "We are still in that kind of relationship-building stage, if you will, coalition-building stage, and that. . . . [B]ut if we don't come around to doing something kind of substantive, then it probably wouldn't be something I'd continue to participate in, just because we have enough of just getting together; there are other opportunities for that."[54] Representative Millie Hamner also added, "I would like it to be more in terms of 'What are some of the issues that can improve quality of life?' 'What are the issues facing women in Colorado?' And then 'What are some bills that we might be able to sponsor or things that we might be able to promote?'"[55] Senator Giron (D) had this expectation for the future of the caucus: "I would, at a minimum, expect that we are in a more organized or agenda format talking about issues that are relevant to women and how do we stack up in Colorado with women in general across this country and other countries. I think women and children don't fare very well."[56] Representative Deb Gardner (D) shared this expectation:

> My hope would be that if either we initiate attention to some issue or if there were an issue that came from the outside, that we could come together as a group and talk about it and figure out if we wanted to kind of operate as a group in terms of, support or not support, and the ideal I think would be if as a group we identified an issue because the women's caucus is bipartisan and what a great opportunity to, even just the social piece is a way to form relationships with people across the aisle in a way that you maybe wouldn't normally, and so that part's good.[57]

Representative Ryden agreed, identifying her goal for the newly formed caucus as ultimately including policy: "I think it would be to identify some really serious issues that we can agree on, some real meaningful issues beyond just socializing and getting to know each other."[58] Ryden hypothesized the kind of conditions that would have to be present for that to occur:

> I think we had a lot of building to do before we could get to that point where [we] could all buy in on something. So I think at some point we probably could, and, again, it depends on what's going on around us. If suddenly there's a whole lot of discrimination cases that come up or there's a real big issue that comes out into the media, I think we could probably get women on board to do a women's caucus kind of bill.[59]

She identified choice and other health care issues as policy issues that would definitely need to be avoided. Other legislators agreed with this assessment of "hot button" issues. The caucus staffer concisely explains the impasse: "When you are a Democratic liberal woman, you have this perspective that everyone is going to be on board with you for something, and when you are a conservative woman, you have this perspective that 'of course, this makes sense; this is perfectly reasonable.' But then when you sit in the room together, even the obvious isn't going to get that kind of support."[60]

Representative McCann pointed out the limitations of a social-only caucus: "It's not seen as powerful. It's really not. It's more social."[61] One former Democratic male leader indicated that, from his point of view, an agenda would be important for the caucus if it was to be successful, as he did not see a social networking factor as a substantive objective: "I think there are so many other meetings and things that elected officials have to do during the session, so if there is a reason not to go to a meeting or to a gathering, you don't go. So I think they have to give reason and give action to the caucus."[62]

The one subject who identified as a nonparticipant explained her ambivalence in this way:

> We have made progress in certain areas, but we kind of get stuck in the same "Oh, these are women's issues." And, of course, I mean, I have two kids who are now grown, but I've taken care of a dying parent. I would want us to be able to acknowledge that women do typically have a little bit different role in the family than the man does. And I welcomed that and I . . . but sometimes it seems like we have limited ourselves to just those kinds of issues or, say, pay equity. And while pay equity is important, there are other factors that as time has gone on . . . sometimes I think we undermine our own power because we don't advance to some other issues.[63]

It was this perception of feminism more broadly that turned her off to the idea of a caucus in general, despite the fact that the caucus was only social in nature. It is clear from the evidence gathered from these subjects that, while an agenda would be important for gaining influence within the institution and satisfying some Democratic legislators' expectations of a women's caucus, it would have been detrimental to the attempt to create a women's caucus in this state. Republican women were reticent in the first place and were much more inclined to participate once the decision to stay away from policy was made. When women make a decision about whether or not to work collectively, political party affiliation shapes their calculus. Republican women are concerned they will be asked to take positions that oppose their political views, and Democratic women are concerned they will waste valuable time and capital without a policy payoff. Although there is hope among some Democrats that relationship building will lead to policy achievement, for now the focus of the caucus remains celebrating women more generally as admired historical heroes and as potential present-day friends within the legislature.

LOOKING TO THE FUTURE

In April 2011, the Colorado Women's Legislative Caucus launched a website (Colorado Legislative Women's Caucus 2011). The site offers the historical research that caucus staff has done and shares the press coverage of the present-day caucus. In May 2011, the sitting board members and paid staffer decided to expand the board from four to eight members. Sitting members were concerned about term-limited board members and wanted to establish security for the transition. Without formal bylaws, it was determined that each of the sitting board members would approach a woman from their party caucus to serve, indicating again that institutional party norms shape the strategies of even bipartisan groups. A priority for this recruitment was diversity both ethnically and geographically. In 2011 the eight members were Representative Labuda, Representative Cindy Acree (R), Senator Spence, Senator Williams, Representative Kathleen Conti (R), Senator Giron, Senator Jean White (R), and Representative Angela Williams (D).

At an October 2011 meeting, these eight legislators set the agenda for the upcoming year. The priorities were establishing with the College of Denver that they would continue to serve as the 501(c)3 and arbiter of funds for the caucus; placing an emphasis on social networking between women legislators, including holding a Welcome Back Lunch in January 2012 featuring a talk by Senator Spence regarding her off-session trip to Turkey to visit women in Parliament there; presenting the possibility of member dues to fund lunch meetings; hosting the annual reunion event in March with the first lady of

Colorado, Helen Thorpe, as speaker, highlighting her recent book on women and immigration; holding a book signing event with former State Senator Patricia Pascoe (D), who had recently published a book featuring Helen Ring Robinson (D), the first woman state senator in Colorado; expanding the current senate program, Girls with Goals, to the house so that fourth-grade girls can shadow women legislators in both houses; publishing the historical research on women in the legislature in booklet form; and continuing to facilitate Colorado College women students' shadowing of women legislators as they had in 2010.

In 2011, there were some behind-the-scenes rumblings by some of the board members who were frustrated with how leadership positions in both parties are selected. After two incidents of men being selected for leadership vacancies with no significant consideration of women legislators, some board members would have liked to see the caucus take up the issue. Advocating for more women in leadership is a potential place for action by the caucus in the future, although nothing formal was discussed in 2011 when the last of my interviews took place.

Staffer Laura Hoeppner attributes the success of the caucus to the institutionalization of staff and structure. Founder Representative Middleton was careful to have a replacement when she left office so there would not be a vacancy on the board. Anticipating turnover from term limits, Hoeppner and the board planned to expand the board of directors for the 2013 session to ensure stability. Hoeppner added that the annual reunion event and back-to-session gatherings, where women legislators gather socially at the beginning of new sessions, are common now and in place. These recurring events, in conjunction with the two-year survival of the group, are to what Hoeppner attributes the increased participation by women legislators from both sides of the aisle, but particularly among Republican women who are more determined to approach those in their party who are resistant.[64]

Like New Jersey, Colorado had a motivated entrepreneur and staff available to organize the logistics of a caucus launch. The staffer from New Jersey volunteered that her time while in Colorado was funded by the Women's Foundation in Colorado. Their work was vital to the success of both launches. Similarly, these entrepreneurs seized a political opportunity when in New Jersey a large influx of women were elected and when Colorado's proportion of women was reaching the highest in the nation. Entrepreneurs seized this opportunity differently. In New Jersey, women had long established relationships across the aisle, at least among the caucus leadership, and were able to agree to set policy as a priority. In Colorado, relationships themselves were the top priority because of a legislative environment in which legislators did not know each other well.

Political party in both states proved important. In the case of Colorado, in order to have bipartisan participation and get a caucus off the ground, the women agreed to leave policy off the table entirely. In New Jersey, initial policy advancement was successful and an important unifying frame used to launch the caucus. Party differences, however, challenged caucus maintenance over the long haul. Analyzing whether or not women experienced any pressure from party leaders or male colleagues not to participate in a women's caucus is complicated in this case by two factors. On the one hand, Democratic women perceive pressure on Republican women that Republican legislators themselves do not admit receiving. This issue was also present in the New Jersey case. Whether this indicates that Republican women are reluctant to report pressure or Democratic women are eager to perceive it among Republicans is not clear. What is clear from this evidence, however, is that the decision about how to structure the caucus as a social network had both positive and negative consequences. On the one hand, it meant that women could avoid any real opposition from colleagues. On the other, it meant that the men and party leaders did not take it very seriously.

External organizations were useful to both caucuses as they were initiated. In the case of New Jersey, nonpartisan institutions were able to offer meeting space. In Colorado, they offered financial support and legitimacy as well as information. In both states, Democrats controlled the legislature when the caucuses emerged, but women in neither case indicate that it was a factor for them. Similarly, the existence of other caucuses within the legislatures and party competitiveness do not seem to have been important to their success as they perceive it. Term limits in the Colorado case seem to have intensified the need for a venue to build relationships among legislators and complicated the maintenance of the caucus. In New Jersey, while there are no term limits, their effects are seen in the importance of the role of senior women legislators. Had those women been termed out, they may not have had the experience and relationships established which enabled them to launch a women's caucus.

While women in both New Jersey and Colorado acknowledged women's difference and women's unique approaches to political life, it manifested itself differently in the two cases. In Colorado, gender consciousness was not employed prominently as a frame for the caucus explicitly. Instead, entrepreneurs focused on recognizing women's historical exclusion from political acknowledgment as an objective to be accomplished by women legislators. In New Jersey, both political parties had recently inflicted wounds on women, which they referenced as they banded together to achieve common goals, including party reform.

Democratic women in both states were suspicious of male Republicans pressuring Republican women either not to participate in the women's caucus or to undermine its effectiveness. Republican women in both states did not acknowledge this pressure. Interestingly, women in both states also stated that age as an accompanying identity factor affected how much bias or ill treatment women in both parties received from their male counterparts.

In Colorado, where participation by Republican women legislators was a concern, Representative Middleton and her Democratic colleagues prioritized bipartisan participation over any potential policy objectives. How long this social mission will satisfy Democratic participants remains to be seen. While branding the women's caucus as social in nature enabled it to get off the ground, it is clear to both participants and their colleagues in the legislature that this decision has limited their ability to contribute substantively to the legislative agenda or to women's representation more broadly. The state's long history of women in public office contributing to the large proportion of women in the legislature in 2009 created both a political opportunity and served a mobilizing frame in this case. The particular attention on ethics in this state also created a dissatisfaction among legislators that Middleton and Hoeppner were able to use as a frame for recruiting participants who lamented the diminishing occasions to socialize. The high ethical standards, however, were also an obstacle that could have prevented the caucus from getting off the ground had Middleton been less persistent, the ethics board ruled differently, or the College of Denver been unwilling to partner. The ability to raise funds through a 501(c)3 was crucial in securing the staffer who played a vital role in succession planning, ensuring the caucus would survive beyond Middleton's term.

When comparing the New Jersey and Colorado cases, certain variables seem irrelevant in both: party control, party competitiveness, and the presence of other caucuses. Women's proportion in the legislature was a political opportunity seized by entrepreneurs in both cases. Also, both states had the largest Republican women proportions of all four cases. Similarly, caucus founders in both cases cited the existence of staff and external resources as important, although they came by them by different means. The major difference in these two cases is the frames employed. In New Jersey, caucus creators exploited women's shared discrimination by party organizations and rallied them around common policy priorities to recruit participants. In Colorado, caucus creators had to establish a social networking purpose in order to secure bipartisan participation. Party leaders and/ or male colleagues in neither Colorado nor New Jersey saw women's caucuses as a threat to traditional legislative norms or organization, which allowed them to emerge.

In New Jersey, the decision to address public policy challenges the women's ability to maintain the caucus. While there was initial consensus, new issues and balances of power, exacerbated by Chris Christie's election, have come between the legislators. In Colorado, Democratic legislators would prefer that the women's caucus evolve to be policy oriented. If that process takes too long, it is not clear how long Women's History Month celebrations will satisfy them.

In the next chapters, I consider the two attempts to create a women's caucus that occurred in Pennsylvania and Iowa. These two caucus attempts were not successful in that they did not meet consistently over the course of a year. By comparing these two states to each other, I identify which factors are common to both and therefore detrimental to a caucus launch and what separates these attempts to create a women's caucus from the successes in New Jersey and Colorado.

6

THE PENNSYLVANIA ATTEMPT

TIMELINE

Early 2009: Democratic caucus letter sent to legislators encouraging the creation of caucuses.

During 2009 session: Representative Venessa Lowery Brown and Representative Karen Boback organize first meeting of women legislators on energy issues.

Beginning of 2010 session: Representative Brown refiles petition to form women's caucus with her party.

During 2010 session: Several informal meetings among Democratic legislators take place. One fundraiser for Haitian women suffering from the earthquake included Republican women legislators but no subsequent bipartisan meetings occurred.

In Pennsylvania, a representative newly elected in 2008 attempted to organize women's voices to impact public policy. With the explicit encouragement of party leadership, but without consultation of more senior women in their own party, Democratic representative Vanessa Lowery Brown and her Republican counterpart, Representative Karen Boback, were facing an uphill battle in 2009. In an unfriendly environment, without previously established friendships across the aisle, women legislators in Pennsylvania were not moti-

TABLE 6.1. PENNSYLVANIA INTERVIEW SUBJECTS (10) DEMOGRAPHICS		
Party affiliation	Legislative leaders	Gender
5 Republicans, 5 Democrats	1	1 male, 9 female

vated to participate in an organization they did not acknowledge as important to them or their constituents. This case demonstrates the importance of accurately assessing the motivations of women legislators within a highly partisan environment and acquiescing to legislative norms like seniority. (For additional demographic details about the interview subjects cited in this chapter, see Table 6.1.)

A POLITICAL NOVICE MISREADS POLITICAL OPPORTUNITY

Representative Brown was elected in 2008 and one of her first priorities was to create a bipartisan women's caucus. Like Representative Middleton in Colorado, Brown was a new legislator who was dissatisfied with the lack of a cohesive voice among women. Her motivation for the caucus was very similar to Middleton's:

> I'm listening to legislation as being proposed, and, to me, I see a lot of it affects women, children, families. And I didn't see a real strong voice that was arguing those bills on the floor, even though there are women in the House. And I looked at the number of women that are in the House, and we're in the minority, so I thought that we needed a venue [where] we could strengthen our voice, review legislation, and then try to come up with certain women to be leaders on the issues.[1]

Gender and Political Party

Pennsylvania has been historically on the low end in terms of the proportion of women in the legislature, never being ranked nationally over thirty-eighth. As in New Jersey, party leaders in Pennsylvania controlled the paths to political office in detriment to women's political participation (Collins 2018; Kennedy 1999). Legislators acknowledged this as a challenge to organizing. Representative Sheryl Delozier (R) said, "The numbers are so miniscule percentage-wise, which is pathetic."[2] While this was certainly not the deciding factor, according to these legislators or my other interview subjects, it was cited as a challenge to organizing. In 2009, during the first attempt at a women's caucus in the state, women held 14.6 percent of the seats in the legislature, and Pennsylvania was ranked forty-sixth in the nation. In 2010, at the time of a repeat attempt, women inched up to 15.4 percent; however, they remained at forty-sixth in the nation. No women were serving in the highest legislative leadership positions and in terms of committee chairs, Pennsylvania ranked forty-fifth in the nation, with women holding 14.6 percent of chairmanships (7/48 chairmanships) (CAWP 2009a). (For additional demographic details about the state, see Table 6.2.) Despite women's low status in Pennsylvania politics, they were unable to come together and create an organization that might address some of their grievances in part because of a lack of gender consciousness or a belief that collective action was legitimate but also because of the poor strategy of the caucus entrepreneur.

To address the lack of a voice of these women legislators, Representative Brown filed a formal request with her Democratic leadership. The presence of other caucuses did encourage Representative Brown in her attempt to create a women's caucus. A letter sent by her party leadership, which listed the existing caucuses and encouraged the development of others, triggered her action. She noticed that on the list were a number of important caucuses but did not see a women's caucus. This omission and the explicit approval of her party leadership spurred her to action.

In Pennsylvania, there are a number of identity and issue caucuses, including Job Creation Caucus, Fire Caucus, Black Caucus, Early Childhood Learning Caucus, Italian-American Caucus, and an Autism Caucus, among others. Representative RoseMarie Swanger (R) described these caucuses as fleeting and emerging only when a salient issue came onto the agenda: "[They meet] very, very infrequently, and . . . if, say, a certain piece of legislation comes forward that that

TABLE 6.2. PENNSYLVANIA DEMOGRAPHICS (NCSL 2010; U.S. CENSUS BUREAU 2011)	
2010 population	12,702,379
Population size	Ranked 6th in the nation
Political culture (Elazar 1984)	Individualistic
Party control—assembly (2009)	Democrat
Party control—senate (2009)	Republican
Party of the governor (2009)	Democrat
Proportion of women—legislature (2009)	14.6% Ranked 46th in the nation
Proportion of women—legislative leadership (2009)	0% Ranked 24th in the nation
Party competition—assembly (2009)	5-seat difference
Party competition—senate (2009)	8-seat difference
Professionalization (Squire 2007)	Ranked 6th in the nation

caucus would be interested in, they might hold a meeting and bring in a speaker to talk about it."[3] Other legislators indicated that these caucuses were not very powerful and did not compete with party caucuses: "You know, they're not able to do anything really meaningful."[4] "Some of them do some work; some of them don't do anything; some of them, when the issues are important at that point in time, there's a conversation here in Harrisburg about subject matter . . . within that caucus, [and] then that activity kicks up."[5]

The Democratic leadership in the House did not discourage Representative Brown in her attempt to create a women's caucus. As a legislative leader, Senate Minority Leader Jay Costa did not object to the idea of alternative mechanisms for organizing outside of party caucuses:

> We encourage folks to participate in the caucuses because it does a number of things. Obviously, it [t]akes them further, [gives them] a deeper awareness of the issues related to that. I think that's always important. So I think knowledge about these areas within the caucus are important. . . . I think there's a value. The value that these caucus conversations have outweigh[s], I think,

the impact it would have on leadership's ability to convince members to do something or, I guess, to control members.[6]

Having interviewed only one Democratic leader in the senate, where the women's caucus attempt did not take place, I cannot make any definitive conclusions about Republican leadership opposition to the attempt made in Pennsylvania. This one Democratic leader seems to see the value in caucuses and participates in many himself. However, as in New Jersey and Colorado, Democratic women, in this case, suspect that Republican women are objects of pressure from their party leaders not to participate in bipartisan activity. As in those cases, no Republican women themselves report such pressure. Representative Brown said, "I appreciated being able to be in a room with the women on the opposite side to hear their side of the story, but then it was discouraged by leadership again that that wasn't approved by them, it wasn't sanctioned by, especially from the Republican side, and some of the women chose not to come back."[7] Again, this was not confirmed by Republican legislators.

Representative Mauree Gingrich acknowledged that while there may be some benefits to a formal caucus, it could raise the ire of men within the party:

> There are advantages and disadvantages; I like the communication part, opportunity part of it, so that you can talk about policy. . . . I do not know that a formal caucus is the way to do that, because that scares men beyond belief. If they see two or three women talking, they go, "What are you talking about? What are you doing? What are you trying to accomplish?"[8]

A Republican legislator also told of another attempt at women's caucus creation outside of my time frame. She said, "There was a newer legislator that came in sometime after I did and she was very assertive about putting together a female caucus and, boy, she was knocked down a few pegs by the caucus chairman. He said no, we wouldn't be doing that. So that's part of the reason why maybe Pennsylvania doesn't have one."[9] Although there is no evidence of Republican leaders opposing the attempt to create a women's caucus in

2009, this story indicates a historical objection to gender organizing. Other legislators argued that party leaders would not object because they would not be threatened. Senator Jane Earll (R) commented, "I can say unequivocally there wouldn't be pressure from the leadership. They wouldn't care. . . . The current day leaders wouldn't do anything to . . . they don't feel threatened by that."[10] Senate Minority Leader Costa even indicated that he would be interested in participating in a women's caucus as a way to become better informed on those issues.[11] Male leadership was not the only veto point, however.

Women also spoke of a long serving Republican woman legislator who was very influential in the party and among women in the legislature more broadly. She was philosophically opposed to any sort of gender organization, and her opposition was cited as a reason for the historical lack of a women's caucus in the state. Representative Gingrich explains:

> She was definitely not interested in doing it and was an obstacle to doing it. . . . I think she had fought so long and hard as a woman several generations before me and the rest of us that she just had a different attitude about it: I want to be treated like a woman. I don't want to be anything exclusive because I'm a female. . . . I want to be one of the decision makers at the table. And gender was irrelevant, so, you know, she was not interested in doing so, and it definitely was an obstacle.[12]

The departure of this particularly opposed member created an opportunity for Brown. She would have been shut down much earlier in her attempt had this legislator still been in office in 2009, which indicates that powerful individuals, especially more senior ones, have a lot of influence especially in preventing action.

Freshman women legislators were as important in Pennsylvania as they were in New Jersey and Colorado. It was in New Jersey that senior women took advantage of an influx of new women; in Colorado a newly elected legislator was motivated by her initial disappointment of how little women voiced their political power. The same was true in Pennsylvania. A newly elected Representative Brown was disappointed to learn that inside the institution women were not as vocal as she would have expected. This perception motivated her to attempt a women's caucus by enlisting another relatively new legislator, Representative Boback, elected in 2006, to organize women for change.

Representative Boback recruited Republican women legislators to participate. Like New Jersey, Pennsylvania is a place where "politics is a business like any other" but where relationships are primary (Elazar 1984, 116). Representative Brown violated this state political norm and it sank her caucus attempt. Being new to the legislature, she and her cochair did not have the benefit of seniority or existing ties that Senators Weinberg and Allen had in New Jersey. While Representative Middleton in Colorado was also a newcomer, she read and deferred to informal norms, giving her speaker a heads-up and seeking permission from the senior women in the legislature. This political maneuvering served Middleton well and got everyone on board. Brown and Boback may have followed the formal rules going through the formal channels of the Democratic Party, but they misread or ignored the informal rules of the power of seniority.

Political Culture

Relationships in political cultures like Pennsylvania's are largely expressed through political party ties. Pennsylvania is noted for close competition and frequent turnover of control, which contributes to partisanship (Kennedy 1999, 6). In the legislature, the margins of victory are historically very close. The state political geography is described as a "T" with Republicans controlling forty-three of the state's sixty-seven counties from the Maryland border to the New York border and branching off to both east and west borders (Kennedy 1999). Democratic strongholds are in the urban centers of the state, Pittsburgh and Philadelphia, but the deciding votes in Pennsylvania's party battles are those in seven counties that share the characteristics associated with the rust belt (Kennedy 1999). In 2009, when the women's caucus in Pennsylvania was attempted, the houses of the legislature were split, with Republicans controlling the senate and Democrats controlling the house, and a Democratic governor was in office. The house partisan ratio was 104 Democrats to 99 Republicans, and the senate was 20 Democrats to 29 Republicans (*Book of the States* 2009).

In the case of Pennsylvania, it appears as though there is histori-cal evidence of Republican opposition to a women's caucus, although evidence in the 2009 women's caucus attempt is not corroborated by Republican women legislators. There is evidence of Democratic Party leadership encouragement of the establishment of extraparty caucus-es, and they did not oppose this attempt in any way.[13] Sixteen percent of the Republican Party in Pennsylvania's House of Representatives was women in 2009. Of the four cases, this is the smallest propor-tion of Republican women and the closest to what Rosabeth Kanter (1977) calls a skewed sex ratio in which the Republican women would be "tokens" (966). In this case, a smaller proportion of Republican women correlates with a failed caucus attempt. Women in the inter-views did not mention their numbers with the Republican Party as a factor in their decision to participate in the caucus or not, but because of their smaller numbers, Republican women may have been more susceptible to party leader pressure than their counterparts in New Jersey and Colorado.

Caucus entrepreneur Representative Brown stated explicitly, "It wasn't an easy task [organizing], because, you know, you have Demo-crats and Republicans, whose leadership discourages from working together, so . . . I could hardly get any Republican women to come, because I was a Democrat."[14] Senator Jane Earll (R) attested to strong partisanship: "I would say that there is definitely a partisan flavor to the debate. I mean, I think the legislature is a reflection of the society that we oversee, and I think that it mirrors the polarization of what's going on in the world, in the United States."[15]

Several legislators indicated that the 2011 Republican takeover of the Pennsylvania House, which directly followed the caucus attempts, had led to a rift between legislators, with Democrats feeling as though Republicans were acting more partisan than they had during their majority and Republicans feeling as though they were acting like any majority party by moving forward their agenda using the mechanisms any majority would have. While subjects did not specifically mention party competition in terms of its effect on caucus organizing, I think the intense party competition in this state discouraged women from developing strong ties across the aisle.

Despite this development, women indicated that bipartisan work was being done by women on certain issues. "It's fair to say that it's congenial, even though it's partisan. I think that there's still a level of civility that rules the day the vast majority of the time," said Earl (2011). Representative Louise Williams Bishop (D) put it this way: "I think that women who feel very strong[ly] about the issues, their issues are stronger than party. It's not often that you do run across that, but when they feel strongly about something, they don't care what party you belong to; they will work you for it and try to get you on board."[16]

The Pennsylvania caucus attempt highlights that similar political opportunities are not necessarily successfully mobilized by caucus entrepreneurs. As in New Jersey, the women legislators in Pennsylvania cited strong evidence of discrimination among parties (although there is not unanimity on this point). In New Jersey, powerful senior women were able to leverage this condition to mobilize newer members. This conversion did not take place in this case, in part because of the political inexperience of the entrepreneur. As in Colorado, Republican women may have been under pressure not to participate in a bipartisan group, and Representative Brown, interested in giving women a voice in policy, did not choose, as Representative Middleton did, to roll back her expectation in order to coalesce a group before attempting to bring policy into the picture. However, the highly partisan and hierarchical norms in this state meant Brown had her work cut out for her. The Pennsylvania attempt demonstrates how crucial strategy is in leveraging the political opportunities available to women legislators.

FEW RESOURCES TO GET THE JOB DONE

In Pennsylvania, unlike Colorado and New Jersey, a legislator's job is full time. Although legislators in these other states balanced sometimes two jobs in addition to their familial obligations, in Pennsylvania where legislators were dedicated to the position solely, time was still a factor cited as an obstacle to a women's caucus. Legislators cited priorities other than a women's caucus and did not see an organization as complementing this work but rather as competing. Further, the caucus entrepreneurs did not secure a full-time staffer, as those in New Jersey and Colorado had, to manage the logistical details. These two factors contributed to the failure of this caucus to launch.

Professionalism

Pennsylvania has undergone significant change over the past three decades, transitioning from a part-time to a full-time legislature, and this professionalism has significantly affected legislative norms and behaviors (Kennedy 1999). Many legislators in Pennsylvania noted that because they were a full-time legislature, always in session, that there simply was not time for their participation in a women's caucus. Representative Kate Harper (R) said she "didn't need another commitment."[17] Representative Babette Josephs (D) added, "We're a full-time legislature—there is no time; we're always in session, always on emergency mode."[18] She indicated, however, that under the right circumstances she might find the time: "I will participate if it doesn't take too much time or ask me to compromise any positions. . . . [I] wouldn't put a lot of time into head scarves."[19]

Here, Josephs is referring to the second attempt made by Representative Brown in 2010. By again, putting a formal request to the Democratic leadership, with the same Republican cochair and attempting to organize the women on a bipartisan level, Brown was only able to organize a subset of Democratic women to have an informal party caucus that met for informal breakfasts and dinners until summer 2010. This attempt featured charitable activities, including when a speaker presented information to women legislators about the conditions in Haiti following the 2010 earthquake. Legislators were asked to contribute headscarves for Haitian women who were unable to afford them after the disaster and were sacrificing other important needs for their families in order to obtain them. Representative Josephs indicates in her quote that she would be willing to participate only if the caucus dealt with issues she felt were substantive and relevant. This attitude mirrors that of many Democratic legislators in Colorado and New Jersey who feel frustrated by the watering down of purpose necessary to get bipartisan participation in a women's caucus. Following this event no additional meetings were held or attended by women from both parties. Because neither attempt to create a women's caucus resulted in legislators from both parties meeting more than once over a period of one year, these attempts do not meet my criteria for a successful caucus creation.[20]

There are other conditions, however, that also challenge women's participation. Representative Delozier, indicating her role in the family as a complicating factor, said:

> I prefer to be home with my kids if I don't have something in the district. So if something in the district isn't calling me, I tend to go home. But sometimes having that social outlet and being able to have a conversation that's not related to a bill or related to something that's going to committee, maybe you can learn something about those that you're working with, which is kind of getting to know people better.[21]

While this representative acknowledges the positive that comes from her participation, she has to balance that against her other role as a mother. It is interesting that she juxtaposes her participation in a women's caucus against her obligations as a district representative rather than seeing one as an extension of the other. This example demonstrates how historical conceptions of representation within legislatures intersect with gender. Representing women or approaching policy with a gendered lens is perceived as distinct from their responsibilities to their district, which is perceived as gender neutral.

In Pennsylvania, as in Colorado and New Jersey, there is no legislative support for caucuses despite having the largest staff size (2,919) of any of the four cases examined in this project.[22] As Senate Minority Leader Jay Costa described it:

> I think they're on their own. There's no, to my knowledge, there's no allocation that I know of that give[s] to a particular caucus. It's just getting together and meeting and having a conversation. And to the extent that it's a meeting where [they] may want to serve coffee and snacks, they take it out of, members take it out of their own individual account, whoever serves

as chairperson of that particular caucus. The staffing work that is done is typically the existing staff that exists for a particular member, who sort of takes the lead on a particular caucus.[23]

In the New Jersey and Colorado cases, both caucuses secured a staffer (either volunteer or from outside funds) who was completely dedicated to the organization of the women's caucus. It did not depend on the spare time a legislative staffer could dedicate to this one interest of her legislator. In the case of Pennsylvania, it appears that a lack of time on the part of the legislators themselves prevented more widespread participation. This issue was compounded by competing priorities. A large number of legislative staffers were not able to ameliorate these problems. Representative Brown did not complain that the lack of a dedicated staffer was a challenge to the caucus, but the lack of a dedicated staffer is a factor distinguishing it from the two successful cases.

Entrepreneurs

In Pennsylvania, senior Democratic legislators did not like how Representative Brown went about creating the caucus. Unlike Representative Middleton in Colorado, Representative Brown did not consult with senior women in her caucus. These more senior women resented that Brown named herself cochair of the caucus and proceeded without their input. This resentment was evident under the surface as Representative Bishop explained that less-experienced legislators may have time for such things but that she did not, and she did not need a caucus to accomplish her goals:

> Let me just say this to you: there are so many of us moving in many different directions. [Being] chairwoman of Children and Youth . . . takes up most of my time, and it makes it extremely difficult for me to be an active member in the women's caucus. Some of the other women are doing the same thing. Maybe [it's possible] for some of the newer women, who have not been here that long, because you have to be here ten terms before you

can become a chair. So you will find that the women's caucus was usually made up of the women who were here but didn't serve in leadership and they did not have a chair, so that gave them the opportunity to advance some of their issues. I've been here twenty-two years, so long past the time when I've really had time to associate and to move women['s] issues, because I use the committee to move women['s] and children['s] issues rather than a caucus to do it.[24]

Representative Brown (D) herself admitted her political naiveté cost her. In her own analysis of what went wrong in recruiting women to participate, she identified informal political rules such as deference to seniority, which she violated:

The only problem we had is I had to learn we had to respect the leadership. And there are women who have been here a long time, who've tried to form this caucus, and it was expressed to me—and I won't name who they are—that they would have appreciated if they had been the chair before I had a chance to be the chair, which coming from their perspective, I can appreciate it, but coming from young and progressive and ready to go, I didn't appreciate it.[25]

This lack of consultation of her own party set Representative Brown up to fail in many ways. On the one hand, she did not have the benefit of information about previous attempts to create a women's caucus and what pitfalls to avoid. Had she known, for example, that partisanship had been a problem in the past, she and Representative Boback may have used a different frame to motivate participation. Representative Brown may have tried to shore up Democratic support first and then reach across the aisle. Similarly, by not deferring to the more senior women in her party, she alienated women whose influence may have helped her recruitment of participants on both sides of the aisle. This political naiveté was a key factor in the failure of this attempt to create a women's caucus, as Representative Brown herself identifies it as "the only problem."

FRAMING THE TASK AT HAND

In Pennsylvania, the caucus entrepreneurs wanted to give women a voice in public policy. Despite the marginalization of women within the institution and the highly partisan environment, Representative Brown persisted in trying to galvanize women around issues. She initially held a meeting in the beginning of 2009 regarding energy policy that may have drawn opposition from Republican men. Next, she proposed a charitable activity for Haitian women that fell flat when her colleagues perceived it as irrelevant or unsubstantial. The entrepreneurs in this case did not adequately read their political context and, when opposition arose, their alternative course was not compelling to other women legislators. Due to the highly partisan environment and the territorial senior women in this state, it was very unlikely for a policy caucus to be successful. It is questionable if even a social caucus would have been possible under these conditions, but this case points to the importance of matching the right frame to the specific political context when trying to recruit participants to organize.

Gender Consciousness and Party Dissatisfaction

I have hypothesized that gender consciousness correlates with successful women's caucus attempts. Recognition among women legislators of common interests was expected to be associated with a successful attempt to create a women's caucus because I predicted it would be a useful argument for why a women's caucus would be necessary. In this case, women's perceived collective identity was complicated. While they recognized women's difference, many did not see collective organizing as appropriate legislative behavior. Representative Delozier put it this way:

> There's many women that . . . , throughout their children's [lives]—however old their child is—ha[ve] always worked. Yes, is an elected official's position and job, tougher and longer hours and even though people think we're part-time. . . . Are they weird times? Are they Saturday morning at nine o'clock

and Sunday afternoons at two and dinners on Saturday nights? Yes, so my kids are used to me getting dressed in a suit at five o'clock on a Saturday night. So it's different, yes, but I think that because more women are getting involved, and I think that they're doing it successfully, you're seeing Michelle Bachmann at the national level and you're seeing Hillary Clinton . . . , and I may or may not agree with their particular policies, but I think it's a good example to show that women can do what it is that men have always done.[26]

Here, Delozier indicates the challenges she faces as a mom and a legislator; however, she admires women's ability to "do what men have always done" without acknowledging it is wives who in large part have made that possible for men. She went on to talk about her initial campaign. She was questioned by voters and party leaders about her children, despite the other male candidates' similar positions. She said:

There were seven of us running. . . . [I]t was me and six men, and one of the men had just had an infant; they just had a baby. And another one of the men had four children, two of which were younger than my children. My children at the time were young, but they were—what were they when I ran, five and seven, I guess—no, seven and nine . . . seven and nine. So they were young, but you know, it was something we had worked out family-wise, and it was not something we weren't willing to adjust to, but they were asking me the question but not asking my two opponents, who had children younger than me, which is just one of those perceptions.[27]

She explained that she was prepared for those questions and felt she just had to "bite her tongue" to move on.

Senate Minority Leader Costa, as a male legislator, likewise acknowledged women's difference yet disregarded the double standard that women face:

I think there are different life experiences. . . . I would suggest that, no, they're members first and then their respective genders second. That doesn't preclude them or give them an upper hand or put them in a different place, but their life experiences that they bring to the job and bring to the legislature are different than men have to deal with. . . . [I]t has impacted members. I can think of a couple of members from Allegheny County, one in particular, who left the legislature after, I think, two or four years because she wanted to go back home and have her family. Another member from Allegheny County just, Representative [Chelsa] Wagner [(D)], has now a second child, I believe, [and] ran for county office in part to be back at home, raising a family, as opposed to coming back and forth here. So for those reasons primarily, the role that a woman plays in their own family, I think, is different than typically what men do and as a result has an impact on the ability, they believe, to do the job. . . . [B]ut it doesn't give them, they're not at a disadvantage because of their gender or at an advantage.[28]

Representative Gingrich characterized women's different contribution in this way:

Well, there have been times that I feel an issue, a critical issue could be better—let me just put it this way, better understood possibly by the female mentality and experience in life. . . . [I]f I need a level of understanding on issues that I don't think necessarily the guys come by naturally, then I will pull the women together informally, almost like it's an informal whip count. . . . [B]ut, yeah, we haven't done anything about formally creating a female caucus and, again, a lot of—there's party differences, there are personality style differences, there's the demographic, geographic differences, where even the women just can't agree on what's best for their constituency.[29]

Senator Earll agreed:

Women aren't monolithic either. I mean, I have colleagues who I get along with personally, female colleagues who are more to my liking than others. I mean, I don't necessarily, like, relate to them or have things in common with them by virtue of gender as much as issue orientation or philosophical orientation, and I think that's probably true for most of us women in the Senate. And I think you probably hang out with people or gather with people who are more to your personal liking based on those factors, not gender.[30]

Other legislators explicitly explained that gender separation was against their political ideology: "That's not why I got into the legislature; it's not how I want to deal with things; it's not a Republican argument; it's not a good strategy."[31] Senator Christine Tartaglione specifically noted a lack of gender consciousness: "The problem is women normally don't like women. I don't know what it is."[32] She indicated that individually she tried to combat that by taking other women legislators under her wing and mentoring them. Representative Delozier explained:

I don't think that there is an interest, and the reason I say that is because we are one body. And, yes, there are caucuses. I know there's a black caucus, as you mentioned, which certainly is, you know, a racial version of dividing. But I honestly think that in many ways, because a lot of the barriers have come down for women over the years, that by making a caucus just for women, they're almost putting them back up again. . . . I also think that, my personal opinion is that, by putting up more divisiveness . . . you are saying that there is a difference, per se. . . . I think that's the opposite of what we're trying to do.[33]

Senator Earll agreed: "I've just personally . . . never been of a mindset to participate in that type of thing. I mean, I don't—it's always been my personal philosophy that you don't make yourself equal by segregating yourself . . . , and I don't believe that issues relevant to women are relevant to women by virtue of our gender."[34]

While the women legislators in Pennsylvania acknowledge that women bring a different life experience to the legislature, face unique challenges as a result of the gender roles outside of the legislature, and may have specific policy interests, they do not have a strong gender consciousness that lends itself to a belief in collective action, a view that is reinforced by party leadership who do not see a problem. In this case, I attribute the failure of this caucus launch in part to a lack of belief on the legislators' part that gendered organizing is an appropriate form of legislative behavior or a solution to the challenges presented by their gender.

Women in Pennsylvania reported instances of discrimination based on their gender within the legislature or their party specifically. Here, unlike in New Jersey, this bias did not unify women in a caucus. Many legislators told of the different experience of the institution as a result of their gender. Despite Costa's perception that gender is not a disadvantage in Pennsylvania, women's voices tell a different story.

Senator Tartaglione shared this anecdote: "When I first got there, I wore a pantsuit on the Senate floor, and I was told I should have worn a skirt. . . . Well, what are you gonna do? Throw me off the floor? I'm elected. . . . I was a trailblazer."[35] A senior woman in Representative Gingrich's party told her not to bring a purse into the legislature. She warned that it would draw attention to her difference. Representative Gingrich joked, "Do you know what? I don't carry a purse. I laughed heartily when she said that to me so many years ago, and I'll be darned, I do not carry a purse. I make sure that anything I need in the day is in my binder."[36] When asked if there was an old boys' network in Pennsylvania, she admitted there was:

> Oh, yeah. And that probably will never change. . . . [B]ut I think mature women coming into positions like mine—and most of us are, most of us don't do this until our children are at least, a little bit older . . . I don't have a real problem with the men being good ole boys style, because most of them are all about the same age. The old guys, yes. That's enduring. The guys who are up there, that have been there for thirty years, they'll pat you on the back and do all that stupid stuff that drives women nuts, but the younger guys don't. They've worked with women professionally, and I see them definitely looking at us as intellectual, capable equals. Do they have cigar-smoking caucuses? By far. Do they all play golf together and never think of inviting you?

By far. Are many of the leadership decisions made outside of the chamber . . . and in more social settings . . . all guys? Absolutely. And I don't see any sign of that changing at all.[37]

Gingrich's statement demonstrates the multifaceted challenges that women in the legislative environment face, and she acknowledges that age is a mitigating factor in gender discrimination, as was the case in New Jersey. Similarly, she notes that younger men react differently to women in the workplace than older men. She acknowledges the challenge posed by women's role in the family. Ultimately, however, she explains away any consequences of these issues. She has dealt with it as an individual and, despite an informal male caucus that still maintains control, she does not see organized women's action as a solution to the problem. Representative Delozier also blamed the lack of women in politics on individuals:

I don't think that's a [gender] barrier anymore. It's a barrier by the individual feeling that they can do it more than I think the acceptance by voters of it being a woman. . . . I think the candidates themselves have to get past the fact that they are gonna have to fund-raise and they are going to have to go ask for money, and I think that that's very difficult. And I also think that the difference is—and I've said this before to others—is the fact that women wait to be asked to do something.[38]

Some legislators pointed to specific problems with male dominance within political parties. Even Representative Delozier, who explained the lack of women in office as an individual choice, pointed out discrimination in committee assignments:

I think just about every Republican woman was on the Human Services Committee. And that's not necessarily something we choose. Like that was not one of my choices, but that's where they assigned a number of us. And we kind of laughed about it and said, "My goodness, here are all the women in the legislature."[39]

Representative Bishop added:

> The number of men on all the committees and in all the leader-
> ship roles are so overpowering they basically can make the deci-
> sions. But there are times when they really do need women's
> support, and there are some leaders who are concerned about
> women's support, and so they do have an opportunity to make
> some input. . . . Is it as often as we would like? No, it isn't, but
> they do involve us.[40]

Bishop's comment indicates that women are not running parties or
committees. Women are outsiders, tapped when useful; they are not
the deciders. Despite this, other legislators did not report any dissatisfaction with the party or their influence within it. Representative
Swanger said, "I feel very strongly that we're part of the decision-making process, and I don't, I've never seen the women treated any differently than the men as far as being able to run bills, getting support,
getting assistance from the legislators that have been there in office
longer. I was very pleased at the demeanor of the men toward the
women."[41] Senator Jane Earll agreed: "I can't point to an example of
where I've been discriminated against in my caucus because of my
gender."[42]

Some women legislators in Pennsylvania acknowledged that women
face unique challenges as a result of their gender within the legislature,
but they did not identify a women's caucus as an effective solution to
this problem. Similarly, this dissatisfaction with political party's attention to issues or with respect to women more broadly was not unani-
mous among women legislators. Without a shared understanding of
gender bias as systemic, there was little hope of mobilizing women to
act collectively. The frame that worked in New Jersey and Colorado did
not resonate with the women legislators in Pennsylvania.

Most women indicated that individual action was the preferred
way to work in a bipartisan manner. They often mentioned that going
directly to someone on the other side who had an interest in the subject, or was on the relevant committee, was a good strategy, as opposed
to a more formal group where there was a fear of having to compromise their principles or agree to some sort of consensus across party

lines. There was particular hesitation among more senior Democratic women to trust Republican women. Representative Brown said:

> I also had a challenge with the fact that I was a new freshman and I didn't know the history of the House and the history of the women. And I came in very excited, enthusiastic, with lots of passion, and I didn't think about going back to the history. And [I overlooked] that formerly, in the past they have tried to have a woman's caucus, but it was so partisan that it was never successful.[43]

It appears that in Pennsylvania there were real ideological divides between Democratic and Republican women that kept them from participating in a policy caucus. While this did not prevent them from acting individually in a bipartisan manner, historical distrust prevented even a social caucus from gaining the support necessary from participants across the aisles. While Democratic Senate minority leader Jay Costa indicated that his party did not keep a tight leash on members and allowed them to vote their conscience on bills, women still cited leadership expectations of strong party loyalty despite a collegial atmosphere and occasional social interactions with women from different parties.

I hypothesized that states with low levels of women in leadership positions may be more likely to have successful women's caucus attempts because this status would be a frame women could use in organizing. If women felt excluded from leadership, a bipartisan group that could advocate for women's selection for leadership posts might be a compelling argument to organize. The caucus founder did not use this frame in recruiting women to participate, although women did acknowledge a problem with the lack of women in leadership positions. Had Representatives Brown and Boback used this frame, perhaps their attempt would have been more successful. It is possible, however, that those senior women still would not have been mobilized by collective action—preferring instead to act independently to secure leadership positions rather than advocate for and as a group.

Representative Swanger and Senator Earll both pointed to a lack of women in leadership positions. Swanger said, "I think that needs to be worked on, because I think it is harder for a woman in the state legislature to move up into leadership."[44] Senator Earll attributed the lack of women in leadership in part to their different style:

> I think women just play differently than men, and that's why women don't necessarily rise to leadership. . . . I think that we're more interested—and this is just a broad generalization— but I think it's been my experience that women are more action oriented in terms of wanting to get results as opposed to being driven by the need to accumulate power or personal ambition. I don't think women are motivated by those factors as much as men, and I think that probably has more to do with the end result of women not being in leadership.[45]

Here, again, women's disadvantage is explained as a result of their different style rather than institutional structures or male bias. The responsibility for the lack of women in leadership is not tied to a problem with men or the institution. It is attributable to a difference in women—not a neutral difference, but one cloaked in compliment: women want to accomplish things, they are not motivated by ambition, and so forth. The positive attributes women bring as legislators are the same ones preventing them from having positions of power. Representative Delozier said:

> We have our chairperson of our caucus [who] is a woman. We joke that the quota, that there's only one woman allowed in leadership, because there's one Democrat woman in leadership and then Sandy Majors, our caucus chair. But last go-around for leadership of this session, a number of other women ran, so I thought that was encouraging, because that just means that maybe next go-around, or something like that, maybe we'll have more than Sandy. I mean, there's only five leadership positions. It's not like there's two dozen or something like that. So proportionately, I guess, we're well represented.[46]

In fact, this quote indicates that women are ambitious, in that at least in the most recent leadership elections, women ran and yet were not selected. Representative Delozier also endorses a proportional representation of women in the leadership. In a state at the bottom of the list in terms of female proportions in the legislature, it seems discouraging that this would be an appropriate measuring stick instead of say 50-50 allocation of leadership positions between men and women. From the party leadership perspective, Senate Minority Leader Costa said, "It's not a closed shop, and I think women play a significant role in our caucus."[47] This is despite no women as senate president, pro temp, majority or minority leaders, or house speaker, pro temp, majority or minority leaders at the time of the caucus attempts.

Gender consciousness and dissatisfaction with party, including women's lack of leadership positions, were not successfully used frames in the launching of this caucus. The focus of this women's caucus attempt was the impact women could make collectively on policy; these other frames did not appear in the discussion. As the data indicate, women are divided on women's difference and whether or not women are experiencing bias as result of their gender. Similarly, they are divided on the appropriate explanation and response when bias is perceived. It would be difficult for any organizer to mobilize women under these conditions.

Caucus Type

In Pennsylvania, Representative Brown and Representative Boback wanted to create a caucus that was policy based in order to impact women's issues. Representative Brown felt that these issues were not receiving the attention and consensus by women that were appropriate:

> I wanted women to have a voice in the House. I wanted the women of the Commonwealth to be able to speak up for themselves, because, so often, when we get to abortion rights, we get to welfare reform, anything to do with health care, with families, it's the men—they're up there and they're arguing back and forth for hours, for days. And I just saw that women were invisible and voiceless, and why are men governing our bodies, governing how we raise our children, governing where we go for health care, governing how we educate our children? And

> I know I serve a district that's predominantly female head of
> household. There's very few men who run the house—it's the
> women. And so, to me, I have more than a responsibility to any-
> one else in this House to make sure that women are represented,
> and this was a vehicle that I used to do that.[48]

Here again, Representative Brown is referencing the dichotomy between representing a district while also representing women. By cit-
ing the particular nature of her district, she does not perceive the
two roles as contradictory—but for other representatives without her
demographics—would there be a contradiction? Representative Delozier's comments seem to indicate so.

Brown faced challenges because, as has been observed previously,
women legislators in Pennsylvania did not see a need for collective
policy action and preferred to handle issues on a case-by-case basis,
relating as individuals. As Representative Harper said, "We hold very
different views, couldn't agree on issues. We can agree on some things;
without a group, we do that."[49] In this case, as has been noted, a policy
caucus was unlikely to be successful because of partisan differences
and a lack of consensus that women have unique policy issues that
should be addressed collectively. As Representative Gingrich put it,
"It's funny how women can find their way into being very effective
without this 'I am woman, hear me roar!' thing, you know? Caucus
or no caucus."[50] These differences were exacerbated by a lack of trust
between women across and within party lines.

I hypothesized that caucuses that set socializing as the top priority for organizing were more likely to succeed than those that set
public policy as their primary function. From the start, the purpose
of the Pennsylvania Women's Legislative Caucus was to affect public policy. When in 2010 this did not work in a bipartisan manner,
Representative Brown attempted to create such a policy caucus with
other Democratic legislators, but again saw limited success because of
a division between more senior women legislators and more recently
elected women. Many women legislators acknowledged that socializing occurred in a bipartisan or intraparty fashion on occasion but
not with any regularity. "So you have a lot of stumbling blocks, I will
tell you that. I've organized dinners, more social times together. . . .

[W]e're not making any decisions, of course—an informal discussion on some of the policy issues before us. And generally they go really well, but then there are times when somebody will say, 'Well, who's going?' You know, 'If she's going, I'm not going.' You know, that kind of thing. And that's not pettiness; that's just extreme policy, different perspectives on things."[51] Representative Gingrich (R), indicated, for example, that from her perspective as a Republican, an attempt to create a women's caucus might have been more successful if a within-party caucus had been established while Republicans were in the majority, with invitations then expanded out to Democrats. Representative Brown or Representative Boback did not adopt this strategy, however.

LESSONS LEARNED FROM PENNSYLVANIA

In Pennsylvania, as in Colorado, a newly elected representative was motivated to create a caucus because of her disappointment with the status quo of women's influence in the body. She was inspired by the existence of other caucuses, including the Black Caucus, to create an organization for women legislators. Unlike in Colorado, however, Representative Brown did not vet the idea of a caucus with more senior members of her own party. This mistake cost her in many ways, including valuable information that could have altered her and Representative Boback's strategy, as well as legitimacy in the recruitment of participants. Unlike in New Jersey, where the attempt to create a women's caucus was by senior women taking advantage of an influx of new women, this case appears to have suffered from a lack of political experience on the part of at least one of the founders.

Party posed a big challenge in this case from the beginning. Unlike in New Jersey where women legislators had longstanding relationships with each other across the aisle, there seemed to be little social interaction among the Pennsylvania women and a history of mistrust. Tight party competition, frequently shifting party majorities, and ideological differences among women all contributed to an environment unlikely to result in a successful launch of a caucus. Even among women who expressed dissatisfaction with their status within their party and with a lack of women in leadership, legislators did not view collectively identifying with other women as an appropriate response. This state also had the smallest women's proportion of the Republican Party of all four cases, indicating likely increased pressure on them to affiliate with their party rather than their gender. I characterize the subjects interviewed here as having very low gender consciousness in regard to acknowledging women's difference and the benefits of acting collectively.

Institutional factors in Pennsylvania, including professionalism and term limits, had unexpected effects in this case. As a full-time legislature, most women admitted that time was an issue discouraging their participation in a caucus. Similarly, there was no staff or financial resources available for the launch either from the legislature itself or external organizations. While the Pennsylvania legislature is not term-limited, this institutional factor may have had a positive influence on an attempt to create a women's caucus in this state by eliminating the members who had served for a long time and opposed caucus formation, differing from New Jersey, where senior members' experience was key.

Finally, the frame that Representatives Brown and Boback used in creating this caucus was public policy. Without the benefit of history or the experience of their more senior colleagues, Representatives Brown and Boback did not anticipate how partisanship and a lack of gender consciousness on the part of their potential participants would negatively affect the launch. In this case, framing the caucus as a social networking opportunity would have been a starting place, but with the lack of gender consciousness and limited time, it is unlikely that even this frame would have been successful. While it is unclear here how much opposition there would be from the Republican leadership at the present time, it is clear a historical opposition did exist in this state, and the lingering effects of this opposition may have negatively impacted even the launch of a social caucus.

Several institutional features within this case inhibited women's organizing. Women legislators cited a full-time, year-round legislature that was limiting the time available for what they perceived to be superfluous work rather than creating the space for a caucus. High polarization between the parties and a lack of collegiality also contributed to the failure here to organize. Additionally, senior women were able to use their power and influence to shut down attempts here, whereas in New Jersey they used them to create a caucus. Senior women legislators were able to wield informal power to thwart representatives Brown and Boback despite the formal support of Democratic leadership.

In the next chapter, I consider the attempt to create a women's caucus that failed in Iowa in 2007. By comparing Pennsylvania and Iowa, I identify which factors are common to both and, therefore, detrimental to a caucus launch and what separates these attempts to caucus from the successes in New Jersey and Colorado.

7

THE IOWA ATTEMPT

TIMELINE

1980s: Formal caucus.

Late 1980s: Formal caucus declines.

1990s: Informal social caucus.

2001: Women's caucus created as an organization of women legislators, staff, lobbyists, business and community leaders concerned with the election of women to public office.

January 12, 2007: Patty Judge's term as lieutenant governor begins.

March 2008: A reception is held for all the women legislators at the governor's mansion, hosted by First Lady Mariclare Culver and Lieutenant Governor Judge, organized by Rachel Scott, administrator at the Iowa Commission on the Status of Women.

The original Iowa's Women's Caucus was featured in the documentary film *Not One of the Boys,* produced by CAWP in 1984, which documents the experiences of Iowa women legislators (Economou 1984). The film highlights the social and political nature of the caucus and ultimately its decline as partisanship and lack of participation take their toll on the group. This chapter analyzes a women's caucus attempt by former legislator and Lieutenant

Governor Patty Judge (D), who was a participant in this caucus, to reinstate it in 2007 following her election to executive office.[1]

Despite a history of women's caucuses in the state legislature, an experienced former legislator lending her support, and the support of the Commission for the Status of Women, the women legislators of Iowa were not successful in launching a caucus in 2007. Women legislators perceived the attempt to caucus as coming from the outside and, while the purpose of the caucus was left open for discussion, legislators did not take advantage of the external support offered them. Although there was more openness and interest from newly elected women, more senior legislators were cynical, and possible discouragement from party leaders on both sides cooled any initial enthusiasm. In Iowa, I learned that adequate resources and outside support are not enough to motivate apathetic or discouraged women legislators who do not recognize a shared identity.

Women legislators in Iowa did not report any dissatisfaction with their party or any exclusion from leadership opportunities, and therefore did not have any motivation to right any wrongs despite outsiders identifying problems unique to women. Women admitted that women make a difference in the legislature, but it was not a frame that was highlighted by organizers or an identity held passionately by the legislators themselves. Similarly, women felt that individual action on behalf of women's issues was more likely to achieve results, as was the case in Pennsylvania. I attribute this view, in part, to party differences and ideological differences that pushed the women's policy goals and votes apart. Neither social networking nor a policy agenda were tempting enough to encourage participation.

Issues of partisanship, party control, and party competition (resulting in increased party discipline) were problematic for the founding of this caucus. Term limits may not have negatively impacted this caucus launch, but, as in Pennsylvania, the presence of experienced women legislators was significant in that their suspicions toward women outside their party limited their participation. Unlike the other three cases where other caucuses existed in the legislature, at the time of the women's attempt in 2007, no caucuses outside of party caucuses existed, likely due to party leadership opposition. As in other states, the time necessary to participate in any extracurricular

TABLE 7.1. IOWA INTERVIEW SUBJECTS (7) DEMOGRAPHICS		
Party affiliation	Legislative leaders	Gender
1 Republican, 5 Democrats, 1 nonpartisan staffer	1	0 male, 7 female

legislative activities was limited because of women legislators' familial obligations, something they recognized as a negative gender expectation uniquely facing them.

While Iowa may have met any potential threshold for enough women to caucus and the election of a Democratic lieutenant governor sparked the attempt, a lack of a caucusing culture in Iowa and high distrust across party lines were enough to sink the attempt in 2007. The women legislators of Iowa had one bipartisan event in March 2008 and no further activity. The failed attempt at caucusing in Iowa in 2007 can be explained by a political culture that delegitimized organizing outside of political parties and women legislators with no interest in collective solutions to their challenges. Whereas in Pennsylvania a political novice made missteps largely without outside support, in Iowa, a very experienced politician with staffing support from the Women's Commission was still unable to overcome the partisanship that separated women legislators. (For additional demographic details about the interview subjects cited in this chapter, see Table 7.1.)

FEW POLITICAL OPPORTUNITIES FOR EXPERIENCED ENTREPRENEUR TO SEIZE

In 2007, former State Representative Patty Judge was elected lieutenant governor of Iowa. Shortly after, she was contacted by then representative Swati Dandekar (D), who was interested in creating a caucus much like the one Judge had participated in during her legislative tenure in the 1990s. She explains:

> We did have a women's caucus at that time. . . . [I]t was kind of a loosely affiliated thing, and we did not really take positions, hard positions on particular pieces of legislation. At that point

in time, we talked about things where we could find some common ground. . . . [W]e did a lot of socializing and created some pretty good friendships that have endured the times through, friends on both sides of the aisle. So it was—that was a good experience.[2]

Senator Dandekar remembers the initiative coming from Judge:

I think it was her idea; it was her idea that she would do that, and she's an extremely bright person, so it was her idea that "let's focus on issues that are important to us women and let's work on it."[3]

In 2007, when this conversation between Judge and Dandekar took place, the Democratic Party controlled both houses of the Iowa legislature, and a Democratic governor was in office. The Iowa legislature is a place where

the majority floor leader holds a great deal of power . . . although some minority leaders have demonstrated great agility at frustrating the majority party's goals. . . . The amount of power and influence exerted by these leaders depends upon many factors including the relative strength of each party in the chamber, the political strength of the leader, and the amount of loyalty and discipline the leader has developed. (Schenken 1995, xiii)

The development of women's caucuses as challenges to party leadership power and control suggests that strong party leaders are something women would have to contend with in the development of an alternative organization to party. In fact, in the two successful women's caucus attempts examined in this project, party leaders had no such objections and the caucuses proceeded. In Pennsylvania, there is historical evidence of objection by Republican Party leaders, both formal and informal, but no direct evidence of their interference in the 2007 failed attempt to create a women's caucus.[4] Iowa is a unique case because of two previously existing women's caucuses in the state despite strong norms of party loyalty.

While party competition specifically was not something mentioned in the interviews, party majority was something considered very influential in the behavior of legislators. Party discipline, too, was very important. Like the other three cases, there is hearsay evidence of leadership opposition. For instance, Rachel Scott reported that when she attempted to schedule a second reception of legislators, she learned of the Democratic Party's opposition:

> We tried kind of pulling together another event later that year and then asking around about an event for next year, and people had started to kind of dig in a little more. By the second year, I was told that the leadership of the Democrats said, "We don't want you being in any caucuses of any kind." Potentially they didn't want anything. I don't know that they had anything against women necessarily, though some might argue with that, but I think that they didn't want anything that was going to shake up their control of their own caucus or have any kind of rogue voting—that sort of thing.[5]

While two women served in leadership positions during this session, it is unclear which leaders were sending this message. The legislators themselves, however, did not express any concern that party leadership had opposed the attempt to create a women's caucus or would challenge any future attempts. Representative Linda Upmeyer reported no perceived opposition from the Republican side: "No, I don't think there would be. . . . No, I never heard any push back on it at all."[6] On the Democratic side, Representative Phyllis Thede said, "Honestly, I think they would be okay with it. I think they would see us as an organized group, and it would be beneficial to them. . . . I have never heard a man say anything negative or, really, positive either, but I think the support would be out there."[7] Representative Deborah Berry agreed: "I don't expect that. . . . I don't think there would be backlash."[8] This assertion, however, contradicts a story she told about investigating the possibility of an African American caucus:

> When Democrats, when we were in the majority, we wanted to make sure that it was okay with our leadership. I mean, there's

a process for all of those things and for all of that. I mean, you want to make sure that you could get things done as a caucus too. I mean, it wouldn't make sense to do. I'm African American, and we had talked about an African American caucus at one time, but that one particular year, that was not, we were, we were told that there wouldn't be any—that our leadership wasn't interested in caucuses, other caucuses, because we had too much on the agenda. It would be a little too much to have to deal with.[9]

This statement indicates Democratic Party leadership opposition to the development of any alternative caucusing and lends support to the hearsay alluded to by Scott when she was told Democrats were discouraged from caucuses with other women. Here, Berry alludes to an informal process that needs to be followed. Like Middleton, Berry tried to defer to this process but, in the case of an African American caucus, she was rebuffed by party leadership.

Iowa is not a state of legislative caucuses, and I hypothesized that the existence of other caucuses within a legislature, particularly a black caucus, could positively affect a caucus launch by normalizing alternative organizing outside of party structures. The two party caucuses are the only caucuses in existence save a bipartisan Rural Caucus created in 2010. There were no other caucuses at the time of the women's attempt, despite precedent for alternative organizations. On the basis of these interviews, it appears that party leadership may have discouraged the development of these groups.

The evidence here indicates that Democratic opposition to alternative organizing supports the description of Iowa as a place where the majority party holds onto power through party discipline (Schenken 1995). This fact obviously hurt Scott's ability to recruit at least Democratic participants, the legislators most likely to be motivated to participate in a women's caucus. This evidence indicates it is not only the Republican Party that can thwart women's initiative, despite my hypotheses, which anticipated their party norms and ideology would present a particular disadvantage. Controlling women's legislative behavior by discouraging bipartisan activities is a political party issue, not a Republican one. There is also a suspicion on Judge's part that Republicans were discouraged as well. Not substantiated by any evidence from Republican legislators, Judge's comment was "I believe, because they were instructed on the other side of the aisle, the Republican side of the aisle, not to mingle, it never went beyond that point. Again, it was not my role to make it go on, because I was not a legislator at that point in time."[10] Again, as in New Jersey, this remark depicts women as not leading the parties or even as peers. Instead women are instructed by party men—at once indicating women's outsider status while preventing them from ameliorating that through alternative organizing.

In describing the environment of the Iowa legislature, Representative Berry said:

> Politics are so partisan right now. It's kind of tragic, and I think that it's that way because of national politics and feeling the effects of that division. So, yeah, I don't know if I can even say that I could see a women's caucus getting off the ground. I know you'd have women on both sides pretty interested in, again, the issues, and in the end those are the things that bind us. . . . I'm thinking that maybe I'm the one to approach the majority party women and the minority women, party women, and say, "Hey, you know, we've got a lot of issues coming up before us again. We need to b[i]nd together as women." But as I said, I just feel it's just so partisan anymore, politics these days, the climate of it all.[11]

Scott went on to explain the distrust between Republican and Democratic women in this way:

> There's an organization called 50–50 in 2020 in particular that's made up of these kind of mostly elder statesmen from both parties who, they're all about "let's have a high-level campaign training school," and one of the things that I have seen is the Republican women are very interested in this because they haven't had an infrastructure within their party to support that. The Democratic women are extremely suspicious of it because they have to a lesser degree, I mean, not to the degree that they

would want, but they have had some of that infrastructure within their party and so kind of the higher, like if you're talking about, like, "Oh, run for the School Board" or whatever, people are all fine and good, but, "let's lock arms" and "this is a great thing for women," but the higher you get up into policy issues and strategy and all of that kind of stuff, then the less interested people are in working together.[12]

This comment indicates that party competition hinders women's ability to act collectively in a bipartisan way. Representative Phyllis Thede (D) disagreed:

We currently do work across the aisle, when it comes to issues that really do matter to all of us, so I think there's a strong effort to do that. And, there are groups that are out there, currently out there now that work together trying to initiate women to become more active in politics anywhere from helping out with campaigns to actually running for a particular seat of some sort, whether it be city or State, and so there's a lot of work to be done out there. And, I think there's some effort among different groups to enlist women to get involved.[13]

In explaining the failure of the caucus, Scott reported the feelings of the legislators she had approached about next steps: "At the end of the day, I had women legislators tell me, 'I wanna spend—my social time is precious, I'd rather spend it with my family or people who have like interests rather than spend it trying to build a relationship with somebody that I don't know has my best interests at heart.'"[14] Representative Berry agreed with Scott's assessment: "I don't think it got off the ground much, though. We really don't get together women of both parties. It's, unfortunately, it seems to be more just party. Party members just kind of stick together."[15]

Representative Upmeyer described partisanship contextually, explaining that on budget issues, Iowa legislators are prone to partisanship, especially with newly elected majorities. She did concede, however, "I think when it comes to just good public policy, I think pretty regularly I want to work together to achieve good public policy."[16]

She did not clarify how public policy and budgeting could be distinguished or why they would be distinct.

Lieutenant Governor Judge mentioned that stricter lobbying laws in Iowa had limited the time legislators had to socialize. The case in Colorado was similar. Each was a political opportunity, a perceived problem that a social caucus could have addressed, that was not, however, successfully seized by organizers. The women legislators themselves did not want to spend their time together, but rather with their families or working on policy with like-minded individuals.

It appears, in this case, that while individual legislators may be interested in working together across the aisle on issues when agreement could be reached, a collective effort was unlikely to succeed in this case. More senior legislators on both sides were suspicious of each other and, despite success in the past; they were not interested in devoting time to an organization that included both Democratic and Republican legislators. These attitudes proved fatal for the Iowa attempt at a women's caucus. Despite the political opportunity created by Judge's election to lieutenant governor, it did not parlay into a successful caucus attempt.

Women in Iowa Politics

Iowa in 2007 was in the middle of the pack as far as the proportion of women is concerned, but it does not appear to have been a major influence in this case. Public opinion polls indicate "something of a glass ceiling" for Iowa women politicians (Schenken 1995, 163). Only one woman has served as governor of Iowa, and only one has represented Iowa in Congress. In 2007, Iowa ranked twenty-fifth in the country according to gender proportions with women making up 22.7 percent of the legislature. The state ranked twenty-fourth in the nation in terms of the proportion of women serving in legislative leadership positions with 25 percent held by women (2/8 positions), and Iowa ranked thirty-fifth in the nation with women holding 17.6 percent of committee chairmanships (6/34 chairmanships) (CAWP 2007). (For additional demographic details about the state, see Table 7.2.)

The organizers did not cite women's share of seats in the legislature as a factor in their calculation to create a caucus. Representa-

TABLE 7.2. IOWA DEMOGRAPHICS (NCSL 2010; U.S. CENSUS BUREAU 2011)	
2010 population	3,046,355
Population size	Ranked 30th in the nation
Political culture (Elazar 1984)	Moralistic
Party control—assembly (2009)	Democrat
Party control—senate (2009)	Democrat
Party of the governor (2009)	Democrat
Proportion of women—legislature (2009)	22.7% Ranked 25th in the nation
Proportion of women—legislative leadership (2009)	25% Ranked 24th in the nation
Party competition—house (2009)	9-seat difference
Party competition—senate (2009)	10-seat difference
Professionalization (Squire 2007)	Ranked 22nd in the nation

tive Deborah Berry (D) mentioned that at the same time a women's caucus was being discussed, African American legislators were also considering caucusing. She cited their low numbers as a reason not to continue (in addition to the previously discussed leadership objection). Representative Berry saw the women's numbers as favoring the development of a women's caucus, however: "[Regarding] women in the Iowa Legislature . . . I thought we had about thirty-plus total. But I think this last election it went, the numbers went down a bit, but we'd have a better chance of forming as a group."[17] Unfortunately, that did not turn out to be the case.

In 2007, women made up 20 percent of Republicans in Iowa's State House of Representatives. Of the four cases, this is the third-largest proportion of Republican women, and I hypothesized that Republican women, who represent a smaller percentage of the total Republican Party in a state, may feel more pressure to conform to legislative norms and less likely to join a bipartisan group. In this case, the proportion of Republican women is almost the same as in Colorado, which had a successful caucus attempt, but slightly above Kanter's (1977) line of 15 percent for a skewed sex ratio. Women in the interviews did not mention their numbers with the Republican Party as a factor in their decision to participate in the caucus or not, but there may be something to the possibility of breaching the 20 percent mark within the Republican Party freeing women to act in a more bipartisan way.

Many of the women who attended the event in 2008 organized by Rachel Scott at the Governor's Mansion were newly elected legislators, especially on the Republican side. More-senior Republicans were less likely to attend. Contrary to this greater enthusiasm among newly elected women, a Democratic legislator explained that a new influx of legislators (of all stripes, not just women) would discourage caucus formation. She said of the 2011 session, "It was just a pretty interesting legislative session with all the new people and different sectors of folks coming into the legislature, so we've just been not focused on that."[18]

As in Pennsylvania, there seems to be a lot of baggage for more senior legislators in Iowa. Rachel Scott explains:

> We had a bunch of Republican freshmen who were just nice women who wanted to see what this was all about. I mean, we didn't have any of the, kind of the older Republican women did not come. We did have some of the older Democratic women, but they tended to have, I think, a more cynical view of what can happen. I don't think anybody was around from old women's caucus days or at least those weren't the ones who showed up.[19]

During the actual attempt to create a women's caucus in 2007, it was difficult to even recruit women who had previously been active in the women's caucus of the 1990s. Scott again explains:

> There was a woman. . . . [S]he was a Republican, and I remember . . . she had been in that kind of initial women's caucus with Patty Judge. And she's somebody that Patty Judge really had a lot of respect for, so I went out of my way to invite her to be a part of the caucus. And she was famous for not mincing words, and she just said, "I'm too tired for this."[20]

More research is necessary to address both generational and tenure differences among women and how that affects their willingness and interest in caucusing. Age differences have been found to divide women legislators in other states (Brown 2014) and countries (Erickson 2017). Observing differences among women new to the legislature and those who have long served indicates that the institution is shaping women's motivation to caucus.

RESOURCES TO GET THE JOB DONE

As in New Jersey, Colorado, and Pennsylvania, women legislators in Iowa have limited time to govern due to the expectations placed on them through the social roles of wife and mother. When time is constrained, priorities are more sharply defined and, in Iowa, a collective women's group was not important for most of the women. The staffing support provided by the Commission on the Status of Women indicates that while these types of resources are necessary conditions for a caucus to emerge, they alone are not sufficient. Framing is as important as resources for caucus formation. Legislators themselves must perceive the caucus to be of value in order to devote any of their limited time to it.

External Organizations

Newly elected Lieutenant Governor Patty Judge asked the Commission on the Status of Women, an executive agency in the state, to play a supportive role for the women's caucus. Judge requested Rachel Scott, Administrator at the Iowa Commission on the Status of Women, support the organization. Scott then organized a reception for all the women legislators at the Governor's Mansion, hosted by First Lady Mariclare Culver and Lieutenant Governor Judge. Scott explained:

> She [Judge] said, "When I was in the legislature, we had a women's caucus, and that's when this caucus did all kinds of great stuff and really worked together in unexpected ways and kind of got around some of the men." And she told me stories about there's—I don't know if they have this in every state—but there's

this area called the Well that's right up in front of the Speaker or the majority leader's seat in the chamber. And when people wanted to speak privately, they would go up to this Well—even during senate debate—and that's where people would be called who were arguing with each other and that sort of thing. So she talked about sometimes women in different parties would be called up to the Well, or they would go up to the Well and talk. And they weren't on microphones, and it would make the men very nervous. . . . So she asked if I would take that on as a role, and it was something that I was very happy to do.[21]

This story indicates men's suspicions about their women colleagues, which likely transfers to women's attempt to organize as well. Women legislators are aware of these dynamics and their outsider status and it is within this environment that they must decide to caucus together or not. Weighing men's reactions is a part of that calculus that would be unique to an identity caucus. It is unlikely suspicions like the ones described here would be present for colleagues interested in establishing a rural or coastal caucus.

Both Democratic and Republican legislators attended the event hosted by the commission in March 2008. The event's function was primarily social in nature, although the women had a conversation around a large table to discuss the possibility of creating a caucus. Scott informed the women that some legislators had suggested a social network style caucus, while others were more interested in a policy-based group. Judge and Scott report that positive conversation followed and women in general got to know each other better at the event. No subsequent events were held. One year later, Scott attempted to organize another reception but could not generate any interest in such a function from the women legislators themselves, and ultimately she gave up once legislators made it clear they were uninterested in pursuing an organization.

Entrepreneurs

The lieutenant governor, and former legislator, Patty Judge, asked the commission to play this role. While Lieutenant Governor Judge remembers Senator Dandekar asking her to instigate the group, the senator recalls it as Judge's initiative. Representative Berry also perceived it in this way: "We had the lieutenant governor kind of spearheading it, so it didn't necessarily come out of the legislature—you see what I mean?"[22] For her part, Judge made a conscious effort to leave the decision making up to the legislators the night of the reception. Commenting on her role, she said:

> It was bait to get them to come, because many of them were new legislators and had never been inside the Governor's Mansion. They had never had an opportunity to socialize with me or with the First Lady, and so it was kind of a "come and see us and have a glass of wine" and so forth. And a good number of them did come, but for whatever reason—and, again, I was not upstairs on that floor and was not part of any discussions that they had beyond that night. It just did not gel beyond that night.[23]

Again, this evidence is not clear. Did the initiative come from the legislators themselves (Senator Dandekar) or from the executive branch? The executive branch did all of the organizing, and none of the legislators, in their comments about the caucus, took any ownership of its launch. There was at least the perception that it had come from outside the legislature. This seems to have been a negative factor on the chances of success in this case. Here, it is not just the frame being deployed but who is doing the framing that matters.

Professionalism

In Iowa, time was definitely a challenge. In one sense, it was not clear that with limited time a women's caucus was a priority. "People just told me individually, 'Eh, I don't know. I'd just rather spend my time in other ways,'" said Scott.[24] Similarly, the additional responsibilities of women in the home limited the time they wanted to spend. Scott added:

> It was also an issue because many of the women in the legislature are from the Des Moines and Ames area, both within driving

distance to go home each night, and they have, a lot of them have families. And I heard directly from women, "I'm not gonna go to that. I want to be, I want to get home [to] my family." . . . So scheduling was definitely a challenge.[25]

Representative Janet Petersen (D) is one of those legislators:

I think the women get along pretty well actually. There's always room for more opportunity to get to know people outside the legislature, and I'm, once again, probably not the best person in the world to ask because I don't hit a lot of the reception circuits after work because I go home to my family, since I live in Des Moines and I have three young kids. I go home and cook dinner. So I'm not one that does a lot of the social circuit after we leave the chamber. When we're at the state house, I feel like I get along well with the majority of the women up here, even if we completely disagree on issues.[26]

Senator Dandekar also attributed the problem to time issues:

I think it was a great idea, and I really think it's a time commitment. Even though we are legislators, we are moms, we are grandmothers, and we are wives, we have so many other hats to work with. . . . But in Iowa it's a part-time legislature, so people have, on top of all the family commitments you have, you also have your work commitments. And the majority of the women work outside the home, so it was, to me, when I look at it, I really think it had a lot to do with, it was a great idea, but the reason it didn't go anywhere [was] because of the time commitment.[27]

Representative Upmeyer was a legislator who had conflicting feelings about a caucus. On one hand, she thought it was worthwhile, but time was an issue:

I think it was primarily a function of everybody was really busy and it was just really hard to find a time when we could get

together and do that, so I don't think it was so much an unwillingness to do that, but more just a function of time.[28]

Time was even an issue for women who felt a women's caucus was
worthwhile. Representative Thede said, "I do think it's necessary. I
think the problem is always finding the time to get something like
that together, but, no, it's definitely necessary. I think the more
women we have involved in politics, the better it is. There's so many
women's issues, and so I think women are best represented by women.
And so it would absolutely be beneficial if that could be done in
Iowa."[29]

Representative Berry indicated that time had to be prioritized
for policy: "I don't recall it getting off the ground much, for whatever reason. I think it was, more or less, it was just a busy, a hectic
time in the legislature at the time. So everyone was just pretty much
busy with policy and issues and things like that."[30] This legislator is
making a delineation between the caucus and policy and issues. If a
caucus is not doing policy, Democratic women have a hard time justifying participating. This view dovetails with Republican representative Upmeyer who made a distinction between budgeting and public
policy. It seems as though there is a disconnect between organizing as
women and official legislative business.

Scott acknowledged that women legislators, again because of their
role in the family, face different challenges than male legislators.
While this should bind women together, in her depiction, it is just
a condition that prevents women from having time to support one
another. Senator Dandekar's previous statement demonstrated this. It
is difficult to judge from this evidence if time, as a consequence of the
level of legislative professionalism, was really an issue for this wom-
en's caucus attempt. There is the evidence supporting the challenge
women face balancing legislating with their familial commitments
once again highlighting the gendered nature of the legislature and its
influence on women's ability to organize. There is further evidence,
however, that women in Iowa were not sure that a women's caucus
was a worthwhile expenditure of their time, even while at the Capitol.
They do not perceive that organizing as women would increase their

ability to fulfill their legislative duties. This perception hurt participation in the fledgling caucus.

Time was not the only professionalism issue mentioned. Administrator Rachel Scott of the Commission on the Status of Women, charged by Lieutenant Governor Judge with offering support to the women's caucus, connected the level of professionalism of the Iowa legislature with restricting the number of women who could even participate in the legislature:

> I think the institutional factors impact—they're a part of why there are so few women in the legislature to begin with. There are not many women, especially under fifty-five, who can up and leave their household and come to Des Moines and be there during the week and then have their time not their own. . . . The salary is low for a legislator. I mean, you have benefits, but I think it's something like in the ballpark of $25,000 a year, so most women can't afford a job like that.[31]

Iowa has the fewest permanent staffers of all four of my case studies with 191 positions. Although legislative staff may have been few, Administrator Scott made herself available to the legislators through her role at the Commission on the Status of Women. Although she could have offered the same support that was available in the New Jersey and Colorado cases, women legislators in Iowa did not use this resource.

FRAMING THE TASK AT HAND

While observers of the legislature may see gendered difference in the experience of women in Iowa, legislators themselves do not acknowledge this. They certainly do not see collective action as a valuable tool in mitigating the challenges they face due to social and professional role conflict. Due to this lack of gender consciousness and no perceived dissatisfaction with political parties to unite them, Lieutenant Governor Judge was unable to convince legislators to pursue even a social women's caucus. Without a perceived problem for which a caucus is a solution, even an experienced politician with staff support may be unable to organize women within legislatures.

Gender Consciousness

I expected recognition among women legislators of common interests to be associated with a successful attempt to create a women's caucus because I hypothesized that it would be a useful argument for why a women's caucus would be necessary. Representative Berry definitely acknowledged women's difference and connected that frame to the justification for a women's caucus. She said, "Obviously women bring a whole new, different perspective, and, I mean, that would be common ground for both Democratic and Republican women. We could probably get a lot done as a caucus, as it relates to children's issues, family issues, and even women's issues. I think it would be much easier to work as a unified force."[32] Representative Thede indicated that women had more experience with certain issues, such as elder care, because of gender expectations: "We are caregivers from the time, I think, basically, we are born until the time that we die. We take care of our families and our friends and people that we know."[33] For her part, Scott was reluctant to say gender consciousness was very strong in the Iowa legislature—at least not enough to support a caucus. She told this story:

> I think that there was potential to feel commonality, but I don't believe that they had enough interaction to know if there was. . . . There was a woman who was in the Iowa House, and then she retired, and then she's now back in the Senate, and she was a Republican. And a younger Democrat told me that, when she was elected, that this woman came up to her and said something like—she's kind of talking, gesturing to this male environment around—and said something to the effect of "If you're having any trouble, let me know. I castrate hogs at home." There's a little bit of that camaraderie on one level, but I don't think it goes very deep, and I think it's gotten far worse.[34]

So while legislators in Iowa may feel as though women are different and have important perspectives on political policy, acting collectively is a challenge both practically and politically. As we have seen, women's familial obligations limit the free time they would have to socialize, get to know one another and caucus, while at the same time they disagree on matters of public policy and the best way to represent women despite their shared challenges.

Party Dissatisfaction

In Iowa, women legislators did not express dissatisfaction with their party or party leadership. They did not feel bias or report any discrimination as far as party decision making was concerned. Administrator Scott, however, indicated that she had heard frustration from women about a lack of attention to their agenda items:

> I have heard some frustration in terms of bills that had bipartisan support that were for women's issues that women from both parties were working together on that just didn't get moved onto the calendar. And, nobody really knows why. Just some disappointment in what the priorities are versus are not.[35]

In addition to this agenda control, Administrator Scott did mention that the culture of socializing was something that women did not feel comfortable with in Iowa. She said, "The social life of legislators, there's not a lot of it that is not revolved around alcohol, and a lot of these women don't want to put themselves in that situation."[36] Whether these fears are related to being physically vulnerable or risking social stigma related to women and alcohol is unclear, but it is a calculus men do not have to make.

Former lieutenant governor Judge also mentioned that men did a lot of socializing on the basketball court. She explained that women's isolation from this type of activity instigated the caucus formation of the 1990s:

> They play basketball. There's been a running basketball game every—I've been up here twenty years, and I know they were playing basketball when I came, and they're still playing basketball on Tuesday nights. Those kinds of things are never available

to women, and—at the time that we formed a women's caucus in the nineties—the president of the Senate, Mary Kramer, who's a Republican, and I and a few of the other people in the Senate decided that we would have a good time doing this and get to know each other a little bit out of the confines of the Senate.[37]

Women legislators did not mention any personal dissatisfaction with their party organizations in individual interviews; however, there appears to be a discomfort with the lobbying environment and social events as described by outsiders. Party dissatisfaction was not a frame specifically employed by caucus entrepreneurs despite a clear need for a safe space for women to socialize. However, due to women's lack of acknowledgment of these issues, it is unclear if it would have resonated.

So while there are few women in leadership in Iowa, only one respondent commented on the phenomena and despite indicating that it was a structural issue—women's socialization limiting their opportunities—this was not a frame that was used by organizers or one that resonated with potential participants. Representative Upmeyer commented that it was not party leadership that explained the few women in leadership positions but rather women's socialization and subsequent behavior:

Women that step forward, if you're willing to step forward and you're willing to do the work, I think you get equal recognition. I would argue I've had lots of opportunities—my chair of the House Human Services Committee, I've been an assistant leader, I'm now Majority Leader—and it's because I stepped forward and said, "I'm willing to do this. I'm willing to work hard." And my colleagues observed that, and I think they gave me the same consideration they would a man. If women don't get as many opportunities, I think it's often because they've been sort of encultured to wait to be asked or to be invited. . . . If you wait to be asked or invited in many, many areas, you'll never get the opportunity.[38]

This individual explanation for the lack of women in leadership indicates the frame within which women in Iowa perceived their position. Rather than blame institutions, like political parties, or seek collective redress, Upmeyer places responsibility on individual women eliminating any potential role for a women's organization. When matched with opposition from party leaders on both sides, a caucus in Iowa was unlikely to be revived.

Caucus Type

In Iowa, the reception event at the Governor's mansion was an opportunity for legislators to come together and discuss their interest in creating a group and decide on the purpose of the caucus. Senator Dandekar remembers Judge wanting the caucus to be focused on women's policy, but Administrator Scott put it to the group that some women preferred a social caucus for building relationships, while other legislators had indicated an interest in addressing policy. There was no decision made that night, and no subsequent discussion led to the abandonment of the attempt.

Despite the failure, there was some support for the need for a caucus. Representative Berry said, "I think we could probably get a lot more done as women, and if we had our own agenda and if we had a set of priorities, I think that it would be beneficial to women, the women of Iowa, if we did form a women's caucus."[39] Representative Thede agreed: "There's lots of issues surrounding women, and I think this would be a good way to get those done is to have more women involved."[40]

While Representatives Berry and Thede recognized the potential influence a women's caucus could have on issues, particularly those pertaining to women, Representative Petersen acknowledged the challenge partisanship would present for such a caucus:

There's a pretty strong political divide on issues that I, as a woman, am interested in working on, so trying to find issues that women on both sides of the aisle want to rally behind has not been real easy. . . . I don't know if I'd necessarily call it partisanship, but yeah, completely philosophically different opinions on women's issues, anything from child care to reproductive health.[41]

She continued:

> I don't think a women's caucus would necessarily benefit us here in the state. I mean [for] the issues that I want to work [on] on behalf of women, I try to build consensus among the people I need to get the votes I need. And having other women who aren't necessarily going to be with you on what you want to do to advance women's issues isn't necessarily helpful.[42]

While she wanted consensus and support from other women, she did not have faith that collective organizing would necessarily lead to that end. Republican representative Upmeyer agreed:

> The other thing I would note is that for the most part, I don't know that most of the women currently serving—and I certainly can't speak for everyone—but of the women that I know relatively well ultimately don't feel a particular need for a solely women's group in that on both sides of the aisle, no matter who is in the majority, women frequently are committee chairs, women frequently are doing heavy lifting for hard bills. I'm not sure that they don't, that they feel like they need a special caucus to make their issues stand out.[43]

In addition to party problems, Republican representative Upmeyer indicated that women's issues were not the sole domain of women and that she would understand male opposition to a women's caucus: "I was thinking about the question on push back; that might be the only push back is sometimes perhaps the arrogance to assume that the issues belong to women because I think men care very much about many of those issues."[44] Despite men legislators excluding women on the golf course and basketball court, women cannot carve out a legislative space for themselves, according to Upmeyer, who characterizes that exclusion as arrogant. This perception is further evidence of the narrow political path women legislators must traverse.

In this state legislature, organizers of the women's caucus left open the decision of what type the legislators would pursue. Having a policy caucus was one option on the table, but ultimately there were not enough legislators interested in pursuing an organization for this or any other purpose to make this women's caucus attempt successful.

Relationship building was a motivator for the women's caucus attempt in Iowa in 2007. Lieutenant Governor Judge described the conversation with Senator Dandekar, in which she was asked to sponsor a women's caucus: "She thought that it would be something that would be beneficial to them at that time, because they didn't seem to know each other as well as they should, and everything was so very partisan and divided. And she asked if I could help her a little bit."[45] They were presented with the option to create a caucus strictly to socialize and develop relationships. In other states, women legislators, particularly Democrats, have been frustrated by the lack of substantive legislative accomplishments by social caucuses. One of the organizers, Scott, expressed this feeling. Despite telling the story of how social interaction can ameliorate partisanship and benefit the whole legislature, ultimately she sees little value:

> One of the commissioners on the Commission on the Status of Women was a former House Republican. And she talked about when the women's caucus would do a retreat, and she found out that . . . she's going to be rooming with Minnette Doderer, who was this complete powerhouse. . . . [S]he was the first powerful woman in the legislature in Iowa, who worked on things like comparable worth and domestic violence, and, I mean, people shook in their boots around this woman. And so when this Republican House member found out that she was rooming with her, she was terrified. But she said she found out that they had a lot of common ground and all that kind of thing, and . . . I would be so shocked if anything like that could happen again. I hope that it can, because I think people, even men from both parties who were around when the women's

caucus [members] were around, had really a lot of respect for what they were able to accomplish. I don't think that there's no value in a social caucus, but I think it's a pretty small value.[46]

Representative Petersen as quoted earlier does not spend after hours at the legislature and indicated that a social caucus would be a good idea despite her own decision to spend her extra time at home. She said, "There's always room for more opportunity to get to know people outside the legislature."[47] Judge pointed out that there are more social opportunities for male legislators:

I think there is very little social opportunity for women in the after-hours of the legislature . . . , particularly for the women who do not live in Des Moines, beyond the perfunctory cock-tail parties. . . . But beyond that, there isn't a lot of chance to interact with each other. The guys have always had more. They've played cards for years. They play basketball. . . . Those kinds of things are never available to women.[48]

As in Colorado, Judge cited stricter lobbying rules as contributing to the lack of opportunity: "We have some pretty strict campaign finance and gift laws in Iowa, which is fine, except that there just isn't a lot of opportunity to socialize with each other."[49] As in Colorado, the women legislators in Iowa had a political opportunity through restrictive lobbying rules to justify a social women's caucus. This seemingly gender-neutral institutional feature has potentially gendered effects by creating a space for women legislators to make a claim—we need this organization to ameliorate what is lost by this ethics change. However, the pressure from party leaders in Iowa that was not present in Colorado caused women with the same opportunity to have two different results.

Like the other frames, a social networking opportunity was not successful in motivating participants. Despite few opportunities for women legislators to get to know each other, it appears they have other priorities both personally and politically. Although organizers identified relationship building opportunities as sorely needed within the legislature, this frame did not motivate participants.

LESSONS LEARNED FROM IOWA

In Iowa, women were unable to reinvigorate a once successful women's caucus. Legislators did not see a need for a women's caucus in order to accomplish their legislative or personal goals. They admitted that there was a lack of opportunity to get to know one another and that they had unique experiences to share as women, but collective action was not an outgrowth of this. As in Colorado, lobbying legislation in Iowa was blamed for damaged relationships among legislators, but that was not enough to garner participation. As in Pennsylvania, there is evidence here, although somewhat unsubstantiated, that party leaders on both sides of the aisle opposed the bipartisan effort. Regardless, senior women legislators in the Democratic and Republican parties were reluctant, even independent of possible pressure. In contradiction to Beckwith's (2007) hypothesis that new women would be averse to a caucus, the new women legislators of both parties in Iowa were the majority of the ones present at the only event the organizers were able to host. This difference in participation among women indicates that the institution is shaping women's caucusing motivations. More senior women are jaded by the legislature and its norms.

Iowa is a state in which a women's caucus had previously existed but had died out. New Jersey and Colorado were states in which much less formal caucuses preceded the attempts to create a women's caucus examined within this project. I have categorized those cases as successes, whereas this Iowa women's caucus attempt in 2007 was a failure. Judge's disappointment about the outcome is clear. Recognizing the limitations of her position as an outsider, she laments the difference a women's caucus could have made. When asked about the potential of a future attempt, she said:

> I'm not hopeful. I wish I could tell you something different. I don't think under the present leadership, Republican Leadership in the House and actually the Senate has a new Republican Leader, so I really don't know how that's working out yet. But I know that they're not being encouraged to do that, and until that dynamic changes, I don't think they will. . . . When you can put the partisan part of it down for a little bit and talk to each

other as mothers and grandmothers and working women and so forth, the common threads that we have, I think there's a real benefit in that, and I'm sorry that they didn't feel like they could do that or that they could establish enough trust to do that. I don't understand why—like I said, I was really on, just kind of on the edge, on the outside of that, so I don't really have a very good sense of why that kind of decision was made.[50]

Despite Judge's lack of "a very good sense," her comment highlights partisanship as a divider of women and women's lived experience as a unifying force. In reality, women's lived experience does both. Because of the additional homework women legislators do, they have less time than their male counterparts to do the informal legislating that comes through social interaction. In Iowa, women lacked a shared understanding that gender bias is present and therefore they had no need for a collective solution. While formal support from the executive branch was present in Iowa, informal pressure not to organize was more powerful. Despite the history of a women's caucus, organizers were not able to revive within the current climate that was closed to caucuses of any kind.

In the final chapter, I briefly discuss the factors that did not play as important a role as expected. I reaffirm the importance of examining women's organizing within state institutions and suggest the impact my findings have on the field of political science broadly and the implications for women and politics specifically. Finally, I suggest future steps for further study of women's caucuses in state legislatures.

8

EXPLAINING
WOMEN'S CAUCUSES

> God made me a woman and thank God that he made
> your mother a woman because you men wouldn't be
> here. Lawmakers, as we are, have an opportunity to
> shape the attitudes of the public—and those attitudes
> can be positive toward women, they can be nega-
> tive toward women, or they can be both. That falls
> within the gamut of all our possibilities.
>
> —REPRESENTATIVE SENFRONIA THOMPSON,
> *Texas Impact*

Despite the challenges to their organizing, both among women legislators themselves and from their colleagues, women have still attempted to make a space for themselves in state legislatures. Although women created the first women's caucus in Connecticut in 1927, these organizations continued to emerge, even in unlikely places. In July 2011, Texas legislators reported that they were in the process of forming a caucus. A volatile incident mobilized organizers in Texas in May 2011, when the Texas Civil Justice League circulated a flyer that featured an "infant nursing at a woman's bare breast." The flyer was a political comment on the nanny state, but women legislators were outraged (Ramshaw and Galbraith 2011). Like the women in Maryland in 1972, these Texas legislators mobilized around affronts to their status as women within the institution (see Chapter 1).

Representative Senfronia Thompson (D) testified on the Texas House floor in protest, flanked by women legislators from both sides of the aisle. She spoke, as a woman, for women, invoking her gender identity and accepting her responsibility as a lawmaker to "shape the attitudes of the public" (Thompson 2011). Representatives Thompson,

Beverly Woolley (R), and Carol Alvarado (D) immediately sent a letter to all women legislators, requesting their participation in a caucus that would "create the framework for current and future women legislators to get their messages heard, to seek guidance from experienced leaders, and to unite on issues important to us" (Tuma 2011). In its initial stage, this caucus was similar to those formed in the 1970s, in that it was a reaction to a triggering incident of perceived bias and focused on policy issues at least in part of its purpose. Unfortunately, by the time the Texas House came back into session in 2013, Representative Woolley had retired and no other Republican women legislators stepped up to take her place. As a result, the women in Texas have gathered annually to have their photo taken on the Capitol steps, but they have not established a caucus.[1]

In the same year, Democrat Representative Jessica Farrar created the Texas House Women's Health Caucus (TWHC). With one Republican member, this bipartisan caucus corrected inaccurate medical information that was being circulated and produced by state government.[2] While the mission of the TWHC was to address a range of women's health issues, in practice the organization has primarily played defense for reproductive rights. Unlike the general women's caucus proposed by Thompson, Woolley, and Alvarado, which would ideally include all women legislators, the TWHC includes predominantly Democratic men and women. Representative Sarah Davis, who represents the Houston medical community and serves as secretary of the TWHC, is the only Republican member. In these divergent outcomes within one state, we observe that the mobilizing frame and Republican participation are vital to caucus success.

Looking ahead, I predict that, in the short term, any women legislators' attempts at bipartisan caucus creation on the state level are more likely to occur in states with lower levels of party polarization. Two examples are Delaware or Mississippi, which did not have women's caucuses as of this writing and have political parties with less distance between their ideological means (Shor and McCarty 2015). I reported in Chapter 3 that Delaware and Mississippi women legislators had concerns about male opposition to a women's caucus. How these women ultimately choose to deal with any opposition may, in part, determine whether or not an attempt succeeds or fails. I expect this to be the case even when the purpose of the organization is only social in nature, and I expect policy caucus launches to be fewer and less likely to succeed. While Texas was able to establish the TWHC in 2013, it is not a broad-based coalition, and if Representative Davis were ever to lose her seat it is unlikely that any other Republican legislators would replace her in the caucus.

The brief vignette of the state of play in Texas illustrates both the opportunities and challenges that face women legislators as they contemplate both their role within legislatures and the strategies they pursue to represent their constituents. Women are marginalized in many states through a range of practices, including unique electoral challenges, leadership selection, and in daily interactions between legislators, staff, and advocates. To address this marginalization or to increase their own influence, some women legislators have turned to collective action and have attempted to create women's organizations within the legislature. This action is more likely if the women share a sense of gender consciousness and view caucusing as a legitimate strategy. Women develop gender consciousness (or not) and determine actions' legitimacy in a specific political climate. Caucus attempts are more likely to be successful when undertaken by savvy caucus entrepreneurs who accurately perceive and navigate the informal rules of their legislature. Partisanship is a primary concern for these entrepreneurs, who must develop trust across the aisle with other women without drawing ire from party leaders or from resistant women. It is especially difficult for women when colleagues closely monitor their behavior, a phenomenon that I have documented in some legislatures (see Chapters 3, 6, and 7).

NONFACTORS

New Jersey

There were several institutional-level factors that I hypothesized would affect the establishment of a women's caucus that did not play a major role in the New Jersey case. Term limits did not impact this caucus launch, but the presence of experienced women legislators was important. I found no evidence of outside pressure for the women to organize in this case, although outside support did matter as an available resource. Similarly, although the existence of other caucuses, including a black caucus, in New Jersey normalized the practice, the women legislators themselves did not see other caucuses as influential factors in their case. Nor did they acknowledge the great racial diversity among women legislators as a positive or negative influence on their ability to organize.

Of all four case studies, New Jersey in 2009 had the largest proportion of women legislators of color. Fourteen women of color made up 39 percent of all women legislators in New Jersey (CAWP 2009c). One of these women, Representative Spencer, serves as one of the four caucus board members. Her inclusion was important to Senator Weinberg, who wanted the board to reflect the diversity of women legislators in the state.[3] No mention was made that diversity influenced the women's ability to caucus positively or negatively in any of my interviews. Women legislators of color were no more likely to participate in the caucus than white legislators, nor were they more enthusiastic in their support of the launch than their white counterparts. Two women legislators of color were a part of my interview sample. They were asked if their participation in the women's caucus would cause any conflict with their participation in any other identity caucuses, and they reported that they did not anticipate any such conflict. They, in fact, reported that they anticipated a consensus between the two groups on many issues.

Colorado

The frame of gender consciousness, while present among women legislators in Colorado, was not cognitively connected to caucus creation. Neither was dissatisfaction with political parties, including any arguments for an increase in women in leadership positions, despite the fact that some women felt left out of the decision-making process and others perceived women's leadership roles as largely symbolic. In this case, the influence of freshmen women legislators appears to be concentrated in the caucus entrepreneur as opposed to the energy that a new freshman class brought to the New Jersey case. Term limits were marginally relevant. Colorado is a term-limited state, and these laws were cited as hurting women's ability to get to know each other, but were also cited as positively affecting women legislators' ability to exert influence in the legislature because of reduced male power.

Party control and party competition (resulting in increased party discipline) were not problematic for the founding of this caucus. Similarly, the presence of other caucuses did not positively affect this launch. Nor was diversity among women legislators a positive influence, as their numbers were small in 2009. The three women of color in the Colorado legislature in 2009 made up only 8 percent of all women legislators, the smallest percentage in any of my four cases (CAWP 2009b). One Hispanic woman legislator I interviewed mentioned an interest in participating in a caucus based on race identity but thought that small numbers were an obstacle to creating such a group. For her part, she was very enthusiastic about the possibility of influencing public policy on women's issues but was not hopeful that such influence would be possible through the women's caucus created in Colorado because of its social-networking focus and aversion to taking positions on public policy.

Pennsylvania

For Pennsylvania in 2009 and 2010, there is no evidence that term limits negatively affected the caucus attempt. Further, there is no evidence of any external organization that supported or initiated a women's caucus. In this case, however, generational differences hurt the prospects of the caucus, and a long-serving Republican woman legislator was cited as opposing any kind of gender organizing for many years. Her continued presence and influence in the legislature discouraged any attempts to create a women's caucus. Similarly, Representative Brown's naiveté offended senior Democratic women, and their lack of participation also hurt the chances of this caucus's successful launch. In this case, term limits may have removed some of the opposition facing this caucus launch by removing some opponents with seniority.

In Pennsylvania, women legislators did not contact external organizations for support, nor did any organizations express to legislators a need for the establishment of a caucus. One legislator indicated that women's organizations often brought legislation to her as a member of the Health and Human Services Committee but they did not express an interest in the establishment of a women's caucus. This lack of external participation is a distinguishing feature of this case. Although the founder, Representative Brown, did not indicate it as a challenge, external participation was present in the two successful attempts to create women's caucuses in other states.

Iowa

In Iowa, term limits were not an integral factor in the caucus attempt because, like Pennsylvania and New Jersey, Iowa is a state without them. As was the case in Pennsylvania, in Iowa more senior legislators were reluctant to participate or see a caucus as a worthwhile endeavor. In this sense, term limits may have termed out women with more cynical views; however, there is no evidence in this case that newly elected women had the inclination to instigate a caucus or were very aware of the previous successful caucus and its legacy. Iowa had little racial diversity, with only 9 percent of women legislators being of color. Representative Berry discussed the difficulty in launching either a women's or black caucus in such an environment.[4]

When considering the racial diversity of caucus entrepreneurs, I find both white women legislators and women legislators of color initiating these women's caucus attempts. In New Jersey, white women were the entrepreneurs, as was the case in Colorado. In Pennsylvania, an African American legislator and a white legislator were cofounders of their failed attempt. While, in Iowa, a white former legislator and lieutenant governor Patty Judge (D) was perceived most widely as the caucus attempt leader, while she credits the idea to an Indian American women legislator. The racial diversity of caucus founders did not feature in the interviews of either white women legislators or women legislators of color. The founders did not specifically mention their racial identity or lived experience as motivating their decision to organize a women's group. However, Representative Brown (D) in Pennsylvania expressed that from her perspective, with a black caucus in the legislature, the absence of a women's caucus was an obvious void that needed to be addressed.

CAUCUSING AS LEGISLATIVE BEHAVIOR

Previous research on women's caucuses has been too narrow to appreciate their diversity across the United States and what that diversity tells us about women legislators, parties, and legislatures. By broadening my analysis to include any and all collective action by women legislators I was able to map the universe of strategies employed by women working together across party lines. By acknowledging all the priorities of these organizations, we are able to recognize the multiple ways in which legislatures and political parties are gendered through the actions women take to counteract its negative effects. My goal in this book was to document women's collective action in legislatures and use caucuses as a lens to analyze gender as it operates within institutions such as political parties and legislatures. By doing so, I have established that women's partisan and gender identity complicate their ability to serve as representatives effectively. Further, I have analyzed the conditions under which collective action as a remedy can be successful.

Whether or not women's caucuses ever address policy issues for women constituents or others, they can serve to bolster women's status in the institution and improve women's experience as legislators. The mentoring and information sharing that occurs when women have relationships with more senior legislators and women across the aisle is a decided advantage to women in states with such organizations. Even without reaching consensus on policies, women can unite to promote the election of more women to leadership positions within the legislature. If the proportions of women legislators are moderate in the majority party, caucuses have proven to be effective in this way (Kanthak and Krause 2012). Some women's caucuses have already accomplished this, for example in New Jersey, where caucus members supported legislation to bring transparency to state political party nominations that facilitated the campaigns of more women for public office. In the absence of more substantive policy focus, these are areas in which women's caucuses could make a real difference in legislatures. Further, women in the minority party in legislatures can benefit from the information sharing provided by women's caucuses. There can be no bipartisan women's caucuses, however, if there are not enough Republican women in office

(Crowder-Myers and Lauderdale 2014). It is vital, therefore, that analyses of the impact of women's caucuses evaluate contributions to women's political mobilization and candidacy beyond the policy process.

By examining how and why women create these organizations, we learn about the informal rules that govern legislatures, such as partisanship. Women continue to feel marginalized from levers of power within legislatures and parties. Women recognize this marginalization when they start out as candidates and as they continue through their time in office. One response to this exclusion is the creation of a women's caucus, which explains why they participate in activities unusual for other caucuses—like campaign training, leadership development, and historical preservation. By documenting these priorities, we are able to make visible the exclusion of women from state politics and the strategies women themselves are enacting to do something about it.[5] By acknowledging these groups and their importance, we are able to see the gendered nature of state legislatures.

Women do not see themselves only as partisans; some see themselves as women, with all the political consequences of that designation. In some environments, some women consider collective action the right strategy to strengthen their hand. What types of skills do entrepreneurs need, what types of frames are successful? This analysis has established the collective action strategies by marginalized legislators within institutions and the conditions under which they are successful. The story of women's caucuses is one about the failure of women to be incorporated into legislatures and parties uniformly across the fifty states. Whether reifying difference through women's caucuses is the right strategy for incorporation is another question. If legislative institutions and their leaders incorporated women and women's concerns, the needs women often cite for caucusing would disappear. For some women, caucusing is a legitimate strategy, and this book explains when and how they can be successful.

WHAT DIFFERENCE DOES A WOMEN'S CAUCUS MAKE?

I have referenced the benefits of caucus participation to individual legislators throughout this book. Women legislators gain leadership and skill-building opportunities as well as information sharing just as any member of any caucus would, whether it be a partisan, an issue, or an identity caucus. These assets position women to increase their legislative power and influence policy outcomes. But in addition to these general positives, women legislators benefit uniquely from gender-focused organizations in legislatures because of the safe haven they create within environments that still disadvantage women (Weldon 2004).[6] But questions remain about the difference women's caucuses may make. Further analysis should address whether and how women's caucuses affect cosponsorship behaviors, strategies for accomplishing feminist policy, and the incorporation (or not) of women into traditional legislative leadership positions.

Beyond the impact for women legislators, women's caucuses may benefit the community at large. Women's caucuses' activities include scholarships for girls and women, campaign training to build a pipeline for the next generation of women legislators, and historical preservation of women's contributions to state politics. Beyond the practical effects of these activities, caucuses accentuate the visibility of women's presence in a legislature. The symbolic effects of such organizations are also worthy of further analysis. Women's caucuses may increase the efficacy of women voters and, more likely, potential women candidates (Clark 2010; Wolbrecht and Campbell 2017). In assessing the gendered power dynamics at play in existing institutions, women may also need to see the potential for institutional evolution and change that caucuses may signify (Dittmar 2015).

While caucuses may announce and legitimize women's presence in the legislature, their necessity reminds us how marked women are in legislatures. Rather than being seamlessly incorporated, women in some states maintain their token status. We know from other studies that leaders constrain women's committee assignments (Bolzendahl 2014; Frisch and Kelly 2008). Whether or not women should call attention to this through the creation of specifically women's groups is a fair one. It is a question answered by women legislators themselves. I do not argue that the goal should be fifty women's caucuses—in fact, perhaps it would be a sign of success if there were none. But for now, in some cases, it has proven a useful strategy for some women. As long as that is necessary, we should study their emergence, their impact, and their demise and resurgence—not just to understand women elites' political behavior but to better understand the unwritten gender rules that govern our political parties and state legislatures.

HOW WOMEN'S CAUCUSES INFORM THE STUDY OF POLITICS

This project has a lot to contribute to the body of work on legislative behavior, as well as the experience of women in political office. My study examines the relationship between gender and the political behavior of elites, as well as the institutional factors that create and reinforce gender dynamics. This analysis specifically engages the tension for women between their gender and party identity in the pursuit of their legislative goals and their lived experience within the legislature.

My findings have moved scholarship on gender and legislative behavior forward by examining more closely women's relationship to each other and their political parties. From my case studies, I have determined that party polarization and party competition constrain women's collective action. When Republican and Democratic women legislators represent women, they do so very differently (Osborn 2012). Similarly, I find that when Republican and Democratic women legislators caucus, they have very different purposes in mind. Throughout the New Jersey and Colorado case studies, it was evident that Democratic women legislators wanted to organize in order to impact public policy. Their Republican counterparts were much more interested in the social support they could obtain through participation, knowing that they did not want to compromise their policy positions in a policy caucus. In the New Jersey case, legislators came to a crossroads, having to decide whether or not a caucus could survive when Republican women voted differently than expected on the Family Planning Grant bill. In Colorado, some Democratic women are frustrated by the lack of substance pursued by the caucus. Their hope of future policy impact keeps them interested, but for how long?

In Pennsylvania, a senior Republican woman legislator enforced opposition to the idea of a women's caucus for years and thus prevented any participation by women within her party even if there were interest. In Iowa, the other failed case, it is possible that party leaders discouraged newly elected women from participating in a bipartisan caucus despite their initial interest. This outcome indicates that women may not be opposed to gender organizing when they are new to the legislature, but may become so under pressure from party leaders or more senior colleagues.

This project also uncovers the double-edged sword of legislative service among women. On the one hand, political experience is vital for relationship-building and proper deference to key players, but this experience comes with a price. When long-serving women are jaded by partisanship, their reluctance to identify with women across the aisle can sink a caucus attempt, as was the case in Pennsylvania. As Kanter (1977) suggested thirty-five years ago and Kristin Kanthak and George A. Krause (2012) have pointed out, women's proportions in legislatures influence their decision to either reinforce the male majority and its agenda or distinguish themselves and their own interests. In this study, the attitude of senior women legislators is important for whether or not a women's caucus attempt is successful. In New Jersey, long-standing women legislators seized the opportunity of their increased numbers after a surge election of new women. In Colorado, a newcomer was deferential to senior legislators and gained their support early in the formation process. In the failed cases, either entrepreneurs did not consult senior women or they were not interested, to the detriment of the caucus attempt.

The importance of newly elected women also emerged from my findings, which runs counter to theories that newly elected women conform to legislative norms and are therefore less likely to participate in caucuses (Beckwith 2007). Instead, I find that legislative norms constrain newly elected women less than their senior colleagues and as a consequence they are more open to bipartisanship. While in New Jersey two senior women legislators initiated the caucus, ultimately Weinberg's suspicions of Allen's deference to party sank the group. In Pennsylvania and Colorado, newer women legislators led the charge. This mobilization is perhaps because of naiveté or enthusiasm to change the status quo, but this hypothesis is certainly deserving of more testing.

My research also updates scholarship conducted in an era of reduced partisan polarization. In the 1990s, women legislators of both parties were more likely to work on women's issues than their male colleagues (CAWP 2001; Swers 2002). My research complicates this blanket finding. *How* women legislators choose to do this work is different for Democratic and Republican women. I find that because Republican women have different policy positions, they are more likely to support social-networking caucuses than those that address women's issues in public policy. My findings echo Osborn's (2012) work, which argues that party affiliations mitigate how Republican and Democratic women represent women. Similarly, Republican women are less likely than Democratic women to see caucusing as a legitimate legislative strategy. This finding corroborates work that suggests institutions can influence the range of possible options women acknowledge when representing women's interests (Katzenstein 1998). In this case, the ideology of the Republican Party as enforced by its members is narrowing the options women legislators see as appropriate legislative behavior. In the case of women's suffrage movements, "Missing an opportunity may be the result of a fully rational and intelligent decision. Movement activists may make decisions without fully knowing all options or discounting certain viable options because of their values" (Banaszak 1996, 222). Republican women legislators may not seize the opportunity to caucus because their political values and the norms of their party prevent it.

My research also reiterates the importance of caucusing for women legislators and their constituents. In addition to providing emotional support for women legislators in sometimes hostile environments, women's caucuses provide information to the public, scholarships to young women, and recruit new women candidates for office. Caucuses allow legislators to signify themselves as experts in certain legislative areas and advocates for certain constituencies, to develop leadership skills, and to build important relationships within the institution (Hammond 1998).

WHAT MORE CAN WE LEARN FROM WOMEN'S CAUCUSES?

I have discovered that many women's caucuses do not set women's representation as a priority for their group. Instead, seven women's caucuses are primarily social in nature, prioritizing relationships among legislators (14 percent of all women's caucuses). This is important because it demonstrates that the effect of these groups on women's representation may be indirect. Relationships are important for the achievement of legislative success and, therefore, these groups may be affecting the legislative process in unexpected ways. Previous research on the effects of women's caucuses has focused on bill sponsorships and passage (Thomas 1991; Reingold and Schneider 2001). My findings suggest that a more nuanced analysis of social caucuses is necessary to appreciate the full impact of these groups on legislative life and policy. For instance, how do the relationships formed by women's caucus participation affect bill cosponsorship, legislative strategy, and partisanship in the legislature more broadly? For legislators, what benefits or costs do women face by participating in such groups? Do they have higher feelings of efficacy than nonparticipants? Do they experience more or less gender bias in the institution? Can these types of organizations improve the status of women within the institution? These are all questions that emerge when the definition of a caucus is expanded beyond those with a policy agenda.

More traditionally, fifteen women's caucuses identify as policy caucuses, but even within this group, I found a variety of approaches. Only five caucuses set agendas, whereas ten choose to take on issues as they emerge. This suggests that a more nuanced approach to analyzing the effects of women's caucuses is necessary to fully appreciate whether or not these groups are successful in representing women. My research has identified where scholars should look for this effect, as policy caucuses identified women and children's health as the primary issues on which they focus their attention. Previous research, which looked for effects on children more broadly—at family law, sexual assault and domestic violence, child abuse, daycare and parental leave, welfare, the environment, and other broad areas sometimes categorized as "women's issues"—may have been looking in the wrong places because of assumptions made about women's caucuses or because women's caucuses may have changed their priorities over time (Thomas 1991; Reingold and Schneider 2001). Either way, my findings offer a roadmap for future impact studies.

A majority of the women in this study, even participants in policy caucuses, also reported that abortion rights were too controversial for caucuses and that they table the issue across the country. Texas is a notable exception. This finding is vital to understanding the representation of women across the country, as it indicates that on this very high-profile issue, women are acting individually or as partisans, not as a bipartisan collective as had been the case on the federal level (Swers 1998). How this decision by women legislators across the country impacts the debate and policy outcome is deserving of further study. By investigating the strategies employed and the outcomes achieved by women's caucuses, we can assess the impact these groups have on these issues. My study has narrowed the range of issues where it is appropriate to observe this impact.

Another question that emerges from my case studies is whether there is an evolution from a social caucus to a policy one and under what conditions that would be likely to occur. Similarly, under what conditions might a policy caucus become social and what would that tell us about the institution of the legislature? Because one outcome of legislative behavior is public policy, it is necessary to connect these organizations to their substantive effects, and appreciate their influence on gender relationships inside the institution.

Finally, my work points to the difficulty in obtaining information about women's organizing in the states. Data gathered over time would allow for more sophisticated analyses of state level variables and their relationship to the existence of women's caucuses. These groups are always appearing and fading away, and the disappearance of a caucus in a state is also worthy of attention. While I pose questions about the conditions under which a caucus emerges, the conditions surrounding the demise of a women's caucus can also tell us about the institution of the legislature and its gendering. More attention to the absence of a women's caucus is warranted as well.

Many questions remain to be answered about caucuses: What is their role in policy adoption? How do they affect the legislature's norms and processes? Why do they die or in some cases reemerge? Further questions about their interactions with constituents and advocates and the role they play in representation endure. Last, a full analysis of the impact of caucuses on women's leadership through campaign trainings, scholarships, and historical preservation is necessary to appreciate the complete effect of these organizations. This book opens the door to multiple possibilities for further study.

EXPLAINING WOMEN'S CAUCUSES IN THE UNITED STATES

Legislators are crafting important policy at the state level, including access to reproductive health, resource allocation for health services of all kinds, legislation regarding child and elder care, and many other issues that disproportionately affect women because of gender-role expectations. Therefore, the behavior of legislators and the norms and rules of legislative institutions are of the utmost importance for women's representation. This study examines the specific conditions under which women legislators choose to act collectively as women within state legislatures.

My findings demonstrate that women's caucuses across the country take different shapes based on the needs of legislators in that state. In some legislatures, women feel the need to draw attention to women's political contributions as a way to assert their status. This assertion is often a way for women to rally around a common cause when they cannot agree on political issues and legislation. By discounting these groups, we would be ignoring the political environments and institutional features (such as party differences) that have shaped these legislative choices and the need for women to assert their presence. This is an important finding because it counters those who would argue equality already exists in today's legislatures. Women in some states may not be able to agree on political outcomes, but they are willing to meet together to share information about issues of the day, indicating that women legislators may be able to counteract the highly partisan environment in some states. Doing so could improve the quality of representation for constituents in those states, as well as the quality of life for legislators within the institution. To ignore caucuses that do not address legislation is to ignore important aspects of the experience of women legislators around the country.

Finally, I find that women in states without caucuses most commonly explain that party differences prevent women from finding enough common ground through their shared gender to create an organization. As Osborn (2012) has argued, "The pursuit of women's policy in the states is an inherently partisan endeavor" (7). It is this political climate in which women throughout state legislatures are deciding how best to represent their constituents and women more specifically. In some cases, they do this as individuals, but in others they join with other women to accomplish both personal and legislative goals. While male opposition exists in pockets around the country, women do not cite this as the primary reason they do not organize. This unwillingness may be because it is true or because women are reluctant to admit the power imbalance. They are more likely to cite a lack of time and resources (specifically staff and financial support for events) as explanations for the lack of a caucus. This lack of time in some instances not only is due to the legislative schedule but also is a consequence of their gender. Many women explained that their roles as wives and mothers outside the legislature limited their ability to organize within it. This obstacle is important as it demonstrates the role gender expectations play in the lives of women legislators, which limits their ability to represent their constituents on equal footing with their male counterparts, who do not face the same expectations.

On February 10, 2017, the women legislators of Nevada met for the first time as an agenda-setting women's caucus (Messerly 2017). During the meeting, there were references to gender bias felt within the institution. In addition to a policy focus, they clearly sought a social support system. The local news coverage of this caucus confirms many of my findings. For example, this first caucus meeting showed evidence of a clash between institutional priorities when leaders had to cut it short due to a scheduled floor session. The caucus entrepreneur in this case was a nonpartisan state senator who cited in an interview that this political identity gave her credibility across both parties. While male Democratic Party leaders spoke at the meeting demonstrating their support, Republican leaders were not available or cited miscommunication for their absence. There is also an anticipated partnership between the caucus and the newly reinstated Women's Commission, indicating that in this state, external organizations are an asset.

Women's organizing for equality inside and outside institutions has faced challenges uniting women across categories including race, sexual orientation, class, and age. Many of the challenges that women state legislators faced in the 1970s and 1980s are the same today, as contemporary examples of sexual harassment and exclusion from power mirror the experiences of the women who organized caucuses during the second wave. The first women's caucuses were created because women legislators believed that their voices were not being heard and that their colleagues did not respect them. They determined that acting collectively would improve their chance at effectiveness. Successfully caucusing still requires bridging the divides of race, party, and generation. Women legislators, like women voters, are not monolithic, and collaboration is not inevitable. Today, caucus entrepreneurs face the challenge of convincing some women that gender matters within legislatures and that collective, bipartisan action is an appropriate response. With increased polarization and fewer moderate women legislators, entrepreneurs need tactful framing and a reputation of integrity and fairness. However, in more polarized environments, legislators may be looking for opportunities to increase their effectiveness outside traditional mechanisms of power. My analysis has demonstrated the political opportunities that, when matched with the right resources and messages, can overcome these divisions. Dedicated and politically astute entrepreneurs are crucial for recognizing these opportunities, acquiring the right resources, and strategically framing why a caucus is necessary and worthwhile. These factors have been essential in social movements throughout history and, as I demonstrate, they are central in organizing within institutions as well.

I began this book by arguing that gender influences women legislators' decisions about how to act within legislatures. Their marked identities as women do not always or only act to hold them back from incorporation into the larger political sphere. In some instances, women's gendered identity serves them positively by attributing to them advantageous political skills or expertise. In other cases, however, women's difference harms their ability to act on behalf of their constituents by limiting their access to power or attributing negative group characteristics to individuals regardless of their veracity. Sometimes other identity markers, such as race, age, or sexual orientation, compound these limitations. These conditions shape women legislators' decisions to organize around their gendered identity. It is their status as women that makes possible even the conception of an alternative organization beyond the traditional political party affiliation. The context in which this idea emerges is shaped by the political opportunities available to women, the resources to which they have access, and the frames that are employed by organizers (and their opposition) and whether or not these frames resonate with potential participants. Whether or not women choose to organize and are successful when they do matters for women inside the institution as well as their constituents.

NOTES

CHAPTER 1

1. Scholars have criticized conceptualizing women's activism into waves (Laughlin et al. 2010; Nicholson 2015). I use the commonly understood concept here to emphasize the CCWI founding during a time of heightened attention to women's activism in popular culture.

2. For example, women were divided by length of tenure in office, beliefs about the appropriate role of gender in politics, and their own goals for what an organization might accomplish (Gertzog 2004).

3. Caucus creation and maintenance are further complicated by racial and generational identities. See N. Brown 2014, wherein the Women Legislators of Maryland split over a bill pertaining to expungement of court records related to domestic violence protection orders.

4. Acker (1992) defined gender as "the patterning of difference and domination distinguishing women and men," which, more recently, scholars have expanded to recognize a spectrum of identities beyond two dichotomous, oppositional possibilities (565).

5. This frame was also used in Texas in 2011 and Nevada in 2017, which, though they fall outside my time frame, I discuss in Chapter 8.

6. Hawkesworth (2003) describes the racing and gendering of Congress as involving "the production of difference, political asymmetries, and social hierarchies that simultaneously create the dominant and the subordinate" (531).

7. My findings corroborate those of Hawkesworth's (2003) study of a raced and gendered Congress.

8. For examples of dress code initiatives seeking to regulate women's physical presentation within legislatures, see Montana in 2014, Missouri in 2015, Kansas in 2016, and New Hampshire in 2017.

CHAPTER 2

1. Acker (1992) defines gendered institutions as those in which "gender is present in the processes, practices, images and ideologies, and distributions of power," with political institutions being masculinized in particular, "historically developed by men, currently dominated by men, and symbolically interpreted from the standpoint of men in leading positions both in the present and historically" (567). See also Duerst-Lahti 2002 and Kenney 1996.

2. Dahlerup (1988) defines a crucial act as "one which will change the position of the minority considerably and lead to further changes," including "the willingness and ability of the minority to improve the situation for themselves and the whole minority group" (296). For her, this includes the creation of new institutions that focus political attention on women.

3. For women with families, Hochschild (1989) defines the household responsibilities that a wife and mother takes care of, aside from working her paid job, as a second shift.

4. Of these three state identity caucuses, there is one Republican member of the New York Black, Puerto Rican, Hispanic and Asian Legislative Caucus, Representative Peter Lopez (R).

5. Katzenstein (1998) defines unobtrusive mobilization as feminists' under-the-radar claim making on institutions as a strategy to maintain influence and legitimacy and sometimes as a preference of the actors themselves.

CHAPTER 3

1. According to the Center for American Women and Politics, in 2009, when I started data collection, 70.5 percent of all women legislators were Democrats. This party distribution is reflected in my subject demographics.

2. The creation of the Colorado caucus is discussed in depth in Chapter 5. https://sites.google.com/site/coloradowomenscaucus/?pli=1.

3. Examples of women's health issues that these groups address are getting insurance companies to provide plans that cover health tests common for women, funding health centers for low-income women and families, and promoting awareness resolutions that pertain to diseases common among women.

4. Again, this is not inherent to this type, but it was a common theme in this handful of states. The discussion of alcohol was gendered in that the underlying concern was men's inappropriate behavior connected with drinking.

5. In 2017, Oregon and Vermont were among the top ten states with respect to the proportion of women in the state legislature, with 33.3 percent and 40 percent, respectively (CAWP 2017b).

6. Christine Watkins, telephone interview by the author, Utah, May 11, 2011.

7. Karen Keiser, interview by the author, National Conference of State Legislatures, Louisville, KY, July 2010. This comment not only brings to the surface

the informal rules about gender—how far women can push before they are seen as "rubbing it in"—but also the ideological assumptions legislators make about women's caucuses. This legislator necessarily assumes a women's caucus and a progressive caucus are interchangeable.

8. My research does not find evidence of such intra-party women's caucuses in 2016.

9. The National Order of Women Legislators is a nonpartisan organization of women serving as current state legislators and former state legislators (http://www.womenlegislators.org/about/nowl.php). Emerge America is a national training program for Democratic women that has branches in several states (http://www.emergeamerica.org/about).

10. Sylvia Larsen, telephone interview by the author, New Hampshire, March 11, 2011.

11. Karen Petersen, telephone interview by the author, April 19, 2011. This remark is similar to those that Gertzog (2004) quotes from women in Congress about why they did not form the CCWI earlier.

12. On the stability of elite arrangements and the presence of allies, see my case studies at the end of this chapter.

13. These hypotheses are based on expected behavior of men and women in organizations with disproportionate sex ratios. These behavioral expectations can be found in Kanter 1977.

14. As previously mentioned, Connecticut had the first women's caucus in 1927 but adequate data on the legislative data analyzed here is not available. Further, since subsequent caucuses did not form, Connecticut in 1927 remains somewhat of an outlier.

15. Further research is necessary to determine why caucuses disband.

16. The data on the formation of black caucuses were provided by Chris Clark.

17. CAWP 2017b reports that 94 percent of women of color serving in state legislatures nationwide are Democrats.

18. As Dodson (2006) states, "Lauding women's actions as surrogate representatives of women could intensify the potential costs Republican women face[,] for it may cast their efforts on behalf of women as particularly contrary to institutional norms" (258).

19. While some level of gender consciousness must be present to launch an attempt, the attempt itself may also generate increased gender consciousness among women legislators.

CHAPTER 4

1. Backlash from party leaders in this case appears to be an issue for caucus maintenance, however, as Democratic women perceive that Republican leaders in the state opposed the policy priorities and positions they wanted the caucus to put forward.

2. Alison McHose, telephone interview by the author, April 19, 2010.

3. Jennifer Beck, interview by the author, March 31, 2010.

4. Amy Handlin, telephone interview by the author, May 11, 2010.

5. This is the only state in my research where women in the senate played a vital role.

6. Between 2007 and 2009, five assemblywomen and two women senators took office by election or appointment, filling seats previously held by men who were under indictment for political corruption or criminal charges (Carroll and Dittmar 2012).

7. Diane Allen, interview by the author, July 15, 2010.

8. Ibid.

9. For more on women's historical participation in political reform movements, particularly in the Progressive Era, see Frankel and Dye 1991 and Schneider and Schneider 1993.

10. Mary Pat Angelini, telephone interview by the author, April 11, 2010.

11. Beck interview.

12. Joan Voss, interview by the author, April 15, 2010.

13. Kathy Crotty, interview by the author, March 11, 2010.

14. Angelini interview.

15. Nellie Pou, interview by the author, July 29, 2010.

16. McHose interview.

17. The advantage of political experience is illustrated in the failed Pennsylvania attempt, where a newcomer who lacked institutional knowledge failed to adhere to informal rules. However, retirement removed a longtime caucus opponent from office, allowing an attempt to initiate.

18. Crotty interview (2010).

19. Ibid.

20. Beck interview.

21. Loretta Weinberg, interview by the author, August 20, 2010.

22. Crotty interview (2010).

23. Ibid.

24. Handlin interview.

25. Angelini interview.

26. Here, Crotty is referring to a perceived shortage of gynecologists and obstetricians in New Jersey, which in part prompted the hearings organized by the caucus in June 2010.

27. Beck interview.

28. McHose interview.

29. Voss interview.

30. Allen interview (2010).

31. Ibid.

32. Handlin interview.

33. Voss interview.

34. Handlin interview.
35. McHose interview.
36. Ibid.
37. Handlin interview.
38. Pou interview.
39. Weinberg interview.
40. Diane Allen, telephone interview by the author, December 5, 2011.
41. Ibid.
42. Ibid; L. Grace Spencer, telephone interview by the author, December 12, 2011.
43. Spencer interview.
44. Pou interview.
45. Allen interview (2011).
46. Ibid.
47. Handlin interview.
48. Weinberg interview.
49. Kathy Crotty, interview by the author, November 30, 2011.

CHAPTER 5

1. The Women's Foundation of Colorado is an organization that was founded in 1987 with the mission of building resources and spearheading change so that every woman and girl in Colorado can achieve her full potential (Women's Foundation of Colorado 2016).

2. Amendment 41 regulated public officials' conduct in an effort to bolster public confidence in government and restricted expenditures for events such as dinners and receptions.

3. This has changed somewhat, according to my own interviews in 2010, with several women in the legislature self-identifying as Tea Party members or perceived as such by their colleagues.

4. These chairmanships are not as powerful as in other state legislatures because of institutional rules that limit chair control of the legislative process. Certain rules work against partisanship. For instance, every bill that is introduced has to be heard in committee. Similarly, the committee must hear anyone who appears for the purpose of testifying. This opens up the process and limits control by partisan committee chairs.

5. Su Ryden, interview by the author, March 23, 2011.
6. Ibid.
7. Karen Middleton, telephone interview by the author, March 11, 2011.
8. Carole Murray, interview by the author, March 22, 2011.
9. Ryden interview.
10. Paul Weissmann, interview by the author, March 23, 2011.
11. Laura Hoeppner, interview by the author, March 25, 2011.

12. Beth McCann, interview by the author, March 25, 2011.

13. Weissmann interview.

14. Ibid.

15. Ellen Roberts, interview by the author, March 22, 2011.

16. Ryden interview.

17. Middleton interview.

18. Ibid.

19. Peter Groff, telephone interview by the author, April 5, 2011.

20. Ryden interview.

21. McCann interview.

22. Hoeppner interview (March 2011).

23. Middleton interview.

24. McCann interview.

25. Ryden interview.

26. Hoeppner interview (March 2011).

27. Jeanne Labuda, interview by the author, March 23, 2011.

28. Ryden interview.

29. Hoeppner interview (March 2011).

30. Ryden interview.

31. Murray interview.

32. Angela Giron, interview by the author, March 23, 2011.

33. Ibid.

34. McCann interview.

35. Roberts interview.

36. Weissmann interview.

37. Roberts interview.

38. Millie Hamner, interview by the author, March 22, 2011.

39. Ibid.

40. Ibid.

41. Ryden interview.

42. Groff interview.

43. Hamner interview.

44. Giron interview.

45. I contacted Republican legislative leaders, but schedule conflicts prohibited interviews.

46. McCann interview.

47. Ibid.

48. Weissmann interview.

49. Ibid.

50. Ibid.

51. Labuda interview.

52. Murray interview.

53. Ibid.

54. Deb Gardner, interview by the author, March 21, 2011.

55. Hamner interview.

56. Giron interview.

57. Gardner interview.

58. Ryden interview.

59. Ibid.

60. Hoeppner interview (March 2011).

61. McCann interview.

62. Groff interview.

63. Roberts interview.

64. Laura Hoeppner, telephone interview by author, November 22, 2011.

CHAPTER 6

1. Vanessa Lowery Brown, interview by the author, December 7, 2011.

2. Sheryl Delozier, telephone interview by the author, July 13, 2011.

3. RoseMarie Swanger, telephone interview by the author, November 29, 2011.

4. Mauree Gingrich telephone interview by the author, July 5, 2011.

5. Jay Costa, interview by the author, December 7, 2011.

6. Ibid.

7. Brown interview.

8. Gingrich interview.

9. Ibid.

10. Jane Earll, telephone interview by the author, April 14, 2011.

11. Costa interview.

12. Gingrich interview.

13. Brown, Costa, and Gingrich interviews.

14. Brown interview.

15. Earll interview.

16. Louise Williams Bishop, telephone interview by the author, December 6, 2011.

17. Kate Harper, telephone interview by the author, July 18, 2011.

18. Babette Josephs, telephone interview by the author, April 11, 2011.

19. Ibid.

20. Although Representatives Brown and Boback did make attempts to create a women's caucus in two different legislative sessions, I analyze this case as one attempt, since the characteristics of the observed variables remain the same over the full two-year timetable.

21. Delozier interview.

22. In Pennsylvania, caucuses can use meeting space, but the legislature does not contribute financially to staff or events for the caucuses.

23. Costa interview.

24. Bishop interview.

25. Brown interview.
26. Delozier interview.
27. Ibid.
28. Costa interview.
29. Gingrich interview.
30. Earll interview.
31. Harper interview.
32. Christine Tartaglione, telephone interview by the author, July 13, 2011.
33. Delozier interview.
34. Earll interview.
35. Tartaglione interview.
36. Gingrich interview.
37. Ibid.
38. Delozier interview.
39. Ibid.
40. Bishop interview.
41. Swanger interview.
42. Earll interview.
43. Brown interview.
44. Swanger interview.
45. Earll interview.
46. Delozier interview.
47. Costa interview.
48. Brown interview.
49. Harper interview.
50. Gingrich interview.
51. Ibid.

CHAPTER 7

1. In 2001 Iowa founded another women's caucus, similar to the type that exists in South Carolina today. It was an organization of women legislators, staff, lobbyists, and business and community leaders interested in the election of women to public office (Sanbonmatsu 2006). I was unable to obtain information on its decline.

2. Patricia Judge, telephone interview by the author, February 15, 2011.

3. Swati Dandekar, telephone interview by the author, February 17, 2011. It is possible that Senator Dandekar does not want to be credited with instigating a women's caucus attempt that failed. It is also possible that her recall of the events or Lieutenant Governor Judge's is inaccurate.

4. Mauree Gingrich, telephone interview by the author, July 5, 2011; Vanessa Lowery Brown, interview by the author, December 7, 2011.

5. Rachel Scott, telephone interview by the author, January 19, 2011.

6. Linda Upmeyer, telephone interview by the author, May 5, 2011.

7. Phyllis Thede, telephone by the author, February 17, 2011.

8. Deborah Berry, telephone interview by the author, November 9, 2011.

9. Ibid.

10. Judge interview.

11. Berry interview.

12. Scott interview.

13. Thede interview.

14. Scott interview.

15. Berry interview.

16. Upmeyer interview.

17. Berry interview.

18. Ibid.

19. Scott interview.

20. Ibid.

21. Ibid. These types of comments mirror those in Colorado and Pennsylvania, which indicate that women are highly visible and monitored by male colleagues within the institution. It is likely that, as a consequence, this dynamic shapes women's behavior.

22. Berry interview.

23. Judge interview.

24. Scott interview.

25. Ibid.

26. Janet Petersen, telephone interview by the author, February 16, 2011.

27. Dandekar interview.

28. Upmeyer interview.

29. Thede interview.

30. Berry interview.

31. Scott interview.

32. Berry interview.

33. Thede interview.

34. Scott interview.

35. Ibid.

36. Ibid.

37. Judge interview.

38. Upmeyer interview.

39. Berry interview.

40. Thede interview.

41. J. Petersen interview.

42. Ibid.

43. Upmeyer interview.

44. Ibid.

45. Judge interview.

46. Scott interview.

47. J. Petersen interview.

48. Judge interview.
49. Ibid.
50. Ibid.

CHAPTER 8

1. Jessica Farrar, interview by the author, August 18, 2016.
2. Ibid.
3. Loretta Weinberg, interview by the author, August 20, 2010.
4. Deborah Berry, telephone interview by the author, November 9, 2011.
5. It is likely that similar activities are associated with other identity-based caucuses, although further study is necessary to make this claim. For details regarding black caucuses, see Sullivan and Winburn 2011 and Clark 2010.
6. For example, see Louisiana, where in 2016 legislators proposed joke amendments to important anti–human trafficking legislation and brought a birthday cake in the shape of a woman's body into the Capitol (R. Allen 2016; Ballard 2016).

CITED INTERVIEWS

Diane Allen, personal interview, July 15, 2010.

Diane Allen, telephone interview, December 5, 2011.

Mary Pat Angelini, telephone interview, April 11, 2010.

Jennifer Beck, personal interview, March 31, 2010.

Deborah Berry, telephone interview, November 9, 2011.

Louise Williams Bishop, telephone interview, December 6, 2011.

Vanessa Lowery Brown, personal interview, December 7, 2011.

Jay Costa, personal interview, December 7, 2011.

Kathy Crotty, personal interview, March 11, 2010.

Kathy Crotty, personal interview, November 30, 2011.

Swati Dandekar, telephone interview, February 17, 2011.

Sheryl Delozier, telephone interview, July 13, 2011.

Jane Earll, telephone interview, April 14, 2011.

Jessica Farrar, personal interview, August 18, 2016.

Deb Gardner, personal interview, March 21, 2011.

Mauree Gingrich, telephone interview, July 5, 2011.

Angela Giron, personal interview, March 23, 2011.

Peter Groff, telephone interview, April 5, 2011.

Millie Hamner, personal interview, March 22, 2011.

Amy Handlin, telephone interview, May 11, 2010.

Kate Harper, telephone interview, July 18, 2011.

Laura Hoeppner, personal interview, March 25, 2011.

Laura Hoeppner, telephone interview, November 22, 2011.

Babette Josephs, telephone interview, April 11, 2011.

Patricia Judge, telephone interview, February 15, 2011.

Jeanne Labuda, personal interview, March 23, 2011.
Sylvia Larsen, telephone interview, March 11, 2011.
Beth McCann, personal interview, March 25, 2011.
Alison McHose, telephone interview, April 19, 2010.
Karen Middleton, telephone interview, March 11, 2011.
Carole Murray, personal interview, March 22, 2011.
Janet Petersen, telephone interview, February 16, 2011.
Karen Petersen, telephone interview, April 19, 2011.
Nellie Pou, personal interview, July 29, 2010.
Ellen Roberts, personal interview, March 22, 2011.
Su Ryden, personal interview, March 23, 2011.
Rachel Scott, telephone interview, January 19, 2011.
L. Grace Spencer, telephone interview, December 12, 2011.
RoseMarie Swanger, telephone interview, November 29, 2011.
Christine Tartaglione, telephone interview, July 13, 2011.
Phyllis Thede, telephone interview, February 17, 2011.
Linda Upmeyer, telephone interview, May 5, 2011.
Joan Voss, personal interview, April 15, 2010.
Loretta Weinberg, personal interview, August 20, 2010.
Paul Weissmann, personal interview, March 23, 2011.

REFERENCES

Acker, Joan. 1992. "From Sex Roles to Gendered Institutions." *Contemporary Sociology* 21 (5): 565–569.

Aldrich, John H., and James S. Colman Battista. 2002. "Conditional Party Government in the States." *American Journal of Political Science* 46 (1): 164–172.

Allen, Diane. 2010. "Senate Republican Response to S-2139." August 3. http://www.senatenj.com/index.php/allen/senate-republicans-statement-on-s-2139/6541 (May 15, 2011).

Allen, Rebekah. 2016. "'Joke' Amendment Causes Outrage." *The Advocate,* May 18. http://www.theadvocate.com/baton_rouge/news/politics/legislature/article_59dc58d7-76d1-5138-abaa-14707b343790.html (August 9, 2017).

Anthias, Floya, and Nira Yuval-Davis. 1983. "Contextualizing Feminism: Gender, Ethnic and Class Divisions." *Feminist Review* 15:62–75.

Arco, Matt. 2018. "N.J. Now has the Strongest Equal Pay Law in America." NJ.com, April 24. http://www.nj.com/politics/index.ssf/2018/04/nj_now_has_the_strongest_equal_pay_law_in_america.html (May 4, 2018).

Ballard, Mark. 2016. "Bikini Birthday Cake at State Capitol Stirs Anger and 'Disgust,' Calls of Misogyny." *The Advocate,* November 18. http://www.theadvocate.com/baton_rouge/news/politics/article_b8bed38a-add5-11e6-bb7d-af2f87ad99d8.html (August 9, 2017).

Banaszak, Lee Ann. 1996. *Why Movements Succeed or Fail: Opportunity, Culture, and the Struggle for Women's Suffrage.* Princeton, NJ: Princeton University Press.

———. 2010. *The Women's Movement Inside and Outside the State.* Cambridge: Cambridge University Press.

Barrett, Edith J. 1997. "Gender and Race in the State House: The Legislative Experience." *Social Science Journal* 34 (2): 131–144.

Beckwith, Karen. 2007. "Numbers and Newness: The Descriptive and Substantive Representation of Women." *Canadian Journal of Political Science* 40 (1): 27–49.

Berkman, Michael B., and Robert E. O'Connor. 1993. "Do Women Legislators Matter? Female Legislators and State Abortion Policy." *American Politics Research* 21 (1): 102–124.

Blair, Diane Kincaid, and Ann R. Henry. 1981. "The Family Factor in State Legislative Turnover." *Legislative Studies Quarterly* 6 (1): 55–68.

Bolzendahl, Catherine. 2014. "Opportunities and Expectations: The Gendered Organization of Legislative Committees in Germany, Sweden, and the United States." *Gender and Society* 28 (6): 847–876.

The Book of the States, 2009 Edition. 2009. Lexington, KY: Council of State Governments.

Bratton, Kathleen A. 2002. "The Effect of Legislative Diversity on Agenda Setting: Evidence from Six State Legislatures." *American Politics Research* 30 (2): 115–142.

Breines, Winifred. 2006. *The Trouble between Us: An Uneasy History of White and Black Women in the Feminist Movement.* Oxford: Oxford University Press.

Brown, Nadia E. 2014. *Sisters in the Statehouse: Black Women and Legislative Decision Making.* Oxford: Oxford University Press.

California Latino Caucus. 2016. "Member Directory." http://latinocaucus.legislature.ca.gov/member-directory (October 1, 2016).

California Lesbian, Gay, Bisexual, Transgender Caucus. 2016. "Home." http://lgbtcaucus.legislature.ca.gov/ (October 1, 2016).

Carlson, Margaret. 2012. "How the Senate's Women Maintain Bipartisanship and Civility." *Daily Beast,* March 4. http://www.thedailybeast.com/articles/2012/03/04/how-the-senate-s-women-maintain-bipartisanship-and-civility.html (March 12, 2012).

Carroll, Susan J. 1989. "The Personal Is Political: The Intersection of Private Lives and Public Roles Among Women and Men in Elective and Appointive Office." *Women and Politics* 9 (2): 51–67.

———. 2002. "Representing Women: Congresswomen's Perceptions of Their Representational Roles." In *Women Transforming Congress,* ed. Cindy Simon Rosenthal, 50–68. Norman: University of Oklahoma Press.

———. 2003. "Have Women State Legislators in the United States Become More Conservative? A Comparison of State Legislators in 2001 and 1988." *Atlantis: A Women's Studies Journal* 27 (2): 128–139.

Carroll, Susan J., and Kelly Dittmar. 2012. "Preparedness Meets Opportunity: Women's Increased Representation in the New Jersey Legislature." *Center for American Women and Politics.* http://www.cawp.rutgers.edu/research/research_by_cawp_scholars/documents/Carroll_and_Dittmar_WomenIncreasedinNJLeg.pdf (June 6, 2012).

Carroll, Susan J., and Krista Jenkins. 2001. "Unrealized Opportunities? Term Limits and the Representation of Women in State Legislatures." *Women and Politics* 23 (4): 1–30.

Carroll, Susan J., and Kira Sanbonmatsu. 2013. *More Women Can Run: Gender and Pathways to State Legislatures.* Oxford: Oxford University Press.

Carroll, Susan J., and Ella Taylor. 1989. "Gender Differences in Policy Priorities of U.S. State and Legislators." Paper presented at the Annual Meeting of the American Political Science Association, Atlanta.

Center for American Women and Politics (CAWP). 2001. "Women State Legislators: Past, Present and Future." http://www.cawp.rutgers.edu/research/topics/documents/StLeg2001Report.pdf (August 3, 2010).

———. 2007. "Women State Legislators: Leadership Positions and Committee Chairs 2007." June. http://www.cawp.rutgers.edu/fast_facts/levels_of_office/documents/LegLead07.pdf (September 9, 2012).

———. 2009a. "Women in State Legislative Leadership Positions." August. http://www.cawp.rutgers.edu/fast_facts/levels_of_office/documents/LegLead09.pdf (June 12, 2012).

———. 2009b. "Women in State Legislatures 2009." December. http://www.cawp.rutgers.edu/fast_facts/levels_of_office/documents/stleg09.pdf (June 12, 2012).

———. 2009c. "Women of Color in Elective Office." December. http://www.cawp.rutgers.edu/FactSheets/Fact2009/F.Color.pdf (June 12, 2012).

———. 2016a. "Women in State Legislatures 1975–2016." December. http://cawp.rutgers.edu/sites/default/files/resources/stleghist.pdf (August 12, 2017).

———. 2016b. "Women in State Legislatures 2016." January. http://cawp.rutgers.edu/women-state-legislature-2016.

———. 2017a. "State Legislative Leadership Historical." Excel data set shared May 12.

———. 2017b. "Women in State Legislatures 2017." January. http://cawp.rutgers.edu/women-state-legislature-2017 (August 8, 2017).

———. 2018. "State Fact Sheet New Jersey." http://cawp.rutgers.edu/state_fact_sheets/nj (May 4, 2018).

Childs, Sarah, and Mona Lena Krook. 2009. "Analysing Women's Substantive Representation: From Critical Mass to Critical Actors." *Government and Opposition* 44 (2): 125–145.

Clark, Christopher J. 2010. "Unpacking Descriptive Representation: Examining Race and Electoral Representation in the American States." Ph.D. diss., University of Iowa.

Collier, David. 2011. "Understanding Process Tracing." *PS: Political Science and Politics* 44 (4): 823–830.

Collins, Eliza. 2018. "Trump Prompts Dem Women to Run for Congress in Pa., but They Face 'Old Boys Network.'" *USA Today,* April 18. https://www.usatoday.com/story/news/politics/2018/04/18/pennsylvania-democratic-women-running-after-trump-still-boys-network/524157002/ (May 5, 2018).

Colorado Legislative Women's Caucus. 2011. https://sites.google.com/site/coloradowomenscaucus/ (August 9, 2017).

Colorado Legislature Assembly. 2006. *Amendment 41.* August 11. http://www.leg.state.co.us/lcs/0506initrefr.nsf/89fb842d0401c52087256cbc00650696/

c1b04aaab700f2b987257188007a733e/$FILE/Amendment%2041.pdf (June 6, 2012).

Connors, Richard J., and William J. Dunham. 1993. *The Government of New Jersey: An Introduction*. Rev. ed. Lanham, MD: University Press of America.

Cox, Elizabeth M. 1996. *Women State and Territorial Legislators, 1895–1995*. Jefferson, NC: McFarland.

Cress, Daniel M., and David A. Snow. 1996. "Mobilization at the Margins: Resources, Benefactors, and the Viability of Homeless Social Movement Organizations." *American Sociological Review* 61:1089–1109.

Crowder-Myers, Melody, and Benjamin Lauderdale. 2014. "A Partisan Gap in the Supply of Female Potential Candidates in the United States." *Research and Politics,* June. http://rap.sagepub.com/content/1/1/2053168014537230 (November 15, 2016).

Dahlerup, Drude. 1988. "From a Small to a Large Minority: Women in Scandinavian Politics." *Scandinavian Political Studies* 11:275–298.

———. 2006. "The Story of the Theory of Critical Mass." *Politics and Gender* 2 (4): 511–522.

Daum, Courtenay W., Robert J. Duffy, and John A. Straayer, eds. 2011. *State of Change: Colorado Politics in the Twenty-First Century*. Boulder: University of Colorado Press.

"The Democratic Party." 2010. *Democratic National Committee*. People Page: Women. http://www.democrats.org/a/communities/women/ (July 22, 2010).

DiMaggio, Paul J., and Walter W. Powell, eds. 1991. *The New Institutionalism in Organizational Analysis*. Chicago: University of Chicago Press.

Dittmar, Kelly. 2015. *Navigating Gendered Terrain: Stereotypes and Strategy in Political Campaigns*. Philadelphia: Temple University Press.

Dodson, Debra. 1991. *Gender and Policymaking: Studies of Women in Office*. New Brunswick, NJ: Center for American Women and Politics (CAWP), Eagleton Institute of Politics, Rutgers University.

———. 1997. "Change and Continuity in the Relationship between Private Responsibilities and Public Officeholding: The More Things Change, the More They Stay the Same." *Policy Studies Journal* 25 (4): 569–584.

———. 2006. *The Impact of Women in Congress*. Oxford: Oxford University Press.

Dollar, D., R. Fisman, and R. Gatti. 2001. "Are Women Really the 'Fairer' Sex? Corruption and Women in Government." *Journal of Economic Behavior and Organization* 46 (4): 423–429.

Duerst-Lahti, Georgia. 2002. "Governing Institutions, Ideologies, and Gender: Toward the Possibility of Equal Political Representation." *Sex Roles: A Journal of Research* 47:371–388.

Eagly, Alice Hendrickson, and Linda Lorene Carli. 2007. *Through the Labyrinth: The Truth about How Women Become Leaders*. Boston: Harvard Business Press.

Economou, Rose. 1984. *Not One of the Boys*. New Brunswick, NJ: Center for American Women and Politics, Eagleton Institute of Politics, Rutgers University.

Ehrenhalt, Alan. 1992. *The United States of Ambition: Politicians, Power, and the Pursuit of Office*. New York: Three Rivers Press.

Elazar, Daniel J. 1984. *American Federalism: A View from the States*. 3rd ed. New York: Harper and Row.

Enloe, Cynthia. 2014. *Bananas, Beaches and Bases: Making Feminist Sense of International Politics*. Irvine: University of California Press.

Epstein, Jennifer. 2011. "Nancy Pelosi Calls GOP Budget 'a War on Women.'" *Politico,* April 8. http://www.politico.com/story/2011/04/pelosi-gop-plan-a-war-on-women-052793 (October 1, 2016).

Epstein, Mike, and Lynda Powell. 2005. "Do Women and Men State Legislators Differ?" In *Women and Elective Office: Past, Present, and Future,* ed. Sue Thomas and Clyde Wilcox, 94–109. 2nd ed. New York: Oxford University Press.

Erickson, Josefina. 2017. "When Age Intersects with Gender: The Marginalization of Young Female Legislators in the Swedish Parliament." Paper presented at the European Conference on Politics and Gender, Lausanne, Switzerland.

Evans, Sara. 1980. *Personal Politics: The Roots of Women's Liberation in the Civil Rights Movement and the New Left*. New York: Random House.

Fox, Richard L., and Jennifer L. Lawless. 2004. "Entering the Arena? Gender and the Decision to Run for Office." *American Journal of Political Science* 48 (2): 264–280.

Fraga, Luis Ricardo, Valerie Martinez-Ebers, Linda Lopez, and Ricardo Ramirez. 2008. "Representing Gender and Ethnicity: Strategic Intersectionality." In *Legislative Women,* ed. Beth Reingold, 157–174. Boulder CO: Lynne Rienner Publishers.

Francis, Wayne. 1985. "Leadership, Party Caucuses, and Committees in U.S. State Legislatures." *Legislative Studies Quarterly* 10 (2): 243–257.

Frankel, Noralee, and Nancy S. Dye. 1991. *Gender, Class, Race, and Reform in the Progressive Era*. Lexington: University Press of Kentucky.

Freeman, Jo. 1973. "The Origins of the Women's Liberation Movement." *American Journal of Sociology* 78 (4): 792–811.

———. 1986. "The Political Culture of the Democratic and Republican Parties." *Political Science Quarterly* 101 (3): 327–356.

Frisch, Scott A., and Sean Q. Kelly. 2008. "A Place at the Table." *Women and Politics* 25 (3): 1–26.

Fulton, Sarah A., Cherie D. Maestas, L. Sandy Maisel, and Walter J. Stone. 2006. "The Sense of a Woman: Gender, Ambition, and the Decision to Run for Congress." *Political Research Quarterly* 59 (2): 235–248.

George, Alexander L., and Andrew Bennett. 2005. *Case Studies and Theory Development in the Social Sciences (Belfer Center Studies in International Security)*. Cambridge, MA: MIT Press.

Gertzog, Irwin N. 2004. *Women and Power on Capitol Hill: Reconstructing the Congressional Women's Caucus*. Boulder, CO: Lynne Rienner Publishers.

Hammond, Susan Webb. 1998. *Congressional Caucuses in National Policymaking*. Baltimore: Johns Hopkins University Press.

Hawaii Senate Majority Office. 2017. "Children's Health and Safety, Access to Healthcare and Violence against Women Focus of Women's Legislative Caucus in 2017." January. https://www.hawaiisenatemajority.com/single-post/2017/01/26/Womens-Legislative-Caucus-2017 (August 12, 2017).

Hawkesworth, Mary. 2003. "Congressional Enactments of Race-Gender: Toward a Theory of Raced Gendered Institutions." *American Political Science Review* 97 (4): 529–550.

Hawkesworth, Mary, Debra Dodson, Katherine E. Kleeman, Kathleen J. Casey, and Krista Jenkins. 2001. *Legislating by and for Women: A Comparison of the 103rd and 104th Congresses.* New Brunswick, NJ: Center for American Women and Politics, Eagleton Institute of Politics, Rutgers University.

Hedlund, Ronald D. 1984. "Organizational Attributes of Legislatures: Structure, Rules, Norms, Resources." *Legislative Studies Quarterly* 9 (1): 51–121.

Hinckley, Barbara. 1971. *Stability and Change in Congress.* New York: Harper and Row.

Hochschild, Arlie. 1989. *The Second Shift: Working Parents and the Revolution at Home.* New York: Viking.

Holman, Mirya. 2014. *Women in Politics in the American City.* Philadelphia: Temple University Press.

Huddy, Leonie, Erin Cassese, and Mary-Kate Lizotte. 2008. "Gender, Public Opinion, and Political Reasoning." In *Political Women and American Democracy,* ed. Christina Wolbrecht, Karen Beckwith, and Lisa Baldez, 31–49. Cambridge: Cambridge University Press.

Jamieson, Kathleen Hall. 1995. *Beyond the Double Bind: Women and Leadership.* Oxford: Oxford University Press.

Kanter, Rosabeth Moss. 1977. "Some Effects on Proportions on Group Life: Skewed Sex Ratios and Responses to Token Women." *American Journal of Sociology* 82:965–990.

Kanthak, Kristin. 2009. "U.S. State Legislative Committee Assignments and Encouragement of Party Loyalty: An Exploratory Analysis." *State Politics and Policy Quarterly* 9 (3): 284–303.

Kanthak, Kristin, and George A. Krause. 2012. *The Diversity Paradox: Political Parties, Legislatures, and the Organizational Foundations of Representation in America.* New York: Oxford University Press.

Katzenstein, Mary Fainsod. 1998. *Faithful and Fearless: Moving Feminist Protest inside the Church and Military.* Princeton, NJ: Princeton University Press.

Kennedy, John J. 1999. *The Contemporary Pennsylvania Legislature.* Lanham, MD: University Press of America.

Kenney, Sally J. 1996. "New Research on Gendered Political Institutions." *Political Research Quarterly* 49 (2): 445–466.

Kingdon, John. 2003. *Agendas, Alternatives, and Public Policies.* 2nd ed. Boston: Longman.

King-Meadows, Tyson, and Thomas F. Schaller. 2006. *Devolution and Black State*

Legislators: Challenges and Choices in the Twenty-First Century. Albany: State University of New York Press.

Kirkpatrick, Jeane. 1974. *Political Woman.* New York: Basic Books.

Krook, Mona Lena, and Fiona Mackay, eds. 2011. *Gender, Politics and Institutions: Towards a Feminist Institutionalism.* Basingstoke, UK: Palgrave Macmillan.

Lawless, Jennifer L., and Richard Logan Fox. 2005. *It Takes a Candidate: Why Women Don't Run for Office.* Cambridge: Cambridge University Press.

Lemi, Danielle Casarez. 2017. "Identity and Coalitions in a Multiracial Era: How State Legislators Navigate Race and Ethnicity." *Politics, Groups, and Identities,* May 24. http://dx.doi.org/10.1080/21565503.2017.1288144.

Lovenduski, Joni. 1998. "Gendering Research in Political Science." *Annual Review of Political Science* 1 (1): 333–356.

Lowndes, V., and Mark Roberts. 2013. *Why Institutions Matter: The New Institutionalism in Political Science.* New York: Palgrave Macmillan.

Mackay, Fiona, Meryl Kenny, and Louise Chappell. 2010. "New Institutionalism through a Gender Lens: Towards a Feminist Institutionalism?" *International Political Science Review* 31 (5): 573–588.

Massachusetts Caucus of Women Legislators. 2018. http://www.mawomenscaucus .com/ (May 15, 2018).

McAdam, Doug, John D. McCarthy and Mayer N. Zald. 1996. *Comparative Perspectives on Social Movements: Political Opportunities, Mobilizing Structures and Cultural Framing.* Cambridge: Cambridge University Press.

McCammon, Holly J., Karen E. Campbell, Ellen M. Granberg, and Christine Mowery. 2001. "How Movements Win: Gendered Opportunity Structures and US Women's Suffrage Movements, 1866 to 1919." *American Sociological Review* 66 (1): 49–70.

McCammon, H. J., C. S. Muse, H. D. Newman, and T. M. Terrell. 2007. "Movement Framing and Discursive Opportunity Structures: The Political Successes of the US Women's Jury Movements." *American Sociological Review* 72 (5): 725–749.

McCormick, Richard P., and Katheryne C. McCormick. 1994. *Equality Deferred: Women Candidates for the New Jersey Assembly 1920–1993.* New Brunswick, NJ: Center for American Women and Politics, Eagleton Institute of Politics, Rutgers University.

McGlennon, John. 1998. "Factions in the Politics of the New South." In *Party Organization and Activism in the American South,* ed. Robert P. Steed, John A. Clark, Lewis Bowman, and Charles D. Hadley, 149–161. Tuscaloosa: University of Alabama Press.

Messerly, Megan. 2017. "Female Legislators Hope to Be a 'Force to Be Reckoned With' at First Caucus Meeting." *Nevada Independent,* February 10. https:// thenevadaindependent.com/article/female-legislators-hope-force-reckoned- first-caucus-meeting (August 9, 2017).

Mueller, Carol. 1984. "Women's Organizational Strategies in State Legislatures."

In *Political Women: Current Roles in State Government,* ed. Janet A. Flammang, 156–176. Beverly Hills, CA: Sage Publications.

Muirhead, Russell. 2014. *The Promise of Party in a Polarized Age.* Cambridge, MA: Harvard University Press.

National Conference of State Legislatures. 2009. "2009 Partisan Composition of State Legislatures." January. http://www.ncsl.org/documents/statevote/legis control_2009.pdf (August 12, 2017).

———. 2010. "Population and Legislative Size." http://www.ncsl.org/legislatures-elections/legislatures/population-and-size-of-legislature.aspx (November 24, 2012).

———. 2016. "Women's Caucuses, Commissions, and Committees." July. http://www.ncsl.org/legislators-staff/legislators/womens-legislative-network/womens-legislative-caucuses-and-committees.aspx (October 6, 2016).

———. 2017. "2017 State and Legislative Partisan Composition." August 4. http://www.ncsl.org/Portals/1/Documents/Elections/Legis_Control_2017_August_4th_10am_26973.pdf (August 13, 2017).

National Journal Almanac. 2011. "Colorado." http://www.nationaljournal.com/almanac/2010/area/co/ (June 12, 2012).

National Order of Women Legislators Records, Sophia Smith Collection, Smith College, Northampton, MA. Webpage abstract. https://asteria.fivecolleges .edu/findaids/sophiasmith/mnsss333.html.

Nelson, Barbara. 1990. "The Origins of the Two-Channel Welfare State: Workmen's Compensation and Mothers' Aid." In *Women, the State, and Welfare,* ed. Linda Gordon, 123–152. Madison: University of Wisconsin Press.

New Jersey Legislature Assembly. 2008–2009. Party Democracy Act. http://www .njleg.state.nj.us/bills/BillView.asp (November 2, 2009).

Nownes, Anthony J., and Grant Neeley. 1996. "Public Interest Group Entrepreneurship and Theories of Group Mobilization." *Political Research Quarterly* 49 (1): 119–146.

Oliver, Leah. 2005. "Women's Legislative Caucuses." *National Conference of State Legislatures LegisBrief* 13 (29). http://www.ncsl.org/documents/wln/05LBJunJul_WomenLegCaucuses.pdf (May 15, 2018).

Olson, Mancur. 1965. *The Logic of Collective Action: Public Goods and the Theory of Groups.* Cambridge, MA: Harvard University Press.

Osborn, Tracy. 2002. "Women's Voting and Coalition Formation in State Legislatures: Examining the Roll Call Evidence." Paper presented at the Annual Meeting of the American Political Science Association, Boston.

———. 2003. "Institutional Context and Support for a Women's Agenda in State Legislatures." Paper presented at the Annual Meeting of the American Political Science Association, Philadelphia.

———. 2012. *How Women Represent Women.* New York: Oxford University Press.

Peters, B. Guy. 2012. *Institutional Theory in Political Science: The New Institutionalism.* New York: Continuum.

Poggione, Sarah. 2004. "Exploring Gender Differences in State Legislators' Policy Preferences." *Political Research Quarterly* 57 (2): 305–331.

Polletta, Francesca, and James M. Jasper. 2001. "Collective Identity and Social Movements." *Annual Review of Sociology* 27 (1): 283–305.

Ramshaw, Emily, and Kate Galbraith. 2011. "Is There a Boys Club under the Pink Dome?" *Texas Tribune,* May 28. http://www.texastribune.org/texas-legislature/texas-legislature/is-there-a-boys-club-under-the-pink-dome/ (September 11, 2012).

Reingold, Beth. 1996. "Conflict and Cooperation: Legislative Strategies and Concepts of Power among Female and Male State Legislators." *Journal of Politics* 58 (2): 464–485.

Reingold, Beth, and Paige Schneider. 2001. "Sex, Gender, and the Status of 'Women's Issue' Legislation in the States." Paper presented at the Annual Meeting of the American Political Science Association, San Francisco.

Reingold, Beth, and Adrienne R. Smith. 2014. "Legislative Leadership and Intersections of Gender, Race, and Ethnicity in the American States." Paper presented at the Annual Meeting of the American Political Science Association, Washington, DC.

Reitmeyer, John. 2017. "GOP State Senator Offers New Gender-Pay Law but Weinberg Won't Support It." *NJ Spotlight,* May 31. http://www.njspotlight.com/stories/17/05/30/gop-state-senator-offers-new-gender-pay-legislation-but-weinberg-won-t-support-it/ (August 8, 2017).

Rhode, D. L., 2016. Women and Leadership. New York: Oxford University Press.

Rosenthal, Alan. 1998. *The Decline in Representative Democracy: Process, Participation and Power in State Legislatures.* Washington, DC: Congressional Quarterly Press.

———. 2009. *Engines of Democracy: Politics and Policymaking in State Legislatures* Washington, DC: CQ Press.

Rosenthal, Cindy Simon. 1997. "A View of Their Own: Women's Committee Leadership Styles and State Legislatures." *Policy Studies Journal* 25 (Winter): 585–600.

———. 1998. *When Women Lead.* New York: Oxford University Press.

———. 2000. "Gender Styles in State Legislative Committees: Raising Their Voice in Resolving Conflict." *Women and Politics* 21 (2): 21–45.

Sainsbury-Wong, Lorianne, Benjamin Wilson, and Alyssa Vangeli. 2011. "The Useful but Overlooked Massachusetts Equal Rights Amendment." *Massachusetts Bar Association,* August. https://www.massbar.org/publications/lawyers-journal/lawyers-journal-article/lawyers-journal-2011-august/the-useful-but-overlooked-massachusetts-equal-rights-amendment (September 11, 2012).

Saint-Germain, Michelle A. 1989. "Does Their Difference Make a Difference? The Impact of Women on Public Policy in the Arizona Legislature." *Social Science Quarterly* 70 (4): 956–968.

Salisbury, Robert H. 1969. "An Exchange Theory of Interest Groups." *Midwest Journal of Political Science* 13 (1): 1–32.

Salmore, Barbara G., and Stephen A. Salmore. 2008. *New Jersey Politics and Government: Suburban Politics Comes of Age.* 3rd ed. New Brunswick, NJ: Rutgers University Press.

Sanbonmatsu, Kira. 2006. "Finding Gender in Political Parties and Interest Groups." Paper presented at the Annual Meeting of the Midwestern Political Science Association, Chicago.

———. 2008. "Representation by Gender and Parties." In *Political Women and American Democracy,* ed. Christina Wolbrecht, Karen Beckwith, and Lisa Baldez, 96–109. Cambridge: Cambridge University Press.

Schenken, Suzanne O'Dea. 1995. *Legislators and Politicians: Iowa's Women Lawmakers.* Ames: Iowa State University Press.

Schneider, Dorothy, and Carl J. Schneider. 1993. *American Women in the Progressive Era, 1900–1920.* New York: Facts on File.

Shor, Boris, and Nolan McCarty. 2011. "The Ideological Mapping of American Legislatures." *American Political Science Review* 105 (August): 530–551.

———. 2015. "Aggregate State Legislator Shor-McCarty Ideology Data, June 2015 Update," Harvard Dataverse, V1, doi:10.7910/DVN/K7ELHW UNF:6:l5O+/whNdgWGB1Vt4nEheA==.

Sigel, Roberta. 1996. *Ambition and Accommodation: How Women View Gender Relations.* Chicago: University of Chicago Press.

Simons, Margaret A. 1979. "Racism and Feminism: A Schism in the Sisterhood." *Feminist Studies* 5 (2): 384–401.

Smooth, Wendy. 2008. "Gender, Race, and the Exercise of Power and Influence." In *Legislative Women,* ed. Beth Reingold, 175–196. Boulder CO: Lynne Rienner Publishers.

Snyder, James, and Tim Groseclose. 2000. "Estimating Party Influence in Congressional Roll Call Voting." *American Journal of Political Science* 44:193–211.

Sorenson, Georgia. 2000. "Our History." *Women Legislators of Maryland,* February 20. http://www.womenlegislatorsmd.org/history.htm#MEETING THE CHALLENGE: 1965–1973 (September 11, 2012).

Squire, Peverill. 2007. "Measuring Legislative Professionalism: The Squire Index Revisited." *State Politics and Policy Quarterly* 7:211–227.

Squire, Peverill, and Gary Moncrief. 2010. *State Legislatures Today: Politics under the Domes.* Boston: Pearson Education.

Stanley, Jeanie R., and Diane D. Blair. 1991. "Gender Differences in Legislative Effectiveness: The Impact of the Legislative Environment." In *Gender and Policymaking: Studies of Women in Office,* ed. Debra Dodson, 115–129. New Brunswick, NJ: Center for American Women and Politics, Eagleton Institute of Politics, Rutgers University.

Steinhauer, Jennifer. 2012. "Olympia Snowe Won't Seek Re-election." *New York Times,* February 28. http://www.nytimes.com/2012/02/29/us/politics/snowe-opts-not-to seek-re-election-in-maine.html (March 21, 2012).

Stolberg, Sheryl Gay. 2015a. "More Women than Ever in Congress, but with

Less Power than Before." *New York Times,* February 2. http://www.nytimes.com/2015/02/03/us/politics/republican-takeover-of-senate-pushes-women-out-of-powerful-committee-posts.html (October 1, 2016).

———. 2015b. "Proof That Women Are the Better Dealmakers in the Senate." *New York Times,* February 19. http://www.nytimes.com/politics/first-draft/2015/02/19/in-the-senate-women-are-better-dealmakers-than-men-heres-proof/ (October 1, 2016).

Stoper, Emily. 1977. "Wife and Politician: Role Strain among Women in Public Office." In *Portrait of Marginality: The Political Behavior of the American Woman,* ed. Marianne Githens and Jewel Limar Prestage, 320–337. New York: McKay.

Straayer, John A. 2007. "Direct Democracy's Disaster." *State Legislatures,* March. http://www.apsanet.org/~lss/Newsletter/july07/Straayer.pdf (June 6, 2012).

Sullivan, Jas M., and Jonathan Winburn. 2011. *The Louisiana Legislative Black Caucus: Race and Representation in the Pelican State.* Baton Rouge: Louisiana State University Press.

Swamy, A., S. Knack, Y. Lee, and O. Azfar. 2001. "Gender and Corruption." *Journal of Development Economics* 64 (1): 25–55.

Swers, Michelle. 1998. "Are Women More Likely to Vote for Women's Issue Bills than Their Male Colleagues?" *Legislative Studies Quarterly* 23 (3): 435–448.

———. 2002. *The Difference Women Make: The Policy Impact of Women in Congress.* Chicago: University of Chicago Press.

Thomas, Sue. 1991. "The Impact of Women on State Legislative Policies." *Journal of Politics* 53 (4): 958–976.

———. 1994. *How Women Legislate.* Oxford: Oxford University Press.

———. 2002. "The Personal Is the Political: Antecedents of Gendered Choices of Elected Representatives." *Sex Roles* 47 (7/8): 343–353.

Thomas, Sue, and Susan Welch. 1991. "The Impact of Gender on Activities and Priorities of State Legislators." *Western Political Quarterly* 44 (2): 445–456.

Thompson, Joel A., and Gary F. Moncrief. 1993. "The Implications of Term Limits for Women and Minorities: Some Evidence from the States." *Social Science Quarterly* 74 (June): 300–309.

Thompson, Senfronia. 2011. *Texas Impact,* May 26. https://www.youtube.com/watch?v=QKf-6WiBq_Q (November 15, 2016).

Tolbert, C., and G. Steuernagel. 2001. "Women Lawmakers, State Mandates and Women's Health." *Women and Politics* 22 (2): 1–39.

Tuma, Mary. 2011. "Texas House Members Form Women's Caucus." *American Independent,* May 31. http://americanindependent.com/186124/texas-house-members-form-womens-caucus (September 11, 2012).

U.S. Census Bureau. 2011. "Population Distribution and Change: 2000 to 2010." *U.S. Census Bureau: 2010 Census Briefs.* http://www.census.gov/prod/cen2010/briefs/c2010br-01.pdf (September 5, 2012).

Welch, Susan. 1985. "Are Women More Liberal than Men in the U.S. Congress?" *Legislative Studies Quarterly* 10 (1): 125–134.

Weldon, S. Laurel. 2004. "Democratic Policymaking on Violence against Women in the Fifty US States." *International Feminist Journal of Politics* 6 (1): 1–28.

Wolbrecht, Christina, and David E. Campbell. 2017. "Role Models Revisited: Youth, Novelty, and the Impact of Female Candidates." *Politics, Groups, and Identities* 5 (3): 418–434.

Women's Foundation of Colorado. 2016. "About Us." http://www.wfco.org/pages/content/about-us (November 3, 2016).

Women's Policy. 2016. "Our Work: The Women's Caucus." http://www.womens policy.org/our-work/the-womens-caucus/ (October 1, 2016).

Young, Iris Marion. 2000. *Inclusion and Democracy.* Oxford: Oxford University Press.

Zald, Mayer N. 1992. "Looking Backward to Look Forward: Reflections on the Past and Future of the Research Mobilization Research Program." In *Frontiers in Social Movement Theory,* ed. Aldon D. Morris and Carol McClurg Mueller, 326–348. New Haven, CT: Yale University Press.

INDEX

ANNA MITCHELL MAHONEY is an Administrative Assistant Professor of Women's Political Leadership at Tulane University's Newcomb College Institute.